JOHN TERRY

FIFTY DEFINING FIXTURES

Garry Hayes

AMBERLEY

For GP, from whom I inherited my blue-tinted glasses.
Thanks old man.

First published 2016

Amberley Publishing
The Hill, Stroud
Gloucestershire, GL5 4EP

www.amberley-books.com

British Library Cataloguing in Publication Data.
A catalogue record for this book is available from the British Library.

ISBN 978 1 4456 6222 0 (print)
ISBN 978 1 4456 6223 7 (ebook)

Typesetting and Origination by Amberley Publishing.
Printed in the UK.

Contents

Foreword

Playing for Chelsea in the 1960s and 1970s was an exciting time for us players. We had a side complete with talented individuals like Peter Osgood and Charlie Cooke, to name just two, but collectively we were an exciting team as well. We would achieve things Chelsea never had and a lot of my teammates since then have rightly been celebrated at Stamford Bridge as legends.

There is plenty to consider for a player to be regarded so highly by fans. You need to give the supporters something they can relate to, like winning trophies and having a bit of character. It helps if you have been a one-club man who has come through the youth ranks and gone onto captain the club as well. Fans like to see total commitment from players, like they are feeling every kick in the same way they do. It is those sorts of players who win the hearts of supporters. No, I'm not talking about myself here, but John Terry.

What John has achieved in the modern game deserves to be celebrated and he has become the perfect example for anyone who not only wants to play for Chelsea, but wants to support the club. He has helped continue the traditions that I was taught and passed on in my career.

I have got to know John well throughout his time at Stamford Bridge, right from when he first started to establish himself in the first team. I think he is a terrific lad and he has led by example whenever he has worn the Chelsea shirt.

Now, with my reputation during my time at Chelsea it is no surprise that I would say this, but I've always liked watching players who are not scared of throwing themselves into tackles and making their presence known. John has been one of those, yet he did it with intelligence.

The Chelsea careers of John and I were separated by two decades, but there have been similarities. We captained Chelsea after coming through the ranks, but it is also that committed side of his character I have respected about John. He is not afraid of mixing it when he has to and it speaks volumes for his commitment that his career has been defined by the heart and desire he has shown on the pitch. When we talk about defenders, he has been a real defender. He has been an inspirational captain for Chelsea.

John Terry and Frank Lampard have been great symbols of the successes Chelsea have enjoyed in the modern era. They were close friends and whenever I or other former players have been around the club, they have gone out of their way to speak with us and get to know us, which I think is nice and says a lot about them.

I remember having a bet with them both a few years ago that neither would beat my appearance record of 795 games for Chelsea. I have seen Frank off and claimed my half of lager from him, but John is still going strong, looking like he is going to run me a lot closer. Still, my message to him is this: John, if you do not make it, you know what I'm having!

Ron Harris, June 2016

Introduction

There are moments that define careers; then there are those that make them. For John Terry, the latter would come before he was even a professional football player.

Before Terry would lift Premier League trophies, FA Cups, League Cups and experience the romance of those European nights that have been dyed by the Stamford Bridge lights, the future Chelsea captain had it all to prove. He was in danger of the club ending his career before it would even begin. Then came a moment of inspiration.

'I walked into the club as a schoolboy, quietly confident. I had a stage where I grew a lot in a short space of time and I was shaking off a bit of puppy fat, as you do when you're a teenager,' Terry once told *Chelsea* magazine. 'I shot up and became gangly. It took about six months to a year for my body to adjust and it wasn't easy. I still hear stories now that the club were umming and ahhing about whether to give me my YTS contract.'

Terry was in danger of not making the grade and it took a starring role from him in the Chelsea reserves side to convince his coaches he should be given a chance to progress to YTS status.

'Mick McGiven was reserves manager at the time and he pulled me into his team for one game a few weeks before he was due to give out YTS contracts,' Terry continued. 'It was the last game of the season at Luton's ground and I was on the bench, but I was the only player from my youth side selected so I thought, "Hold on, something's not right here!" I came on in centre-midfield, scored two goals and, although we lost the game 5-2, I almost got my hat-trick. I remember Dave Lee was playing centre-back behind me and he was pushing me up front, telling me to stay up there and get my hat-trick, but I didn't know what to do, I was a bit scared of Mick and I was only 15!'

Far from being an adult, Terry was starting the habit of a lifetime. When it mattered most, he was showing up. He did not know it at the time, but he was beginning to get a sense for the qualities that would carve out his career at the very top.

More was to come. Terry was a midfielder and, while he could more than hold his own at youth team level, breaking into the first team was a much more difficult challenge to overcome. It was a time when Chelsea's fortunes were changing dramatically for the better and he needed to show something that would separate him from the others who were fighting to be noticed.

Matthew Harding's presence was helping bring about a revolution to help Chelsea realise their potential in the mid-1990s. In his role as vice-chairman – not to mention a personal investment of over £26 million into the Chelsea coffers – Harding's influence would bring a more cosmopolitan feel to Stamford Bridge, starting with the acquisition of Ruud Gullit in 1995. From there, Chelsea would sign such glamorous names as Gianluca Vialli and Gianfranco Zola to help them compete consistently at the highest level in the top-flight for the first time in close to thirty years.

It was exciting to be a Chelsea fan. The club was exiting the doldrums with a promise that the years of feast and famine, promotion and relegation, would be left behind them. The Premier League was here and Chelsea were very much a premier club; they were becoming the new school.

Exciting for fans, it would not prove as much for those young players coming through. Bobby Campbell, Ian Porterfield and Glenn Hoddle had continued to promote from within during their respective spells as manager, while Frank Sinclair, Eddie Newton, David Lee and others would become familiar faces to fans along the King's Road. Gradually, however, time was moving on and Chelsea's youngsters had to be of a higher calibre. If they were not, they would have to chase their footballing dreams elsewhere.

Indeed, aside from the supremely talented Jody Morris, Chelsea would not have another youngster come through at the time and make as big an impression in the same way he did. Morris was a technically gifted midfielder, seen as the heir to Dennis Wise. The comparison was helped in that Morris' diminutive frame all but mirrored Wise's – the latter was 5 foot 5 inches, with Morris shaving an inch off. He had everything in his game, though. Morris was a menace when he had to be in midfield, but was an exceptional footballer. From the eighteen minutes he played on his debut against Middlesbrough in February 1995, it was clear Morris had everything to rival the more exotic signings Chelsea were beginning to attract.

Morris was the standard coming out of Chelsea's youth ranks and Terry's ability in the middle of the park was not going to match him. His game was not as flamboyant and that restricted him. Terry would not be able to compete with the new complexion football that England was starting to embrace if he remained a midfielder. Then came the epiphany.

'At the start of my first YTS season in 1997, I wasn't selected and I was on the bench for the first three games,' Terry remembered. 'Then, in the fourth game, we played Barnsley at home and one of our centre-halves pulled out. The youth-team manager, Ted Dale, asked me to play there, we won 3-0 and I was probably man of the match.

'It just moved on from there for me. Everyone said how well I'd done, I tried it for a little bit in training and it just seemed natural to me. I stayed at centre-half for the rest of the season and I went on a run of about 10 games where I was just doing really well in the position, then I made the progression into the first team.'

Terry had found his calling and by October 1998, he was making his Chelsea debut. It came in a League Cup fixture against Aston Villa, with the seventeen-year-old racing onto the pitch to replace Dan Petrescu with just four minutes remaining in the game. Chelsea were already 4-1 to the good and there was little else for Terry to do other than enjoy the moment. It was a practice more designed for him to soak up the atmosphere and get that feeling for playing in front of a packed-out stadium.

Terry was still cleaning the boots of his more senior teammates despite that first-team appearance, learning his trade and trying to make an impression.

'It was a different era back then,' explains David Lee, who, along with Wise and Eddie Newton, would call upon Terry to ensure his boots were suitably prepared when matchday arrived.

'The kids came in and they had to do jobs. John was big mates with Paul Nicholls, who's his agent now, and they would come into the dressing room where we had Hitchy [Kevin Hitchcock], Wisey and Eddie, and they would literally stand to attention in the morning until you told them exactly what you wanted.

'If it was cold and you wanted gloves or a hat, bottoms or whatever, they just went and got them without a problem. They were good kids with a very good attitude.

'As a boot boy, John was just excellent. Whatever I wanted, whatever I needed, he would be there to get it. At the same time, we used to look after him. I was sponsored by Adidas at the time, so would get him tracksuits and boots.'

Terry has often looked back on those times with a sense of pride, explaining how the likes of Lee had shown him the ropes and helped him learn his trade to become a professional football player. Coming through under those players was as much a part of his apprenticeship as playing football was. He needed to earn respect and he had no qualms with the way he had to go about it.

Those YTS tasks were aimed at giving youngsters a sense of responsibility. They would ground them and build relationships with the senior professionals at a football club. For Terry, it has given him relationships that remain strong today. Wise remains his idol and the player he has shaped himself on, with the way he has approached his captaincy of Chelsea, while the small bonuses Lee would offer during his time at Chelsea are being repaid now.

'He always mentions to me that he appreciates how we looked after him as a kid,' Lee continues. 'It wasn't just me. Eddie and Dennis always helped him and as Dennis was on the most money, he gave him more financially.

'At the League Cup final against Tottenham in 2015, I asked him if I could get a couple of tickets to take my daughter to the game. I asked for two, but if he could get three, I would take my wife. John just said to leave it with him and then called me during half-term, saying I should go to Cobham to collect the tickets. He told me to bring my daughter and he gave her a tour around and had lunch with her. When I went to pay him for the tickets, he said "No, I've never forgotten what you did for me as a kid."'

It is an insight to a side of John Terry and other footballers we do not see outside of the game. As observers, we associate the person with the player and what they achieve on the pitch. That is where they are celebrated most, which is why this book has been written.

Terry's Chelsea career has been an exceptional one. It has been historic, defined by the record books being rewritten over and over with every triumph.

Up to the end of the 2015/16 season, Terry had little else other than Ron Harris' remarkable appearances record for Chelsea to break.

He has come to represent Chelsea for this current generation, which has taken some doing. He is fighting the same battles he did when he was just a teenager – redefining himself at a club that flourishes with overseas talent and the wealth of its owner.

Terry has done that with his refusal to come out second best, something former Blues midfielder Pat Nevin sees as unique, even among elite sportsmen.

'John's a little bit different from your average footballer,' Nevin explains. 'Everyone wants to get to the top, but his desire to be there was almost psychotic.'

Even when he was a youngster attempting to make the grade at Chelsea, Terry was not one to wilt in the presence of some of the club's bigger stars.

By the time Jimmy Floyd Hasselbaink arrived at Stamford Bridge in 2000, Terry had moved on from cleaning the boots of his teammates. He was a professional with a point to prove.

'We always had a few ding-dongs, me and Jimmy, but he was brilliant,' Terry would later say of the Dutch striker. 'He'd get the hump with me in training but afterwards he'd get me in a headlock and say, 'that's brilliant, I love that, make sure you keep doing it!" Jimmy was a real fighter and battler all the time and we had so many arguments during games – well, him telling me what I was doing wrong basically, because I was too young to say anything back to him! I respected him so much but if the ball was there to be won in a training game, I'd go in to win it and that's what we try to encourage all the young boys to do now [at Chelsea]. We're no different now in that respect.'

While tales from inside the dressing room give us some insight to Terry's career, it is what he has achieved on the pitch that lays everything bare. When Saturday comes, the winners and losers are decided; legends are formed; history is made.

By the time Terry was reaching the twilight of his career, he had made over 700 appearances for Chelsea. If we include his England caps, he was close to hitting the 800 mark for club and country.

There have been eleven cup finals in that number, not to mention six Champions League semi-finals and countless decisive games in the Premier League that would prove pivotal in silverware being won and lost.

John Terry's career has been an incredible one, but before he could achieve anything, he had to prove himself capable at Stamford Bridge. He had to join Nottingham Forest on loan and help David Platt's side pull clear of a potential relegation battle.

It was April 2000 and Chelsea manager Gianluca Vialli had thrown down the gauntlet.

Birmingham City 0-1 Nottingham Forest
Division One
15 April 2000

John Terry was still only nineteen years old when he joined Nottingham Forest on loan in the latter stages of 1999/2000.

It was a significant move for him – the sort of temporary transfer that puts hair on the chest of any young player. Moving away from west London was significant as it meant Terry was no longer in his comfort zone. Throughout his entire development as a youth-team player, Terry had always been in the club surroundings. He was with his friends and teammates, not so much pampered, but in a position where he had long known the daily grind. That can lead to complacency in some players as they are not tested on a daily basis. They require tests of character to really push them, to make them realise the challenges of professional football. That is the theory at least.

Loan moves are not always the answer to that. Just ask the hordes of young Chelsea players now who have spent seasons on loan away from the club only to float off into the ether without a trace. In many ways, as Chelsea continue their efforts to unearth the next John Terry, a loan move is part of the test to see if they can emulate him.

Attempting to force his way into Gianluca Vialli's side at the time, Terry was competing with World Cup winners Marcel Desailly and Frank Leboeuf. It was also the ambition of the club that would prevent him from becoming an instant first-team regular. Chelsea had visions of becoming an established Champions League side, so the risk of playing a young defender was always going to be too much for Vialli to take.

It had been the Italian who had given Terry his Chelsea debut two seasons earlier. Aged just seventeen, the defender had replaced Dan Petrescu in a League Cup match with Aston Villa. It was a milestone for the youngster – as it is for any player when they finally get that first-team nod – but joining Nottingham Forest when he did has since proved more pivotal for Terry's career.

Dropping down a division, he was not joining a club where all was fine. Then managed by David Platt, just one win in six matches had severely dented their hopes of a late play-off push.

Instead, Forest were starting to look over their shoulder and Platt needed to inject some inspiration into his side as they attempted to pull free of the relegation zone. With six games to go, Forest were hovering dangerously close, sitting just five points clear of Walsall in twenty-second position.

Most managers would normally turn to a flair player with the ability to win them matches in such circumstances. Platt opted for defence being, well, the best form of defence and called in a favour from his old teammate at Sampdoria.

Vialli gave him Terry and it worked with almost instant results. Keeping just four clean sheets from Christmas to April, the presence of Terry helped Forest to record three in five games.

He had made his debut as a substitute in a 1-1 draw with Charlton Athletic a week earlier, but Platt had clearly seen enough to start Terry when Forest made the trip to St Andrews to face Birmingham City.

Trevor Francis' side were chasing promotion at the time, so a relegation-threatened Forest side had it all to do. With Darren Purse gifting the visitors an own goal shortly before half-time, Platt's side demonstrated a new-found resilience to hold out for a much-needed win. It was no surprise it came with Terry in the line-up.

Jack Lester had joined Forest that January and remembers the instant impact Chelsea's up and coming star made.

'I was impressed from the moment I saw him train,' Lester recalls. 'Even though he was still very young, you could see that he was a leader. I remember going home and speaking to my friends about him, telling them that Forest had this young lad on loan who would play for England. I was totally convinced about how good he was.'

Despite that quality, Terry remained raw. As his career developed, we grew accustomed to this warrior figure at the back who would carry Chelsea onto greatness. Premier League titles, FA Cups and Champions Leagues were all to come, but the player Lester saw was still finding his feet.

'He combined all the attributes you want to see in a defender; he was confident, intelligent and dominant against opponents,' the former Forest striker continues.

'When he came in, we suddenly started picking up clean sheets. For a player of just 19 to have an impact like that, it's very unusual at any level.

'He wasn't a leader yet, though. He certainly had a voice in training and matches, but he wasn't quite the John Terry we've come to know.

'At that age, he wasn't barking out orders, but you could see that would come in his career. He was always organising those around him, which is something he would have no doubt picked up on the training pitch at Chelsea. You've got to remember, he was 19, but had come through at a club where he was playing alongside Marcel Desailly and some other big names.'

Out of sight, Terry was not out of mind at Chelsea. We can only speculate on the Sampdoria Boys Club passing on favours, yet Terry's loan move had a real purpose. Vialli was not just sending him to the City Ground to assist Platt. There was a method to it, which Lester witnessed firsthand when Terry played him a voice message from then assistant manager Ray Wilkins.

'He used to call John a lot,' Lester says. 'One time he left him an answerphone message, which John played me. I can't remember exactly what he said, but Wilkins was just giving him some praise as it was after another game when we had kept a clean sheet. I just thought to myself that if Ray Wilkins is keeping tabs on him, calling him, then Chelsea must really hold him in high regard. I realised then that Chelsea had big plans for John.

'I hadn't heard of him before he came to Forest, so it was things like that which showed who he was and where he was going.'

After drawing with Birmingham on Terry's full debut for the club, Platt's Forest recorded back-to-back draws with Fulham and Sheffield United before defeating Port Vale and Stockport County to finish the season on a high.

When Terry had arrived at the City Ground, Forest were deep in a rut. They were nineteenth, but by the time the season ended and Terry headed back down the M1, they were safely positioned mid-table and free from the drop. His work there was done.

'It's moves to clubs like Forest where you find out if a player can handle it. Players can look good on the training ground, but put them in the first team and in a stadium in front of a crowd and a lot of them buckle under the pressure. John took that very, very easily,' Lester explains.

'In terms of the players I played with in my career, he's certainly the best. For someone so young to come and shore up a defence that had been shipping goals just speaks volumes for his ability as a player. He was lacking experience, so to come in and do what he did was very impressive.'

It may have happened away from Stamford Bridge, but John Terry had taken his first real steps into creating the legend that would define his career. Now he had to make that same sort of impact back in west London.

Birmingham City: Myhre; Rowett, Purse, Grainger, Holdsworth, Charlton; Lazaridis (Hyde, 46), Hughes, McCarthy (Marcelo, 75); Johnson, Furlong (Adebola, 51).
Unused subs: Johnson, Campbell.

Nottingham Forest: Beasant; Scimeca, Rogers, Terry, Calderwood (Hjelde, 58), Brennan; Johnson, Prutton, Bart-Williams, Harewood; Lester.
Unused subs: Crossley, Louis-Jean, Woan, John.

Arsenal 1-1 Chelsea
Premier League
13 January 2001

The corner was whipped in by Gianfranco Zola, delivered teasingly to the edge of the six-yard box. It was the sort of cross designed to entice goalkeepers with thoughts they might be able to claim it. Zola's ball was perfection, carrying enough weight to allow a teammate to capitalise on the indecision that would prove rife.

The goalkeeper stuttered for a moment – would he or would he not? – causing his defenders to go static in anticipation. That hesitancy was futile.

John Terry stole a march on his marker to break free inside the box, connecting with Zola's delivery to head the ball into the ground before it bounced over the line and rippled the back of the net.

There were eight yellow Gillingham shirts surrounding him – nine if we include Vince Bartram in goal – yet none of them could compete with Terry's movement and the leap that powered his header home.

'And John Terry gets his first senior goal,' John Motson cried out from the commentary box.

It was the fifth round of the 1999/2000 FA Cup and the nineteen-year-old had just put Chelsea 2-0 up against their Division Two opponents. The Blues would win 5-0.

'I didn't know what to do, so I just ran into the crowd and hugged the nearest supporter,' Terry later explained, recalling his celebration with those in the Matthew Harding lower. 'It was a really proud moment for me because I hadn't played many games at that point and to score was brilliant.'

A time for feeling proud it may have been, the goal was just as significant in Terry's burgeoning career. Like his debut against Aston Villa in the League Cup in 1998, the young defender was beginning to put a strike through the milestones every rising star relishes.

Debut. Tick. Ten first-team appearances. Tick. First senior goal. Tick.

Another step forward would follow with that loan move to Nottingham Forest where Terry proved to his manager, Gianluca Vialli, that he could cut it in senior football. The early signs were promising.

When Chelsea arrived at Highbury a year after Terry's first senior goal for the club, it was the moment that Blues fans could start to believe in the myth of the player they had coming through.

Before Jose Mourinho's Chelsea rewrote the rulebook against Arsenal, the Gunners had been the dominant team whenever they met the Blues. In the years since the Premier League was formed up to January 2001, they had lost a mere four times in twenty games in all competitions to Chelsea. The Blues' best league result at Highbury during that time was a 3-3 draw in September 1996.

Dennis Wise rescued a point that night back in 1996 with a superb finish, latching onto a chipped John Spencer pass to fire beyond John Lukic in goal. What had made Wise's goal all the more impressive was not that it came in the 90th minute of a massive London derby, but more the way he had plucked the ball from the air and remained composed enough to not panic and draw his team level.

It was a striker's finish, demonstrating the sort of expertise and instinct we expect from those leading the line. Wise's movement across the back four was clever, ghosting out to the left between the centre-back and the full-back, his execution to send Lukic the wrong way even more so.

With time running out and everything at stake, it is your front man who is supposed to be rescuing a result. If that fails, captains prove the heroes. Wise did that time and again in Chelsea colours as he did at Highbury that night.

Earlier in that game, the Chelsea skipper had won the penalty that had put his side 1-0 up. Fouled by Steve Bould, his reaction was Wise personified. Looking back down the field, he showed no hesitancy as he called out Frank Leboeuf's name and pointed to the spot with vigour, demanding the Frenchman step up and put Chelsea ahead.

Wise's performance against Arsenal was about leadership. Indeed, it was symbolic for everything he had to come to represent in west London. He was never seen to shirk his responsibilities, living up to that terrier-like persona he had created from when he had first come through at Wimbledon before joining Chelsea in 1990.

Wise would spend eleven years as a hero along the King's Road. He was a figurehead in the same spirit as those before him who had carved out the pathway he would often tread.

Wise was a connection to the past and also Chelsea's future. John Terry had idolised him as a youth team player, which is why it was so fitting that his first Premier League goal would come at Highbury where Wise had shown the sort of character that would come to define Terry throughout his career.

In terms of Chelsea's season as a whole, a 3-3 draw in north London in 1996 did not shape the campaign. It was another result among many. In isolation, however, Wise's influence on proceedings stood for so much.

That year would see Chelsea win the FA Cup for the first time at Wembley. The last time they had lifted the trophy in 1970 had come at Old Trafford by way of a replay against Leeds United.

Everything positive about Ruud Gullit's side revolved around Wise. The squad was becoming more cosmopolitan – as well as Lebouef, Chelsea signed Guanluca Vialli and Roberto Di Matteo that summer leading into 1996/97 – so Wise's presence was crucial. It was not about the dressing room figure, but also what he contributed on the pitch.

Coming from Serie A and Ligue 1, Chelsea's new recruits needed to be indoctrinated in the traditions of English football and how they should handle themselves. So who better than a rascal with a reputation for celebrating those dark arts?

For all that continental feel, Chelsea maintained an Anglo-Saxon heart at the core. The concern was that when Wise left for Leicester City in 2001 – the same summer that Frank Lampard joined Chelsea for £11 million – that element would be lost.

It was games like Arsenal away in January 2001 that hinted the next generation was beginning to emerge, though.

Unlike his first goal in senior football against Gillingham, Terry's goal meant something against Arsenal. He wasn't proving a flat-track bully, scoring against lower-league opposition in matches Chelsea should be winning. He was helping take points from sides who were a scalp. In the same fashion as Wise five years earlier, the Chelsea youngster was earning his side a point against opponents who were no stranger to getting the better of them. He was standing up in a stadium that was not a happy stomping ground for his club.

Fittingly, in similar fashion to that FA Cup goal, Terry's equaliser against the Gunners came from a corner. In a repeat of Zola's set-piece, Wise had hit the erogenous spot that every player craves from a corner. Standing in front of David Seaman, Terry was expertly positioned to collect any scraps, which he did when Eidur Gudjohnsen's header was not cleared and sat up in front of the No. 26 for him to nod home.

That goal stood for plenty, yet it was at the back we saw Terry mature. Facing Thierry Henry, he had come out on top in the battle with one of the Premier League's finest strikers. The Frenchman would score twenty-four goals that season and already had fourteen to his name by the time Chelsea arrived at Highbury in January. Terry would stop him in his tracks.

It was a sight Chelsea fans would become used to against the rest of the Premier League's most lethal marksmen.

Arsenal: Seaman; Dixon, Stepanovs, Keown, Sylvinho; Ljunberg (Vivas, 87), Vieira, Parlour, Pires; Wiltord, Henry.
Unused subs: Manninger, Cole, Malz, Pennant.

Chelsea: Cudicini; Leboeuf (Ferrer, 46), Desailly, Terry, Harley; Wise, Dalla Bonna, Jokanovic (Gronkjaer, 46), Poyet; Hasselbaink, Gudjohnsen (Zola, 77).
Unused subs: De Goey, Le Saux.

Chelsea 3-0 Levski Sofia
UEFA Cup, First Round
20 September 2001

It sounds like the opening line to a joke, but for those who were in attendance, it would prove anything but.

Five footballers were in a bar drinking, or so the story goes. Depending on the version of events that are to be believed, things got messy from there.

Chelsea should have been playing Levski Sofia in the UEFA Cup at Stamford Bridge on 12 September but, after the World Trade Center terrorist attacks a day earlier, the game had been postponed. Indeed, across all of Europe football matches had been rescheduled by UEFA as a mark of solidarity with the thousands who had lost their lives in New York City when two commercial airplanes had been turned into weapons of mass destruction and flown into the iconic Twin Towers of lower Manhattan.

Young, carefree and with unscheduled free time on their hands, John Terry, Frank Lampard, Jody Morris, Eidur Gudjohnsen and former Blues defender Frank Sinclair decided to make the most of it by enjoying a night out. According to reports in the *News of the World* newspaper, the result was an evening of drunken rowdiness that left American tourists who were there to witness it upset and offended. The red top reported that the four Chelsea players and Sinclair had embarked on a five-hour binge at the Posthouse hotel bar at Heathrow Airport.

'They were causing lots of noise and knocking things over in the bar and upsetting everyone. They were really drunk,' said manager Antonio Parisini.

Not only that, apparently stripping had been involved in their partying, while one player in the group was also reportedly seen vomiting.

When the papers caught wind of the story, it cast the quintet in an unfavourable light. Here they were, a group of wealthy football players, seemingly showing no compassion for the American tourists who had been stranded in the UK after the flights chaos caused by 9/11.

The *NOTW* report also added that Terry and his teammates were later seen at a nearby bowling alley, the Airport Bowl, continuing their drinking session. Some of the group were allegedly disinterested in using the available bowling balls to knock over the pins, instead throwing themselves head first down the bowling lanes.

Regardless of their intentions, the media were not letting the Chelsea players off the hook; not when they should have been in action for their club that night only for an atrocity of such magnitude as the World Trade Center attacks to postpone their match.

It became a story about the modern day footballer and their apparent lives of excess. Right or wrong, the five had lived up to the stereotype. Footballers are held under a different sort of scrutiny to your average young male. Across the country on the evening the Chelsea stars were causing a scene, there would have been other youngsters enjoying an evening out despite the tragedy that struck New York City; on university campuses, in high street bars and nightclubs, drinking and partying would have been rife. However, when you are growing up in the public eye and paid well for the privilege of being a footballer, society holds you more to account. Different rules apply; different questions are asked of you.

Whether they accept the notion or not, footballers are made to be role models simply by the profession they choose. Their lives away from the pitch are under as much scrutiny as they are when they turn up to play on a Saturday. It is the reality they and other sportsmen and women must face, even more so in these times where the emergence of social media gives instant access to lives of celebrities. Back in September 2001, John Terry and his teammates had fallen into the trap and they were going to pay a big price.

It hit the Chelsea players in the pocket. All four were fined two weeks wages – totaling over £100,000 collectively – with the money being donated by the club to a fund set up to help families of the 9/11 victims.

'Obviously we are condemning their behaviour by fining them. We have acted very quickly in this matter,' said Chelsea's managing director at the time, Colin Hutchinson. 'They were loud between themselves but they, like everyone at the club, have been as hurt and moved by what has happened in the United States as anyone else.

'Their behaviour was totally out of order but there is no way that the players went out to insult or abuse anyone.'

Having only recently signed for Chelsea from West Ham United for £11 million, Lampard was a known name in English football. His dad, Frank Lampard Sr, had been a star for the Hammers during his own playing career and, until the end of the 2000/01 campaign, had been assistant manager to Harry Redknapp at Upton Park.

He at least had some credit to fall back on when it came to his treatment by the press. For Terry it was different. Here was a kid trying to make his name at Chelsea and his introduction to the wider public was giving the impression that he was a hapless youngster more interested in the bright lights than he was his career.

The financial implications of the incident were not the important factor in the outcome of it all. Terry's reputation had been damaged severely and he needed to start turning things around. The task for Terry and Lampard was to do that the only way they knew how – by performing on the pitch.

For Lampard, the immediate aftermath could not have gone any worse when he was sent off against Tottenham Hotspur at White Hart Lane on the weekend the *News of the World* ran its story. Chelsea won the game 3-2, but Lampard was dismissed in the 90th minute for throwing a punch at Spurs defender Chris Perry, who had accused him of diving to try and earn his side a penalty. Terry himself came off injured just before the interval in that game.

It was when the rescheduled fixture with Levski Sofia was eventually played a week later than scheduled when Lampard started to make amends, scoring his first Chelsea goal to make it 3-0. A clean sheet was an equally good start for Terry in that regard.

The following week, Terry opened the scoring in the away leg in Bulgaria to get Chelsea up and running. Eidur Gudjohnsen added a second to bring his tally for the tie up to three having bagged a brace in the first leg.

It was all the culprits of that drunken night at Heathrow who had put Claudio Ranieri's side through to the next round.

Still, it remained an unsettling time. Terry had come so far in his early Chelsea career and after all the positivity surrounding him, now here he was getting caught up in the wrong sort of headlines in the national press. It was not in isolation, either. He would have to suffer further public ignominy before he eventually got the message and cleaned his act up for good.

He was making the mistakes of a young man and doing it in the public eye. He was at the crossroads many young sportsmen find themselves; the decisions he would make in the 2001/02 season would go a long way to shaping his career.

Chelsea: De Goey; Melchiot, Gallas, Terry, Le Saux; Lampard, Jokanovic, Petit (Morris, 30), Zenden; Gudjohnsen, Zola.
Unused subs: Bosnich, Di Cesare, Ferrer, Dalla Bona, Aleksidze, Knight.

Levski Sofia: Petkov; Stankov, Markov, Topuzakov, Stoyanov (Angelov, 80); Guenchev, Ivanov, Golovskoy (Telkiyski, 54), Stoilov, Chilikov (Pantelic, 46), Botelho.
Unused subs: Ivankov, Dragich, Trenchev, Tzvetino.

Chelsea 0-1 Charlton Athletic
Premier League
5 December 2001

John Terry says he does not recall much from when he first wore the captain's armband at Chelsea. 'I remember standing in the tunnel to walk out, but I remember nothing of the game,' he told *Chelsea* magazine in a November 2005 interview.

It is probably for good reason as it was a largely forgettable Chelsea performance all-round against Charlton Athletic. Claudio Ranieri's side should have come away with a victory, but after Eidur Gudjohnsen and Jimmy Floyd Hasselbaink squandered some good chances, Kevin Lisbie's 89th-minute header pulled off an upset.

What Terry does not remember from the game many Chelsea supporters will, as Lisbie's goal came from a free-kick that never was. Oh, the injustice.

Running down the right wing, Lisbie appeared to trip over his own feet, although the linesman flagged for a free-kick, pointing at Celestine Babayaro to suggest he had upended him. Paul Konchesky whipped in a fine ball that Lisbie beat his marker Mario Melchiot to, nodding home beyond Carlo Cudicini.

It was two days before Terry turned twenty-one, so he probably felt mixed emotions with it all – a landmark birthday overshadowed by a landmark occasion that had proved bittersweet.

Terry's career has been defined by moments that parallel each other and being named captain by Ranieri that evening is no different. It was a rite of passage that had long been set out for him since his debut. That it came in the same week as his birthday added to the significance of it all.

It is when turning twenty-one that suddenly boys become men. It is when we begin to view them as adults for the first time and expect something different. There is an emphasis on maturity, acting with a semblance of purpose. Becoming Chelsea captain, despite it being a temporary honour at the time thanks to a Marcel Desailly injury, meant a similar step in Terry's career.

Here was a young kid Chelsea were building the future of the club around and the Charlton game was the beginning of the next phase in that process. That the game ended in defeat held little consequence in the bigger picture.

'Initially it meant so much to me just to break into the side. There were people like Frank Leboeuf, Desailly and Emerson Thome in front of me,' Terry would later say, reflecting on how he started to become a more established presence. 'Then, all of a sudden, we weren't doing so well and Ranieri put me in out of the blue. That was a progressive achievement in itself.'

Ranieri had shown a similar sort of faith in Terry to Gianluca Vialli before him.

Despite being a relative novice in management when he succeeded Ruud Gullit, Vialli had demonstrated some of the wisdom he picked up during his time playing at the highest level in Serie A with the likes of Sampdoria and Juventus.

They were massive clubs – and still are – with Vialli lifting the 1996 Champions League as a Juventus player before he joined Chelsea. He had played for some of the finest managers in Italian football, so it was no surprise some of their principles had rubbed off on him.

Managing Terry's game time was just one aspect of that. Vialli utilised his ability well, bringing him in at different stages to continue that progress. When Ranieri inherited the youngster in September 2000, he knew enough to build on what Vialli had started.

The captaincy against Charlton was a step in the right direction, which was later followed by Terry officially becoming the vice-captain at Stamford Bridge to the experienced Desailly for the 2002/03 season.

'With Franco [Zola] and Graeme [Le Saux] still there, to be given the role and for everyone to be told this is the future of the club was a massive thing,' Terry later explained.

'I dreamed of captaining Chelsea, but first things first, I wanted to get in the side. I wanted to be Chelsea captain in the long-term, but for me there was still some reserve-team football and breaking back in. Never did I dream of captaining Chelsea so soon.'

Despite not being a club in the same mould as that which Terry went on to help forge in the reign of Roman Abramovich as owner, there were still some big figures at Stamford Bridge during his formative years.

Playing reserve football with many of them meant Terry rarely, if ever, got the chance to be a captain until he reached the first team.

'I was always captain at school and in my Sunday team, but not Chelsea,' he said. 'We had quite an experienced reserve side with people like David Rocastle, Mark Stein and Dave Lee. Before the games I felt like a young kid, but once on the pitch I felt confident to boss and demand, shout and organise. I think that was down to those players as well, making me feel confident. They were great for youngsters.

'My dad was always captain [in non-league football], loud on the pitch and bossing people about. That's where I got it from.'

If Terry's dad played such an influence in his attitude on how to captain a group of players, the presence of Desailly helped transform that into the professional game. Having the Frenchman at Chelsea undoubtedly played a big part in where Terry's career would go, which reflects well on Ranieri's judgement at the time.

Again, it was Vialli who had the foresight to bring Desailly to Chelsea after France had lifted the World Cup in 1998, but Ranieri made sure he nurtured what he had inherited from his compatriot, not only utilising 'the Rock' as a defender in his team, but as a mentor to Terry. Making the then twenty-one-year-old vice-captain was all part of it, which Terry would later acknowledge.

'I was watching the way Marcel dealt with things,' he explained. 'If the lads were tired, Marcel would tell the manager, "Ask him to take it easy." There were small things that could be explained to the manager for the benefit of everyone.

'I was still one of the lads. But I think we missed the leadership of Wisey a little bit. Times had changed, but when [Desailly] was playing there was a real leader on the pitch.'

When Bob Dylan had sung years earlier about a revolution in society, there was an air of mystery about things. The 1960s were setting a new course in history where an entire generation opened its mind to new ways of thinking. We were not quite sure where it would lead. The song goes:

> Come writers and critics who prophesise with your pen
> And keep your eyes wide the chance won't come again
> And don't speak too soon for the wheel's still in spin

And there's no tellin' who that it's namin'
For the loser now will be later to win
For the times they are a-changin'.

Indeed, it was the case at Chelsea. It was a new era where a cosmopolitan flavour would define the club's future; players were adapting to a new-found modernity. Right at the heart of Chelsea's core was an English heartbeat, though. There was a figurehead getting ready to lead the way. Terry was stepping forward to take charge, which started against Charlton on a December night in west London.

Chelsea: Cudicini; Melchiot, Gallas, Terry, Babayaro; Jokanovic, Dalla Bona, Lampard, Zenden (Zola, 46); Gudjohnsen (Forssell, 79), Hasselbaink.
Unused subs: De Goey, Keenan, Stanic.

Charlton: Kiely; Young, Fish (Costa, 81), Fortune, Powell; Stuart, Parker, Jensen, Robinson (Konchesky, 3); Johansson (Lisbie, 64), Euell.
Unused subs: Roberts, Bart-Williams.

Norwich City 0-0 Chelsea
FA Cup, Third Round
5 January 2002

Outside of those Chelsea fans that had made the laborious trip down the single-lane roads of the A140 that takes you to Carrow Road, few will remember a goalless draw with Norwich City in the FA Cup in early January 2002.

It was the subsequent replay at Stamford Bridge eleven days later that would capture the imagination. Chelsea thrashed the Canaries 4-0 and Gianfranco Zola scored one of those goals that so endeared him to the Chelsea faithful.

In came the corner from Graeme Le Saux at the perfect height for Zola to leap forward and redirect the ball with the instep of his right foot into the net at the front post to leave Robert Green with no chance. The goalkeeper's reaction dive a few moments after the ball had hit the back of the net was more in vain than an actual attempt at stopping the ball. It was one of those goals that plays through a goalkeeper's mind time and again; Green probably spent days wondering what had happened exactly, whether or not he should have positioned himself better to prevent Zola's audacious attempt from ending up successful. Truth is, there was nothing he could have done better; Zola was a master of his craft and few, if any, goalkeepers would have saved his effort.

It was an outrageous bit of skill from the Italian; the sort of strike that has fans who witnessed it inside Stamford Bridge still regaling even now about where they were stood exactly.

The commentator did not do it justice. His reaction was rather underwhelming in fact, simply describing Zola's effort as a back-heel. It was so much more than that.

'Not a good corner, but it's still turned in by Zola,' he said, completely unaware of what he had just witnessed. When the replay came through, he got a bit more carried way. 'That is sensational. Just look at that!' was his cry.

If Zola has fond memories of the cup tie with Norwich for that reason, John Terry certainly does not. He sat out the replay, but was present for the trip to Norfolk when he came on as a second-half substitute for Marcel Desailly.

A Premier League side travelling to face an opponent in the Championship – or Division One as it was known then – is hardly buying into the romance of the FA Cup. Especially when Norwich themselves had been a Premier League side as recently as 1995. Broadcasters and the wider media want to see Premier League stars forced to turn up at ramshackle stadia in the non-league districts for FA Cup matches, playing on pitches hardly fit for Sunday League, let alone millionaire footballers. They want to see them out of their comfort zone and forced to slum it for ninety minutes.

Norwich were hardly minnows, so unless Nigel Worthington's side walloped the Blues, the headlines would be going elsewhere.

But less than two days before the game, something nasty happened; Terry was caught up in a violent incident outside of a night club and suddenly a routine cup game for Chelsea became big news. The focus now was on Chelsea's rising star and what had occurred away from the pitch.

It was the early hours of 4 January and Terry was out with teammate Jody Morris and Wimbledon player Des Byrne. The trio were celebrating the birth of Morris's child when things took a turn for the worse. According to a report in the *Guardian*, a scuffle had ensued at the Wellington Club, a members-only London nightclub, and bouncer Trevor Thirlwell had been assaulted in the melee. According to the reports, Thirlwell 'suffered severe bruising and swelling to one eye, his cheek and nose. He also needed stitches.'

Terry was just twenty-one at the time and seeing his name on the front pages for all the wrong reasons was a major concern for Chelsea. Here he was, one of England's best young prospects, but he was allowing his life away from the pitch to get in the way of his progress on it. It was in stark contrast to a month earlier when he had worn the armband for the first time.

Subsequently, Terry would not be available for England Under-21s duty until the police investigation and court case were complete, which meant he would miss out on eight months of further development with the Three Lions' youth side.

It was a glare Terry was seemingly becoming familiar with after the incident at Heathrow Airport on 9/11. Before then, the wider football public had not known much about him. Chelsea fans were excited by where his career seemed to be headed, but reports of heavy drinking in September, followed by an alleged scrap at a nightclub so close to a game was not the ideal way for fans outside of the club to be introduced to who this young player was. It questioned his attitude; it raised doubts about his character; it put his professionalism and commitment into doubt.

When he came on as a substitute at Carrow Road, it was that previous Friday morning that dominated conversation. It was not John Terry the rising star and future of English football.

Two years after the event, Terry spoke of how it had impacted his career and frame of mind at the time. Speaking to *Chelsea* magazine, it was clear he regretted putting himself and the club under the spotlight, but vitally, stressed the point that he had learned his lesson in the whole affair.

'It helped me grow up a lot and made me a better man,' he said. 'I still maintain that I didn't do anything wrong that night except for being out two nights before a game. I hold my hands up for that and I've apologised for it.'

It took until August 2002 for the clouds to lift over Terry. From the moment the allegations of assault were put against him, he was living with the thought that a custodial sentence could follow if he was found guilty of any wrongdoing. That would have left his Chelsea career in tatters.

Terry had been accused of glassing Thirlwell in the face and wounding with intent to cause grievous bodily harm. He was also up on an unlawful wounding charge, possessing a bottle as an offensive weapon and affray.

Those are the sort of allegations that can terminate contracts with the biggest clubs. Chelsea were having their patience and belief in the young defender well and truly tested. Coupled with his actions on 9/11, it was not looking good for Terry and his priorities where his career was concerned.

The ongoing legal enquiry from January right through to August would have given Terry plenty to consider in that time. He would have been able to think about what he wanted to achieve at Chelsea and what sort of player he wanted to become. In all of it, though, replacing Desailly at Carrow Road carried a symbolism that should not be lost on where Terry's career would eventually take him.

It would be two years before Terry replaced Desailly as captain, being appointed full-time skipper under Jose Mourinho. Being his replacement that day against Norwich was almost timed perfectly, however. Here he was, up on some serious criminal charges and the following day is sharing a dressing room with a player who was respected across the whole of Europe. Desailly had done it all in football, winning major honours with Marseille, AC Milan and France with the World Cup in 1998 before the European Championship two years later.

Terry was experiencing both sides of the game. On that Thursday evening-cum-Friday morning, he was with players who would not fulfil their potential in the game. Morris's decline is a topic the midfielder has spoken eloquently about since his retirement, but that regret should never have come to define his career. He should have achieved so much more in a Chelsea shirt, but instead his time in west London is spoken of now with conversations that start with 'what if?'

Was Terry going to allow himself to be dragged into that? Or would he show the sense to avoid the bright lights that can appear inviting at first, but are laced with temptations that can devalue careers.

All Terry needed to do was observe Desailly against Norwich. Since his arrival in 1998, he had helped Terry develop his game. The Frenchman had been a mentor off the pitch, helping his younger teammate understand how to conduct himself properly. He had developed Terry on it too, using his experience to good effect to set the example of what a great centre-back needs to be. Now here he was, being replaced by the youngster in the FA Cup at a pivotal time in his career.

Given all that was going on in Terry's life, it was a moment about so much more than that game. It was emblematic for what his career could be: would his legacy be a tale of glory or one of the same caution that is told of Jody Morris? As it transpired, it was Desailly's example that would have the biggest impact.

Come August, Terry was found not guilty of affray and all charges against him were dropped, as they were for Morris. Des Byrne was found guilty on one count, but was not given a custodial sentence.

Speaking through his solicitor, Terry spoke of his relief that the case was over and he could get back to focusing on his career.

'I should have never been charged with these offences,' his solicitor, Desmond da Silva, said on the Chelsea defender's behalf. 'I am angry and upset, I have had this allegation hanging over me for seven months ... I have been training every night and I wish to get back to my preparation for the season ahead.'

A big season it would prove, too. Come the end of 2002/03, Chelsea's fortunes would change for ever.

Norwich City: Green; Kenton, Mackay, Fleming, Drury; McVeigh, Nedergaard (Rivers, 75), Mulryne (Russell, 18); Notman, Holt, Libbra (Llewellyn, 89).
Unused subs: Crichton, Sutch.

Chelsea: Cudicini; Ferrer (Melchiot, 46), Desailly (Terry, 46), Gallas, Babayaro; Dalla Bona, Jokanovic, Le Saux; Zola; Forssell (Lampard, 72), Hasselbaink.
Unused subs: De Goey, Keenan.

West Ham United 2-3 Chelsea
FA Cup, Fourth Round (Replay)
6 February 2002

Leaving West Ham United when he did in 2001 to join Chelsea of all teams, Frank Lampard well and truly burned his bridges at Upton Park. Later quotes about his true feelings for the club and how his dad and uncle Harry Redknapp were treated were not needed. He was already public enemy No. 1 by that time.

Moving across London or any other major city to join a rival has never been a popular move for any player. It is as close to usurping Judas as a hate figure that a sportsman can come by trading one club for a rival.

It is not so much that a player has departed; it is more to do with where he has chosen to go that irks supporters. For Lampard to join Chelsea, West Ham fans could not accept it.

His trips back to east London were always an occasion. Being present at Upton Park, it felt like you were witnessing a moment of importance, such was the vitriol. Lampard's visits were often laced with a hatred and bitterness from the terraces. Lampard had not only departed the Hammers for Chelsea, but he had done it at the right time. While his former club would yo-yo between the top flight and Championship, Chelsea were fighting for major honours.

Indeed, it was instant as Lampard reached the first of five FA Cup finals as a Chelsea player in his first season with the club. And, en route, he was part of the Chelsea side that beat West Ham 3-2 with a 90th-minute goal at the Boleyn Ground to end the Hammers' own cup dream that year. The match winner that night? John Terry.

When Lampard scored his 200th Chelsea goal, that it came against West Ham gave the milestone an added poetry after all that history he has with the club. He had grown up in claret and blue, but had moved on elsewhere to truly achieve his potential. Now he was marking career milestones at their expense.

Hammers fans would not accept that, but every time Lampard lined up against his former team, he would remind them of what they were missing. A mere three times he would be on the losing side against them in Chelsea colours, scoring seven of his 211 Blues goals against them. As if to drive home the point, his last ever game at Upton Park for Chelsea saw Lampard score twice in a 3-0 win. He haunted them.

In the eyes of West Ham supporters, Terry is a similar case to Lampard as he is from Barking. He may not have as rich a history with West Ham as Lampard once did, yet his hometown is very much in the Hammers' heartlands. He should have grown up to be one of them too, but instead he chose Chelsea. His legend has been carved out on the opposite side of London, despite being born as one of West Ham's own.

So when Terry scored his header that beat the Hammers in a fourth round FA Cup replay in 2002, he was not just celebrating winning the game at the death; his attempt to run the length of the pitch and soak it up was about something so much more. The boy had returned 'home' as a man and he was showing it.

It was a period of such great consequence to Terry's career. He had it all going on in his personal life with his court case after his ill-judged night out with Jody Morris and Des Byrne, yet on the pitch the player Claudio Ranieri believed in so much was delivering.

There was no doubting Terry's application or focus. While his indiscipline off the pitch had brought an unwanted spotlight on him, the maturity was there to overcome it. He flirted with the devil and it had not taken him long to realise it was a dangerous game that wasn't worth fighting.

Here Terry was, carving out a different memory for the FA Cup. After all, his indiscretions with Morris had come less than forty-eight hours before a trip to Norwich City for a third-round tie and just over a month to the day since that game, Terry was making headlines in the way he should have been before.

It had been an end-to-end game at Upton Park that night. Twice Jermain Defoe had put the home side ahead – the first deflecting off Terry before Carlo Cudicini helped it in - and twice Chelsea had levelled through Jimmy Floyd Hasselbaink and then Mikael Forssell.

It was the FA Cup and, despite having already met each other three times that season, both sides were going hell for leather. It was a London derby, it was a cup replay, the lights were on and the occasion was there. Neither team wanted to lose.

West Ham could have won it themselves when Don Hutchison saw his header bounce back off the post. The home side lacked that nous in front of goal, though. They were not clinical enough and, as simplistic as it may sound, Chelsea proved they were right at the death.

Mario Stanic thought he had won the game when his goal-bound header looked to be in only for David James to tip it to the other side of the post.

The Hammers had not learned their lesson as, from the resulting corner, it was a Chelsea player who was rising highest to win the ball. It was Terry, getting between two defenders to divert Graeme Le Saux's delivery in off the post. Game over.

Come April, Chelsea were in the FA Cup semi-final where they faced Fulham. Despite the clubs being just two miles apart, The FA insisted they contest the game at Villa Park – some 125 miles away. Thanks to Terry, it was not a wasted journey. Chelsea won the game 1-0 and, like at Upton Park two months earlier, he scored the game's decisive goal to book his team's place in the final.

West Ham United: James; Repka, Schemmel, Dailly, Winterburn; Sinclair, Lomas, Hutchison (Labant, 76), Cole; Defoe, Kitson (Todorov, 82).
Unused subs: Hislop, Foxe, Moncur.

Chelsea: Cudicini; Ferrer, Desailly, Terry, Le Saux; Lampard, Dalla Bona (Forssell, 61), Petit, Stanic; Gudjohnsen (Zola, 61), Hasselbaink.
Unused subs: De Goey, Huth, Jokanovic.

Arsenal 2-0 Chelsea
FA Cup Final
4 May 2002

After the season John Terry had endured, an appearance in an FA Cup final was the ideal way to be ending it.

There had been the drinking session at Heathrow Airport that resulted in fines from the Chelsea hierarchy. A few months after that incident, Terry was caught up in the scrap at a London nightclub that would not be resolved until August. All the while he had a potential custodial sentence hanging over his head, his career hanging in the balance.

Sandwiched between those defining moments away from the pitch was something all the more positive: Terry had made his first appearance as Chelsea captain. Despite the game finishing 1-0 to Charlton Athletic shortly before his twenty-first birthday, it was an indicator for how highly rated he was by Claudio Ranieri. It was another step in his rapidly progressing journey.

For a player of his age, the 2001/02 season had been as much defining as it had a rollercoaster and the ride was not finished there. Chelsea had one last corkscrew to negotiate at the Millennium Stadium in Cardiff, where they faced London rivals Arsenal.

It had been two years since Chelsea's last success in the FA Cup at the old Wembley. Dennis Wise had captained the side that day as the Blues brought down the curtain on the famous old venue. A nineteen-year-old Terry was an unused substitute – just weeks after his loan spell with Nottingham Forest had ended – watching on from the sidelines as Roberto Di Matteo scored the game's decisive goal.

He would be on the bench again in 2002, although this time it was for much different reasons. He was sick with a virus that was affecting his balance, so with injury concerns also surrounding Jimmy Floyd Hasselbaink and Graeme Le Saux, Ranieri had erred on the side of caution and decided three would not be the magic number on cup final day.

Being a substitute in no way reflected Terry's true standing at Stamford Bridge by this stage. From young pretender at Wembley in 2000, he arrived in Cardiff a massive a part of Ranieri's strategy to deny Arsene Wenger's side. His illness was a big blow to Chelsea doing that.

Indeed, Terry would make 47 appearances in all competitions that season, which went a long way in proving the manager's wisdom in allowing Frank Leboeuf to leave Stamford Bridge for Marseille the summer leading into the campaign.

In the five years he had been in west London, Leboeuf had been a major success. Brought in as part of Ruud Gullit's 'sexy football' regime that helped get Chelsea back to winning trophies regularly, the French defender was a big figure. So for Terry to have not only taken his place, but then forced him out of Stamford Bridge, was a significant development.

Marcel Desailly had a new partner in defence and Ranieri was pinning his colours to the mast, making it clear to anyone who would listen that Terry was the future of Chelsea.

However, that future would have to wait a couple of seasons. Arsenal were about to stop Chelsea in their tracks and take home the eighth FA Cup in their history – the second of Wenger's reign as boss.

Comparing where Terry was in his career to the Arsenal side is apt for the position of both clubs at the time. The Gunners were on the cusp of reaching their peak; meanwhile Chelsea, much like their young defender, were still maturing. The Blues had a few more rungs on the ladder to climb before they could be taken seriously as a threat to the leading clubs in England. That number sat at two, with Manchester United and Arsenal enjoying a period of dominance that saw them pass the league title back and forth.

In 2002, it was Arsenal's turn to have temporary charge of the Premier League trophy, meaning victory over Chelsea in Cardiff delivered them a third league and cup double. Only Manchester United can match that record in English football.

Two years after claiming the Double, Arsenal would go the entire 2003/04 league season undefeated. It was the crowning moment of Wenger's tenure, although the team would hit a sharp decline soon after.

Chelsea were up against it, facing a side that had an abundance of flair backed up by substance. Wenger's side was superior in every department, even in Terry's preferred position at centre-back.

In their peak years as individuals, it would be a tough call not to declare a Terry–Desailly partnership a better, more talented option than Tony Adams and Sol Campbell. In 2002, however, Chelsea did not have that luxury; those sorts of bragging rights belonged to Arsenal. Desailly remained a fine defender, yet this was not the AC Milan Desailly, as much as Chelsea fans wanted it to be; it was not peak John Terry from 2004 to 2012, either.

What we witnessed in Cardiff was Chelsea being a taught a lesson in how to win the biggest matches against the best teams. Arsenal's know-how was supreme. They were arriving at a moment when destiny – call it what you will – was serving them. Chelsea were on a learning curve, as was Terry.

Ray Parlour's wonder strike had separated the teams after seventy minutes. It was a goal that came from nowhere; an Arsenal break that finished up with Parlour bending a spectacular long-range effort beyond Carlo Cudicini. Even he looked surprised that he had actually pulled it off. Within ten minutes, Freddie Ljungberg was scoring a carbon copy to kill the game off.

Watching highlight reels of Ljungberg's goal now, hindsight does not offer wisdom after the event, but more surprise at just how effortlessly the Arsenal midfielder shrugs off Terry's challenge. The Chelsea defender bounces off him almost, and is floored. It's not a sight football has grown familiar with. Terry cannot blame the illness that impaired his balance, either. If he is looking for a reason to sum up Ljungberg's superiority in that moment, the answer is more to do with his own shortcomings as a defender than it is Ljungberg's brilliance.

Terry was caught out. He had his positioning all wrong and it meant he had to make up lost ground as he tracked back to cancel out Ljungberg's darting run through the Chelsea backline. By this stage Terry is on his shoulder, not exactly level, but positioned well enough to make an attempt at holding his man up at least. Instead he panics, leaning in with his shoulder in attempt to dispossess Ljungberg as the penalty area approaches. We know what happens next.

The game was stretched by that stage and it had given a sense of inevitability that another Arsenal goal would be forthcoming. Terry could have done more to prevent it, regardless. We know that now, as he made a career out of doing exactly what he should have against Arsenal.

That perceived lack of pace has only damaged Terry at times in his career when he allowed it to. When something similar happened against Robin van Persie – again, an Arsenal player – in October 2011, it was for the same reasons that Ljungberg had got free. Terry was punching down on the panic alarm and it got the better of him. He had lost his nerve.

A sign of Terry's quality is that seldom did that ever happen in his career. He made mistakes and errors in judgement. Rather than define him, he learned from them. He did what every great player has to: he got better.

Arsenal: Seaman; Lauren, Campbell, Adams, Cole; Parlour, Vieira, Ljungberg; Bergkamp (Edu, 72); Henry (Kanu, 81), Wiltord (Keown, 89).
Unused subs: Wright, Dixon.

Chelsea: Cudicini; Melchiot (Zenden, 76), Gallas, Desailly, Babayaro (Terry, 45); Gronkjaer, Lampard, Petit, Le Saux; Gudjohnsen, Hasslebaink (Zola, 68).
Unused subs: De Goey, Jokanovic.

MSK Zilina 0-2 Chelsea
UEFA Champions League, Play-Off
13 August 2003

The pressure was on at Chelsea. The manager felt it. The players felt it. The rest of the Premier League felt it.

Roman Abramovich came in with his fortune and in a matter of weeks was changing the landscape of English football. From Premier League also-rans who had squeezed into the top four on the final day of the previous campaign, suddenly Chelsea were expected to challenge to the last in 2003/04. The dominant clubs at the time, Manchester United and Arsenal, were not going to have things all their own way while the Abramovich regime was around.

The ethos that would drive the recruitment strategy was a simple one: if the players Chelsea already had were not good enough, they would simply buy better ones. The same applied to the manager. Everyone was on high alert, their position under the microscope.

'I remember being at home and seeing it on the news [that Abramovich had purchased the club from Ken Bates]. I didn't really know what to make of it at the time, but it is one of those days that I look back on now and realise the significance of,' John Terry would later reveal.

The summer of 2003 really was a new beginning for the Premier League. We had been used to rich clubs and their owners in the past, but this was different. Abramovich was on another level to anything the league and English football had ever seen. In fact, the Russian was unique across Europe when we consider the lengths he would go to make Chelsea an established force among the elite.

Today, it is not unusual for the extremely wealthy to invest in football as a means of earning fame within the media and among their peers. Being the owner of a football club is the ultimate status symbol. It was Abramovich who started it all off in the modern era.

What has struck up a bond with Chelsea supporters and the club's owner is the way he has gone about his business. There have been decisions regarding managers that not all fans would have agreed with – think the appointment of Rafa Benitez, not least sacking some popular faces – yet overall Abramovich's relationship with those on the terraces is a healthy one.

The Glazer family could only dream of having a similar bond with their fans at Old Trafford. We have witnessed the green and gold protests in more recent times that have taken the focus away from the football, putting it firmly on the boardroom. It has been fuelled by how their purchase of the club was financed and what their ownership means for the club's long-term future. It has created a palpable discord, some might say.

Indeed, even a whole new football club has been spawned in protest at the Glazer's perceived actions. FC United of Manchester are a supporter-ran club aimed at maintaining the values many believe have been lost under the Glazers' ownership of Manchester United.

Whether those fans are protesting against anything as profoundly immoral as they suggest is a matter of opinion. Despite the Glazers owning the club outright since 2005, United have gone on to win the Champions League and multiple Premier League titles, not to mention some lavish spending sprees of their own that not only rival Abramovich's early forays into the transfer market, but also top them. Still, the fans remain unconvinced about their intentions, given the debt United have been straddled with.

It is a different story in west London, where Abramovich has funded Chelsea's rapid rise from his own pocket to the tune of over £1 billion. It is quite remarkable. It all started in 2003 when Chelsea had just booked their place in the Champions League for the following season.

Whether it was the view from his helicopter as he flew over London, or the appeal of owning some prime real estate just off the glamorous King's Road, Abramovich took the plunge with Chelsea and has not looked back since. He has not done it by half measures, either. The Russian has not flinched, at times seemingly operating with an open cheque book when it comes to bringing in some of the best players in world football.

His wealth has trickled down the leagues of the English game, too. For instance, West Ham United made £12 million on player sales to Chelsea in 2003 when Glenn Johnson and Joe Cole moved to west London. The Hammers had not long been relegated from the top flight – they lost their Premier League status on the same day Chelsea were beating Liverpool to finish in the top four in 2003 – and Abramovich's money that financed those player sales was desperately needed to get them back up the following campaign.

Blackburn Rovers, Charlton Athletic and Southampton would share £34 million in transfer fees during Abramovich's first season at Chelsea, too. Those three clubs alone would sign players from the likes of Millwall, Huddersfield Town, Nottingham Forest, Leicester City, Birmingham City, Oldham Athletic and Brentford with the proceeds.

It was an exciting summer for all in football. Chelsea were getting the biggest slice of the pie, yet it was allowing others to reshuffle and strengthen in places they perhaps had not considered pre-Abramovich.

Despite spending over £150 million in that inaugural summer, the Russian would miss Chelsea's first competitive game of his tenure, however. It came away to MSK Zilina from Slovenia and Chelsea folklore has it that Abramovich watched from his yacht that was moored off the Alaskan coastline.

The game was a Champions League play-off and Chelsea would cruise to victory thanks to Eidur Gudjohnsen and a Michal Drahno own goal.

At the time, a game of this nature would have been far from the minds of broadcasters. With or without Abramovich, Chelsea would have been expected to defeat minnows Zilina and reach the Champions League proper. It was only a potential giant-killing that would have spiked interest and, lest we forget, some of Chelsea's biggest names of the twenty-first century were already at the club before the Russian had arrived, notably Frank Lampard and the homegrown John Terry. As a news story, Chelsea facing Zilina was not exactly top billing until Abramovich came on the scene.

Such was the interest his arrival would have, BBC Sport purchased the rights just so they could proudly be the first broadcaster to get a glimpse of this new-look Chelsea team. Now broadcast deals and sports channels needing to justify increasing subscriptions fees invariably tack on the 'super' tag in front of the most minor of matches; but this game sat on the dawn of those times. It predated the bidding wars and spectacle the Champions League has become, so the BBC were able to act fast for a major summer signing of their own.

The buzz around Abramovich was not just a media phenomenon. The Chelsea players were attempting to digest it all as well.

'That first pre-season, we were all texting each other about what players were going to come in and stuff like that; I think that was probably the first thing the fans thought of,' Terry explained.

'However, from our point of view, it was a case of, "Who are they going to bring in and is your place in jeopardy?" Then we came back to training, with all the new signings there, and we realised how good they were. The standard in training went from being good to being very good on a daily basis.'

Suddenly those regular spots at Stamford Bridge were not there. Some players had left for their summer holidays feeling confident of their place, but would return to find it was no longer the norm to expect Claudio Ranieri to make their lives easy. This was a new Chelsea and even a young hopeful coming through with his eyes on the captain's armband was going to have to raise his game.

'When we had a big squad of players after the summer of 2003, it meant that you could be in and out of the side from one week to the next,' Terry would tell *Chelsea* magazine. 'So, you had to be performing at the highest level every day to be selected for the next game.'

Ranieri was suddenly the envy of Europe. Chelsea were snatching players from Real Madrid and Inter Milan. It was fantasy football in the third dimension.

'I remember playing in the first game of the 2003/04 season,' Terry added. 'We won 2-0 away to Zilina and put ourselves in a good position to go through to the Champions League group stage.

'A couple of players were left out and they were a bit taken aback by it, but they came back into the fold soon after. I think it took a few games just to find out what the best team and the best squad was for the club.'

What Ranieri did not need clarification on was who his defence was being built around. He had the money to potentially buy any defender in the world. He could have chased a glamorous name like his compatriot Fabio Cannavaro, who at the time was in his prime and one of the world's finest defensive talents; the manager could have gone for any number of bona fide established stars. However, he did not; he continued to show his faith in Terry from the outset. His faith in what the young Englishman could offer the club did not falter in the slightest.

The first game of the Abramovich era was the beginning of the end for Ranieri at Chelsea. Not because the performance would damage the club or show his perceived shortcomings as a manager; Chelsea would cruise through to the group stage and even make it to the Champions League semi-final that year so, on paper at least, the Italian was on-message with the club's expectations.

It was the start of his time as custodian of the manager's seat in the Stamford Bridge dugout, though. Gradually, the intensity surrounding his future would build and come the end of the season, he would depart the club.

It would not be until May 2016 that Ranieri would be seen – in an official capacity at least – back at Stamford Bridge, when he returned as the boss of the recently crowned Premier League champions Leicester City.

The game was as much part of the Foxes celebration tour to see out the season as it was a potential farewell to Terry, who at the time was yet to sign the contract extension that would keep him in west London for the 2016/17 season.

From up and coming star against Zilina in 2003, the thirteen years since then had seen him become one of the most significant figures in Chelsea's history. So it was inevitable that journalists would quiz Ranieri for his thoughts on the player he had helped put on the path to greatness despite the temptation to spend big elsewhere.

'John Terry, you know him as my son,' Ranieri would tell the gathered press pack. 'I believed in him when he was young. I put him in the team when there were a couple of champions of the world and European champions at Chelsea like Marcel Desailly and Frank Leboeuf. But I played John as, for me, it was better to put him in the squad. He made a fantastic career.'

Trophies were not on the line in August 2003; it was something far more significant. It was Chelsea futures and as the club took shape that season, leading into Jose Mourinho's revolution, Terry would become the man everything was built around.

MSK Zilina: Trabalik; Konecny, Stas (Drahno, 65), Labant, Zabavnik; Bazik, Durica (Putik, 66), Strba, Sninsky, Barcik; Varadin (Fabus, 82).
Unused subs: Rzeszoto, Klago, Kosmel, Cervenec.

Chelsea: Cudicini; Johnson, Desailly, Terry, Bridge; Geremi, Veron, Lampard, Duff (J. Cole, 69); Forssell (Gronkjaer, 57), Gudjohnsen.
Unused subs: Huth, Ambrosetti, Melchiot, C. Cole, Hasselbaink.

Arsenal 1-2 Chelsea
UEFA Champions League Quarter-Final
6 April 2004

The curtain was close to coming down on the first season of Roman Abramovich's ownership of Chelsea when they were paired with Arsenal in the Champions League quarter-final. We had grown used to the Russian's outbursts of emotion from the director's box all year, with Abramovich seemingly living every kick of every game, punching the air in delight whenever Chelsea scored. Indeed, it was that regular an occurrence that television broadcasters seemed to have a camera honed in on Abramovich wherever he travelled, just to ensure they did not miss a celebration or gasp of disbelief.

When the Champions League draw was made, Abramovich's reaction would have no doubt been the same as what we had seen from the moment Juan Sebastian Veron had stroked home the first Premier League goal of the Abramovich era against Liverpool at Anfield. The Russian would have been beaming from ear to ear, relishing a massive occasion with the eyes of Europe on his club.

It was because of the Champions League that Abramovich had fallen in love with football in the first place. We are told that it was when watching Manchester United take on Real Madrid in 2003 that Abramovoich was inspired to buy a football club. Now here he was very much in the thick of it all just twelve months later.

For neutrals, the Chelsea versus Arsenal tie whet the appetite just as much. This was two of England's biggest clubs coming head-to-head in Europe at such a late stage and the winner would arguably be favourites to go on and win the competition given that Porto, Monaco and Deportivo La Coruna would all reach the semi-finals – three clubs who could not match the wealth of stars Chelsea and Arsenal could showcase.

No London club had competed in a European Cup final at this stage either, let alone win the competition, so there was so much more than a city rivalry on the line. This was about history, or at least the chance to go one step further at attempting to make it.

It had already been a fruitful campaign from a Chelsea perspective, with hundreds of millions of pounds spent on new players to complement those who were already at the club. Indeed, Claudio Ranieri had managed that side of things rather well given the circumstances. All that money had been spent, yet the Italian had done it as wisely as anyone could when they were suddenly given the keys to the vault of the Central Bank of Russia.

Ranieri was spending lavishly, although the club's business in the transfer market came with a sense of rational thinking not overly associated with the concept of fantasy football.

Despite the fortune he had at his disposal, Ranieri had not allowed it to push his better players to one side. Eidur Gudjohnsen, Frank Lampard and John Terry were all in the Chelsea first team pre-Abramovich and they remained so in that first season, as did goalkeeper Carlo Cudicini and an ageing Marcel Desailly.

The face of Chelsea was changing, only Ranieri was not totally ripping the soul out of the club in the name of progress. Instead he was adding improvements in the key areas where they needed it, notably by signing wide-man Damien Duff and adding Joe Cole's flair to the attack. Ranieri also brought in Claude Makelele from Real Madrid to strengthen Chelsea's defensive midfield.

It was those sorts of decisions that would serve Chelsea well in the coming seasons, regardless of the fact Ranieri was not there to benefit from them. For all the shortcomings he had and would show in certain areas of his managerial approach, Ranieri's strengths in identifying talent and nurturing it was proving as vital to Chelsea as Abramovich's vast fortune.

At the same time as they were grabbing headlines on the continent, Chelsea were also ready to break up the Manchester United–Arsenal monopoly at the top of English football.

They would not go the whole way to doing that by winning the Premier League, but beating United into second behind Arsenal's Invincibles was an accomplishment enough.

Chelsea had ticked a lot of the boxes. They had remained undefeated against United that season, beating them at Stamford Bridge before drawing 1-1 at Old Trafford in the final stages of the campaign. Overall, they were becoming harder to beat and in Europe the Blues were making progress. Not since 1999/2000 had Chelsea been a Champions League club, yet here they were in the quarter-final again.

Back in 2000 it was the might of Barcelona that proved their undoing. Four years on, it was Arsenal standing in their way at the same stage – a side that Chelsea had lost to three times already that season.

On each occasion that they met in the league and FA Cup, Arsene Wenger's men had the know-how to beat Chelsea. They were a slicker unit, more ruthless in every department and had the look of a side that knew victory was not going to be too far off for them against the Blues. That trio of games finished 2-1 on each occasion – they met twice within a week in February and it was the same outcome every time – so Arsenal were the overwhelming favourites in the Champions League. An away goal in the first leg of the quarter-final at Stamford Bridge made them even more so when Chelsea arrived at Highbury a fortnight later.

The pendulum was getting ready to swing in a different direction, though. There is only so much losing elite players can suffer and Chelsea's team of budding stars had finally tasted enough. They were ready to turn the page on this rivalry and set things on a different course.

When Jose Antonio Reyes scored the game's opening goal on the stroke of half-time, the sentiments of Chelsea fans would not have been as positive. After all, Chelsea had not beaten Arsenal in any of the fifteen games the clubs had contested since the turn of the century. Going behind to Arsenal usually meant one thing: defeat.

Psychologically, the goal would change nothing for Chelsea, however. Their task remained the same regardless of Reyes' strike; they had gone to Highbury needing to cancel out Robert Pires' away goal from the first leg and with the score now 2-1 on aggregate, their task remained the same. They needed an away goal of their own.

Perhaps it was that mindset that allowed Chelsea to turn things around the way they did. There was no pressure unless Arsenal scored a second. That is when the tie would have been slipping away from them, when all would have felt like it was being lost. At this moment, they were still in it.

If it was not making light of their predicament, then it was Ranieri's half-time team talk that got them inspired as, within six minutes of the restart, Frank Lampard had pulled the visitors level. It was more than game on now – Chelsea were in the ascendancy.

When Makelele had lined up his shot from 30 yards, few people would have screamed for him to follow through with his intensions. It was a hands-over-the-eyes moment, a time to scream at the French midfielder and ask what on earth he was thinking. He needed some sense shaken into him. Strikes from range were not his forte unless he was closing down the space to stop them being launched at the Chelsea goal. This was uncommon ground at a time when Chelsea needed familiarity to overcome their foe.

Rather than hitting the back of Highbury's Clock End, Makelele's effort was more controlled than even he had probably anticipated. He got his head over it, arrowing his effort right into the corner of Jens Lehmann's goal. The best the Arsenal goalkeeper could do was parry the ball right into the danger zone where Lampard had done what every kid playing under-10s football is told by his manager: he followed up in the hope of a loose ball. He had a tap in.

Rivalries are dominated on such turning points in matches. Chelsea were beginning to believe they had the beating of Arsenal. Lampard had started it and it would be Wayne Bridge scoring his best goal in a Chelsea shirt that would finish it.

The left-back would not register a more important goal in his entire career, but it was the execution under such pressure that should be marvelled. His approach play was excellent, linking up with Eidur Gudjohnsen for a one-two inside the Arsenal box before smashing his shot low and hard into the far right corner.

With just three minutes remaining on the clock, there was only going to be one winner. Arsenal needed two goals to go through and they were never coming. They were beaten. Chelsea were knocking them out of Europe.

Now, when Jose Mourinho would eventually arrive as Chelsea boss three months later, this rivalry between Chelsea and Arsenal would gradually intensify. With a genuine disliking between both Arsene Wenger and Mourinho, the hatred between the clubs was fuelled by the managers.

Mourinho never lost a competitive game to Wenger in his two spells as Chelsea manager (although in 2015 Chelsea did lose the Community Shield 1-0, a game that is technically a friendly) and he would use that statistic to very openly goad his opposite number in public. He would talk of Wenger being a 'specialist in failure'.

Mourinho well and truly left his footprint on the fixture, yet it was with Ranieri when the winds of change started to blow. As much as he was the face of the old Chelsea, it was Chelsea's future that was leading them on the pitch that night at Highbury. In the absence of Desailly, who had been sent off in the first leg, John Terry was wearing the armband to lead Chelsea into battle.

It was all very Dickensian. The time of year was a few months out, yet Chelsea fans were being taken by a reassuring hand and guided through the club's past, present and future. They were seeing it play out before them and the result was one that would not stand out in isolation over the next decade.

Chelsea turned up at Highbury with the world writing them off and they did the impossible. They were the only English team to beat the Invincibles in any competition in London that season. It was a feeling Arsenal would have to get used to when Terry was wearing the armband in a full-time capacity.

As for Chelsea, before Mourinho's arrival and Terry's chance to fulfill his destiny, they were going to Monaco.

Arsenal: Lehmann; Luren, Campbell, Toure, Cole; Pires, Vieira, Edu, Ljungberg; Reyes, Henry (Bergkamp, 81).
Unused subs: Stack, Clichy, Keown, Silva, Wiltord.

Chelsea: Ambrosio; Melchiot, Gallas, Terry, Bridge; Parker (Gronkjaer, 46), Makelele, Lampard; Gudjohnsen, Hasselbaink (Cole, 82), Duff (Crespo, 82).
Unused subs: Sullivan, Huth, Geremi, Mutu.

10

Monaco 3-1 Chelsea
UEFA Champions League, Semi-Final
20 April 2004

From the wild scenes of celebration at Highbury to the heartbreak of the Stade Louis II, Chelsea would prove the masters of their own downfall in the 2003/04 Champions League. Just when it all seemed so promising.

For John Terry and Frank Lampard, their cruel, bittersweet love affair with the European Cup was getting started. The tone was set. It would be a journey defined by heartbreak. Whenever the pair thought they were on the cusp of glory, it would be ruthlessly snatched from them and another group of players would get to revel in the success they thought would belong to them. They would experience six Champions League semi-finals together and this was the first.

For all the money that Roman Abramovich has invested into Chelsea, the club stands as a shining example that success at the highest level cannot be bought. Well, not always at least. Chelsea have suffered enough pain to understand that and in the club's new era of wealth, they came crashing back down to earth against Monaco.

With Jose Mourinho's Porto defeating Deportivo La Coruna in the other semi-final that season, there is every reason to suggest Chelsea would not have won the Champions League regardless of what happened to them against Monaco.

Mourinho's side were UEFA Cup winners a year earlier and, after beating Manchester United in March, there was something about their own pursuit of the Champions League that was gathering momentum to suggest destiny had picked them this year.

The manager had that aura about him and it was infectious. As Terry and Lampard would soon experience themselves, Mourinho had a contagious energy that fed his players and they all feasted on it.

That was Porto in 2003/04: a side thriving on Mourinho's will to win and create shockwaves across the continent. Mourinho was redefining the fault lines of European football. Regardless of names and reputations, the richest club of the four remaining in the Champions League still had a major hurdle, despite the stars appearing to align in their favour.

How Chelsea could have done with Mourinho a few months earlier than when they actually got him. With Mourinho pulling the strings on the sidelines, there is every reason to suspect Chelsea would have been in Gelsenkirchen for the Champions League final. Instead they were defeated by a ten-man Monaco and Claudio Ranieri had sealed his fate as Chelsea boss (if it was ever in doubt).

It had been going so well. Despite Dado Prso's opener, Chelsea had hit right back at Monaco through Hernan Crespo to give them an away goal and leave the game tied at 1-1. As it stood, Chelsea were in command.

When Akis Zikos was sent off after fifty-three minutes for fouling Claude Makelele, Chelsea's grip on proceedings was supposed to tighten all the more. Here they were, a man to the good with Lampard, Eidur Gudjohnsen and Crespo taunting the opposition.

Then something peculiar happened. From nowhere, Ranieri lost his nerve. Chelsea imploded.

The sight of Jimmy Floyd Hasselbaink limbering up just past the hour mark gave the impression that Chelsea were ready to go for it. Monaco were seemingly on their knees and Ranieri was going to strike now to get the tie over and done with. But he replaced Mario Melchiot at right-back and Chelsea looked confused. Hasselbaink? At right-back?

It got better – or worse, depending on your preference – when Robert Huth was then introduced to replace Scott Parker. Hasselbaink was moved further forward to right wing, with Huth, a central defender not ever known for his ability on the flanks, now at right-back. Chelsea had lost their shape and were about to pay for it.

The players were looking to the bench puzzled, not sure of what was going on. Ranieri could have used Joe Cole and Geremi to occupy the positions of his substitutes, but instead opted for players with limited experience of the roles they were being asked to play. All this in a Champions League semi-final.

It was the biggest game of the manager's career; the biggest game arguably in Chelsea's history and Monaco were about to mark it in infamy thanks to the manager's bizarre tinkering.

Out of shape and out of hope, Chelsea found themselves 2-1 down on seventy-eight minutes, despite their numerical advantage when it came to players on the field. That fact mattered little to Fernando Morientes and it was the case with Shabani Nonda, who fired home Monaco's third on the night to complete an amazing turnaround in fortunes. From the depths of despair thirty minutes earlier, the French were now on the brink of a Champions League final.

When they visited London for the second leg, Monaco did something similar to Chelsea. They dangled the carrot by allowing Chelsea to race into a two-goal lead (at that stage Chelsea were going through thanks to their away goal), but Hugo Ibarra's strike right on half-time cancelled out that advantage.

'That changed the match,' Ranieri would say afterwards. 'If the first half had finished 2-0 for us, it would have been another match in the second.'

He was right. The timing of Ibarra's goal, coming so close to the interval and also in the immediate aftermath of Lampard making it 2-0 on the night, had taken the stuffing out of Chelsea.

He was deflecting from the point, though. In the context of the tie, it was already lost in Monaco when the manager unsettled his team to the point that a side with fewer players was not only able to outplay them, but score twice.

Chelsea were on the ropes after that. They were staggering for the rest of the game, the return leg included. Ranieri had brought about a self-inflicted vulnerability that a striker of Morientes' quality would punish at some point. He did it inside the Stade Louis II when he put Monaco ahead in the tie and he repeated his exploits at Stamford Bridge, scoring the equaliser to make it 2-2 on the night, 5-3 on aggregate. That really was the final nail in the coffin.

Ranieri was attempting to appear philosophical about it all, but John Terry's mindset was all the more different. His mentality was solely about winning and Chelsea had just blown their best chance at doing that.

'It's not good enough not winning anything but we need to forget the game as soon as possible.' Terry reflected. He was again wearing the armband due to Desailly's absence, suffering the first major disappointment of his time as a Chelsea captain.

'Even before Roman Abramovich took over everyone wanted to win things and I'm no different. At the end of my career the only thing that I want to have is trophies – one being the league title and second the Champions League. As a player you dream of winning things and when you don't it's frustrating.'

Terry was not calling for the manager's head, nor was he intentionally undermining Ranieri's position. Yet his desire to win things was reflected by the club. Abramovich had not spent the money he had at this stage just to be entertained; his desire was to be winning things regularly and to be as powerful in sport as he was in business. Not only was he investing in players to bring that about, he was also bringing in some of football's lead executives to do it, such as Peter Kenyon. He was attempting to create a behemoth and the only way to do that in football is by delivering silverware. That's where the fault lines of power are truly established.

Abramovich needed a manager who was equally on-message and the debacle of Monaco had confirmed about Ranieri what had long since been reported in the press – that the owner did not trust him with the keys to his kingdom.

Terry wanted to win things. Chelsea wanted to win things. It was not going to happen with Ranieri at the helm.

Monaco: Roma; Ibarra, Givet, Rodriguez, Evra; Bernardi, Zikos, Rothen (Plasil, 89), Giuly (Nonda, 82); Morientes, Prso (Cisse, 57).
Unused subs: Sylva, Oshadogan, El Fakiri, Adebayor.

Chelsea: Ambrosio; Melchiot (Hasselbaink, 62), Desailly, Terry, Bridge; Parker (Huth, 69), Makelele, Lampard, Gronkjaer (Veron, 46); Crespo, Gudjohnsen.
Unused subs: Sullivan, Geremi, Cole, Mutu.

11

Chelsea 1-0 Leeds United
Premier League
15 May 2004

There was a time when Chelsea fans really cared about facing Leeds United. Like so many rivalries in football, it was born out of some nasty scraps in the past. On the pitch and the terraces, Chelsea and Leeds had not got along in the 1960s and 1970s. Well, that is the polite way of putting it at least.

Norman Hunter was the enforcer at Elland Road in his pomp, while Chelsea had Ron Harris. Neither took prisoners, so when they met things would be turned up a notch.

In the 1970 FA Cup final, tales spoken of over forty years since the game often revolve around the scraps than they do the actual football. That says plenty, too, given the wonderful Peter Osgood header that had drawn Chelsea level in the replay at Old Trafford.

The goal is proof of the sense of telepathy that existed between Chelsea's No. 9 and Charlie Cooke. The cross from the latter to pick out Osgood in the box was perfection, with Cooke instinctively knowing how his teammate would drift off his marker to the back post to score.

Osgood had picked the ball up inside the centre circle before passing to Ian Hutchinson. The striker then disappears from the television screen – he is off, stage left, waiting for his cue. When Cooke takes possession off Hutchinson, he hardly looks up. He just drops his shoulder and makes his move past the Leeds players attempting to track him. Then he crosses for Osgood to do the rest.

'And Osgood! A wonderful goal! A fantastic strike by Chelsea,' the commentator declares.

In this age of social media trends, there would not be enough retweets or likes that would do it justice. That Osgood header is one of the finest scored by a Chelsea player in a pivotal moment of the club's history. Osgood was such a special talent.

That game was the sort of clash we remember between Chelsea and Leeds. There was often a sense occasion around them. So it proved on the final day of the 2003/04 campaign for wholly different reasons.

There were not any battles this time. In fact, the football was largely forgettable with Jesper Gronkjaer's goal after twenty minutes, giving Chelsea all three points.

It had been twelve months earlier when the Dane was scoring on the final day at Stamford Bridge against Liverpool to secure a Champions League place. That is the goal many will point to as saving Chelsea's future, given the financial ruin that sat on the horizon. We all know what happened next with Roman Abramovich's arrival.

This time out, a goal against Leeds was far less needed. Being coached by legend Eddie Gray – who incidentally was on the losing side against Chelsea in that 1970 cup final replay – Leeds were already relegated from the Premier League.

Before Chelsea's own financial collapse was even hinted at, Leeds themselves had succumbed to the bank manager and it meant the club would nosedive. From a Champions League semi-final in 2001, they were playing second-tier football within three years. They lost their stars and even that could not cover the overheads.

Chelsea had bigger things on their minds in May 2004, though. Leeds' plight was not their issue to contend with, but the position of manager Claudio Ranieri most certainly was.

The Italian had been forced to front his Chelsea future on an almost weekly basis since the turn of the year. The newspapers had a sniff of Abramovich wanting to replace him and would not relent. At every press conference, journalists would up the ante, probing for a response from Ranieri to give them confirmation either way. From being described as the Tinker Man, it was soon headlines of Ranieri being a dead man walking.

It seemed inevitable he would eventually lose his job at Chelsea. If he could have somehow toppled Arsenal's Invincibles to the title, it may well have given him a stay of execution. The common consensus is not even that would have been enough to keep his head off the block.

As it turned out, Chelsea could not prevent Arsenal becoming champions for a third time under Arsene Wenger and Ranieri would be the biggest casualty of that fact.

'No one knew but everyone had a good idea it was his last game [against Leeds],' Terry once recalled.

'He'd been great for me but also for a lot of players at the time, so on the spur of the moment I got them to form the tunnel and we clapped him [out onto the pitch]. I'll never forget that he gave me my first chance at Chelsea.'

Chelsea were not finishing the campaign as champions, but Ranieri was being given an impromptu send off as though they had. As Terry explained, it was all his doing.

A guard of honour is something unique to British football. It is a part of the game that provides a real sense of pride and honour in those who take part in it and follow the game. It is a sign of respect for newly crowned league champions; a pause for thought to acknowledge a team's achievements over the course of the season.

Things were ending for Ranieri and despite not being Chelsea captain – those duties still belonged to Marcel Desailly at the time – Terry was not willing to let a chance pass for him to thank Ranieri for how he had progressed his career.

'We'd been celebrating with him at Manchester United the previous game when we had secured second in the table, and I was thinking this is what it's all about. The fans showed their appreciation to Claudio, too.'

John Terry was just twenty-three at the time and it had been under Ranieri's watch that he had come to the fore in Chelsea reckoning. The Italian had started to build Chelsea around him, developing what was raw talent into something far more substantial.

Reflected on the pitch in a Chelsea shirt, Terry was making plenty more of it away from the game. He was becoming so much more than a footballer.

We see it plenty in football where new managers turn their back on the work of their predecessors. The ego can be too prevalent, clouding the judgement of the man who has replaced another in the hot seat. Managers are headstrong, believing firmly that their way will always be best to progress a club. Picking up where Gianluca Vialli left off with Terry, Ranieri proved his wisdom. The Italian had observed the work of his compatriot and could see the value in how Vialli had promoted from within.

It is that same quality Ranieri has been lauded for in more recent times. Rather than strip Leicester City back and rebuild the team in his vision, he adapted to the foundations that had been laid before his arrival. There were some tweaks along the way, yet ultimately it was the players signed under Nigel Pearson's watch that won the Foxes the unlikeliest of Premier League titles in 2015/16 season.

Fittingly for Ranieri, perhaps, the season would end at Stamford Bridge with another guard of honour. This time it was more for his players than the man himself, but the sentiment was there given all he had achieved in west London. He hadn't stocked the trophy cabinet with silverware, but Chelsea took something worth so much more from him – they inherited their most successful captain.

In May 2004, all that was yet to come. Terry could not have predicted where his career was headed, but he could not let the chance pass without thanking the man who had helped put him in a position to dream about where it might go.

Chelsea: Cudicini; Johnson (Stanic, 82), Gallas, Terry (Huth, 85), Bridge; Melchiot, Makelele, Lampard (Nicholas, 89); Gronkjaer, Gudjohnsen, Cole.
Unused subs: Ambrosio, Crespo.

Leeds United: Carson; Kelly, Duberry, Radebe, Harte; Milner, Richardson, Matteo, Wilcox (Pennant, 61), Olembe (Barmby, 80); Smith.
Unused subs: Allaway, Kilgallon, McPhail.

12

Chelsea 1-0 Manchester United
Premier League
15 August 2004

It's a line often repeated that Premier League titles are not won in August. Or are they? John Terry found himself asking that question after just the first game of the 2004/05 season.

Jose Mourinho had been appointed Blues boss that summer and the culture around Chelsea was dramatically changed as a result.

'I'm not one from the bottle,' Mourinho had declared at his unveiling, 'I am a special one.'

Mourinho's approach would shake up the Premier League. Fresh from winning the Champions League with Porto, he arrived with a swagger that whiffed of success. He cared for nothing, especially the fact that Sir Alex Ferguson and Arsene Wenger were the statesmen of English football.

The duo were the Premier League's alpha males and they did not take too kindly to any of their peers having ideas deemed above their station. They had the ammunition to end any wars that others started, so if you had the stomach for a battle, you needed to see it through. And you had best come armed to the teeth.

Claudio Ranieri had gone some way to testing that resolve when his Chelsea side had finished second the season before Mourinho's arrival. It was the first campaign of the Roman Abramovich-era Chelsea, but coming up against Arsenal's season of the Invincibles, the best the Blues could achieve was a runners-up spot.

Still, they finished ahead of Ferguson's United, which was progress in itself. Only once since 1997 had the top two not been a Manchester United–Arsenal double. Liverpool had achieved that in 2002. They did not have the stamina to sustain it, however. A year later they were finishing back in fifth, being pipped to the fourth and final Champions League spot by Ranieri's Chelsea.

It was that summer when Abramovich arrived, changing the landscape overnight. Suddenly Chelsea were dictating the transfer market, fuelled by the oil riches of their Russian owner. That meant the stakes were that bit higher for the man in the hot-seat.

The dominance from United and Arsenal was clear, but Ranieri's task was about so much more than simply breaking it up. He needed to crush it and the only way of achieving that would be to win the title. The Italian was close, but it was not good enough – not when Chelsea had spent over £150 million on players in the process.

That sort of investment required a manager who not only had the acumen to outwit opponents, but one with the bravado to champion the whole ideal. It needed a special one so Abramovich appointed the one coach who had no problem labeling himself as such.

Mourinho knew full well what the implications were when he sat inside the media room of Stamford Bridge for that first press conference. Chelsea had that odour that only new money gives off; it breeds a feeling of animosity among some that is influenced by primal feelings of jealousy.

Spending the way they did to attack the established elite, Chelsea were looked at with eyes of envy. They were seen as the cocky new kid on the block and those in the playground did not like it. Mourinho was there to tell them all they did not have to, but they would be forced to lump it.

As much as he was making a statement to the rest of the Premier League that day, Mourinho knew his players would be watching. Before he had even met them, the manager was setting the tone for how the new Chelsea would be under him. That would either breed confidence in the squad or send some running for the hills. Those who fell in the latter bracket would be no use to him anyhow.

'Jose brought that feeling that if you lost in training it meant something; if you lost a competitive game, it was huge – that was the weekend ruined,' John Terry once recalled, speaking of the impact Mourinho made on the dressing room in west London.

'That was the mentality he brought with him and that other players who came in having already won trophies at other clubs brought with them.

'The aim was to get to finals and win competitions, to push for trophies and to push each other as well – Maka [Claude Makelele], for example, was brilliant at that. We had this extra enthusiasm around the place and the feeling of winning and losing was on a different scale.

'When I used to go away on England trips around that time, people were talking about being scared of the Chelsea side, scared of coming up against Didier Drogba, Arjen Robben and Damien Duff, trying to get past Riccy Carvalho at the back and then, if you got past them, trying to beat Big Pete [Petr Cech] in goal!

'They knew coming into the games, whoever they were, that they were coming to get beaten by a very strong Chelsea side.'

The first step to creating that aura came against Manchester United on the opening weekend of the 2004/05 season. From finishing second a year earlier, Chelsea had to set out their stall early this time, so the fixture list proved kind in throwing up a meeting with United at Stamford Bridge.

Mourinho was no stranger to facing Sir Alex Ferguson either. Six months earlier he had dumped his idol out of the Champions League en route to lifting the trophy with Porto. He had run down the Old Trafford touchline like a mad man to celebrate with his players – another moment that introduced him to the wider football public.

This game was different now, though. Porto were not expected to beat United. With few stars and a significantly lower transfer budget, Porto were not United's equals. They were supposed to be the lesser team. At Chelsea, it was all the opposite.

Taking his place in the Stamford Bridge dugout, Mourinho was dealing with players Chelsea had paid millions for. Indeed, his starting line-up that day had cost the club north of £100 million – a significant sum before the Premier League's multibillion-pound broadcasting deals made English football's top-flight its own treasure island.

So the manager had a burden of expectation that he was never used to in his native Portugal. He was the biggest of names at home, but there was nobody there to challenge that ideal. Away with Porto in Europe, though, Mourinho had to shout loud to be recognised and even then he would not always be noticed. It was Porto, an unglamorous side that few expected things of. At Chelsea, the money dictated everything.

For all those riches, Mourinho had turned to the one player who had cost his team zero in transfer fees to be his leader. Terry was his captain who would become the emblem for Mourinho's Chelsea.

'It was different in the changing room,' Terry explained to *Chelsea* magazine in a 2005 interview. 'It's difficult to say in what way, but I felt like a captain.

'After beating [Manchester United], I had a little think to myself. "Flippin' hell, imagine if I am the captain to lift the Premier League."

'I'd be lying if I said I wasn't concerned. I really wanted it, to continue where we left off [the season previous] but not coming second. I wanted to be the captain that won the Premier League.'

As Terry hinted at himself, getting the better of a United team that boasted serial Premier League winners such as Ryan Giggs, Roy Keane and Paul Scholes was a significant step. The belief was starting to build, even if it was just the first game of the season.

For Terry, dreaming of being the captain who would lift the Premier League title for Chelsea did not rest just on that one game, however. A plane journey across the Atlantic Ocean for Chelsea's pre-season tour a few weeks earlier had cemented his position in Mourinho's revolution.

With Marcel Desailly leaving Chelsea as the new manager arrived, Mourinho needed to make a strong appointment for the captaincy.

'Jose said before that it was between me and Lamps [who would take the armband],' Terry continued in *Chelsea* magazine. 'When we went to America on tour he called me to the back of the plane and we had a 20-minute conversation. He said to me, "What do you want more than anything?" Straight away I said, "the Premier League."

'He was certainly happy with that. He told me he wanted me to be captain, that the players respected me, and that he wanted his captain to train hard every day.

'He also said we had a great squad of players, most of whom hadn't won anything. It was time we started winning.'

Eidur Gudjohnsen scored after fifteen minutes against United to get Mourinho's Chelsea up and running in the way he wanted. They had started winning.

Chelsea: Cech; Ferreira, Gallas, Terry, Bridge; Smertin, Makelele, Lampard; Gudjohnsen (Parker, 82), Drogba (Kezman, 70), Geremi (Carvalho, 89).
Unused subs: Cudicini, Mutu.

Manchester United: Howard; G. Neville, O'Shea, Silvestre, Fortune (Richardson, 84); Miller (Bellion, 84), Scholes, Keane, Djemba-Djemba (Forlan, 73), Giggs; Smith.
Unused subs: Ricardo, P. Neville.

13

Manchester City 1-0 Chelsea
Premier League
16 October 2004

From the opening weekend victory against Manchester United, Jose Mourinho's reign as Chelsea manager was headed in the direction pundits had expected it would.

Chelsea were looking a more ruthless side than they had at any point in their recent history. The manager had only been at the club a few months, but he had evolved the Blues into a slick operation. They would eventually start playing with the swagger of the side of the mid-to-late 1990s, but before any of that would come, Mourinho had instilled a defensive solidity that made Chelsea close to impossible to breach.

Come the end of the season, a defensive record that sat at just fifteen goals conceded explained where the title had been won (by mid-October the Blues had recorded an impressive eight clean sheets in ten matches in all competitions). Chelsea's rearguard was the meanest in Premier League history and John Terry was at the heart of it.

In those early days of Mourinho's first season, Chelsea were still developing under the new manager, though. The target was always to match Arsenal, who were hinting they could create an unassailable lead if Chelsea did not keep them within touching distance at the top.

From being undefeated throughout all of 2003/04 in the league, Arsene Wenger's men had dropped just two points in their opening nine matches. They had twenty-five from a possible twenty-seven points on the board, so when Chelsea lost their first game of Mourinho's reign nine games into the campaign, we were not sure what it meant. Were Arsenal running away with it? Could Chelsea last the pace? Was it too soon to expect something from Mourinho and his players?

The Blues had picked up six wins and two draws in their other league outings, meaning the Gunners had a five-point cushion at the top and it was not even Hallowe'en. Given how the previous season had gone, it was not beyond the realms of possibility that Arsenal had enough to maintain that points difference over the course of the season.

That first loss for Chelsea came at Manchester City. In a roundabout way, the game's only goal had an Arsenal influence to it as it was Nicolas Anelka who scored from the penalty spot to give City a 1-0 win.

The scoreline was as much a shock as it was a jolt to the system for Mourinho's players. City were not the club we know now. This was before Sheikh Mansour made a similar impact in the north-west to the arrival of Roman Abramovich at Stamford Bridge. In fact, when Chelsea lost to City in October 2004, it was three years even before Thaksin Shinawatra would invest millions into the club to help change their fortunes.

City were perennial strugglers and the fact that Anelka was at the club was more an indictment on where his career had gone than it was a symbol for City's upturned fortunes.

'I played against [Anelka] a number of times and I got absolutely nothing from him,' Terry once recalled about the striker. 'No trouble at all. With his pace, I thought he might try to get in behind us. But he had no heart. He didn't want to know ... It seemed like a waste of talent.'

City and Anelka were one and the same. They had the potential, but for one reason or another, could never really sustain it. As recently as 2000, City had been a Division One club and would finish 2004/05 in mid-table some forty-three points behind Chelsea. For the manager who was the self-titled Special One, losing to Kevin Keegan's side was not part of the plan. It should not have happened.

'If someone had told me that we would lose one game all season, I think the last fixture I would have picked would have been that one,' John Terry explained later in his book *My Winning Season*.

Even the players knew Chelsea were that superior they should have left Eastlands with a victory. Instead, Arsenal were now pulling away from them at the top.

It was the sort of occurence Chelsea fans had grown accustomed to in the years previous. Chelsea could beat Manchester United in September and then go all the way to Christmas with just two wins in all competitions, losing to the likes of Norwich City and Oldham Athletic in the process. That happened in 1993/94.

Losing to City was not on the same scale as an eleven-game winless streak that had Chelsea in a relegation scrap, but it was still a tough blow to Mourinho.

'At half-time, the manager was livid. It was one of the few times I saw him really angry,' Terry continued. 'We made plenty of chances in the second half ... but City, who aren't exactly famed for their defensive solidity, were rock solid at the back.

'[Frank Lampard] hit the post with a volley that skidded off the surface and Eidur [Gudjohnsen] missed a clear chance late on.'

Those sorts of misses were haunting Chelsea. The Blues had been playing some good football, but with just eight goals in nine games, the knives were out in the press now that they had lost their first game of the season. Journalists had been waiting to carve them up and take a chunk out of the Special One's ego and they finally had their chance.

By contrast, Arsenal had twenty-nine goals already. They were running away with it and the mood around Chelsea was not great. Even the owner was feeling frustrated, despite it being just one loss.

'Roman Abramovich was gutted after the game. I don't think he expected something like that so early in the season ... He came into the dressing room and just said "Why?" There was silence from the players and the staff. It was pretty uncomfortable. I thought then that I didn't really want to experience that again.'

In the Premier League, Chelsea did not. Losing at Eastlands was their solitary defeat for the entire campaign. It got them stirred up instead and Mourinho got the reaction he wanted from his players.

From that moment, things started to click for that Chelsea team. Having struggled for goals in those first nine league matches, come the halfway mark in the Premier League, the Blues had scored thirty-eight times. From October right through to mid-December, they had racked up thirty – that is better than an average of three a game in that period.

The football Mourinho's Chelsea were playing was incredible. He was utilising Damien Duff and Arjen Robben on the flanks and few sides could contain them. In the three of the four games leading up to the traditional Boxing Day fixture, Chelsea defeated Charlton Athletic, Newcastle United and Norwich City all by the same 4-0 scoreline.

Abramovich was no longer asking questions that started with 'why'. The owner was instead asking 'when'. When were Chelsea going to win the title? When was the silverware going to start arriving? When would this team lose another Premier League game?

It was that feeling Terry had spoken of that was driving them. The feeling of regret on the back of the City loss that was being harnessed for Chelsea to go out and not just take the fight to Arsenal, but to completely pummel them in the process.

Those first nine games gave the Gunners a five-point advantage over Chelsea and such was the turnaround at Stamford Bridge after their first defeat, the next nine games saw them now sitting five points clear of Wenger's men on Christmas Day.

With forty-three points to Arsenal's thirty-eight, Chelsea had pulled off a ten-point swing in just two months. It was absurd. Mourinho's side were making a mockery of the title race, dismantling the team of Invincibles with every opportunity that presented itself.

Arsenal slipped further and further back. They would not get that close to Chelsea again until the start of 2005/06 when the points tally was reset to zero. By the end of Mourinho's debut campaign, Chelsea were twelve points clear of second-place Arsenal. Not since Manchester United in 1999/2000 had champions had such a dominant points advantage.

The turning point for Chelsea had been that City loss. Until then they were competing, yet Arsenal were the pacemakers and had everyone else busting a gut to keep up. Chelsea would eventually brush them aside to make the title race about one club – them.

Manchester City: James; Mills, Distin, Dunne, Thatcher; Wright-Phillips, Bosvelt, Jihai (McManaman, 43); Macken (Fowler, 88), Anelka, Sibierski.
Unused subs: Waterreus, Onuoha, Flood.

Chelsea: Cech; Ferreira, Terry, Carvalho (Geremi, 78), Gallas (Bridge, 46); Tiago (Cole, 64), Makelele, Lampard; Gudjohnsen, Drogba, Duff.
Unused subs: Cudicini, Parker.

14

Chelsea 3-2 Liverpool
League Cup Final
27 February 2005

The intention from Jose Mourinho was a clear one. He was at Chelsea to win things and every trophy the club could capture, they would try to deliver.

The manager had his eyes on the big prize. He wanted the Premier League and, if possible, the Champions League soon after. No other coach has won the latter in successive seasons with different clubs, so Mourinho was determined to make that happen. He was a man determined to seek his own personal glory and mark his name in history. Indeed, he still is.

A European champion with Porto the season before he joined Chelsea, Mourinho was inheriting a club on a similar trajectory to his own career. Mourinho was on the up and so too were Chelsea.

There was a big difference between where he stood and Chelsea's position, though. In his own personal trophy cabinet, Mourinho had league titles from his homeland and European cups. What did Chelsea have? Well, nothing was the answer. When he was put in charge, the Blues had not won a trophy since 2000, which meant the end of 2004/05 would signal a half-decade of failure if silverware was not forthcoming. Regardless of what Chelsea had achieved in that time, for a manager with Mourinho's mentality, it was exactly that Chelsea were staring down the barrel at.

He had to set things straight if he was to put the club on a different course. Mourinho had to turn his team of talented players into winners. He needed them to win silverware collectively if he was to harness all of their potential into something more tangible.

He had a captain being hailed as the future of English football, yet John Terry was still to deliver on his promise in a literal sense. Until he had trophies to show for it, there was nothing there to back up the hype. It was more subjective than anything.

It is why the League Cup became so important for Mourinho's Chelsea. Traditionally the first final of the season in the English game, Mourinho needed his players to go out and leave their mark on it. He needed Chelsea to win the competition to give his side the impetus to go on and achieve on the next step of what he was attempting to create, which was to dethrone Arsenal's Invincibles as Premier League champions. Every journey has a first step and this was it for where Chelsea would go.

As vital as defeating Liverpool 3-2 in Cardiff was for Mourinho's legacy in west London, it was equally so for Terry. He was new to the captaincy and in his first season with the armband, he needed to set a precedent. He needed to succeed where his idol Marcel Desailly had not; he needed to justify Mourinho's faith in him. Chelsea had the finances to buy virtually any player they wanted and Terry could not become a victim of that reality.

'I liked Mourinho from day one,' Terry later wrote in *My Winning Season*, his book on Chelsea's historic 2004/05 campaign. 'He sat us down and told us we were going to win things. He turned to Lamps [Frank Lampard] and said he believed he had just taken charge of the best midfielder in the world … He said he believed that I was one of the best defenders in the world.

'He told us he was going to come in and make things happen. We were all playing for our country, he said, but none of us had won anything and he was going to change that.'

Terry explains how Mourinho's sentiments had fired him up to succeed that season. They had a similar impact with the rest of the dressing room, with the Chelsea players eager to go out and achieve success.

As much as Mourinho's long chats with the players were there to motivate them, they were tests of character at the same time. A manager of his ilk, Mourinho has shown throughout his career that he has little time for passengers. He gets every ounce out of those who play for him, drilling them in training and expecting brilliance when it comes to a match day. Those who do not respond to his rallying cries are often swiftly moved on. The player turnover during that first spell at Chelsea tells us that much, with Mourinho selling thirty-six players in three and a half years. There were some big names in that number, too. The likes of Hernan Crespo, Damien Duff, Arjen Robben, Jimmy Floyd Hasselbaink and Scott Parker were all deemed surplus by Mourinho.

In his most recent spell as Chelsea boss, it was a failure to repeat those same successes at Stamford Bridge that ultimately sealed Mourinho's downfall. As talented as the Chelsea squad was that he had inherited from Roberto Di Matteo and Rafa Benitez, the same sort of characters were not present. Mourinho was deploying the same methods to get from Eden Hazard that he had Terry and Lampard before, but he could not do it consistently. There were fundamental differences with the DNA of the squad and it was he who would pay the price by losing his job for a second time. Times had changed and what Mourinho thought he knew about Chelsea had evolved with it.

Arriving at the Millennium Stadium in late February 2005, Terry was on the verge of delivering on the mandate Mourinho had laid out the previous summer. When he had sat down with the players and looked them in the eye, it was about getting a response. What followed in the immediate aftermath had got them this far – Chelsea were also top of the table and in the middle of an epic Champions League last-sixteen battle with Barcelona – but now it was the time of judgement.

Whether Mourinho had been truthful in his assessment of Terry as being one of the world's finest defenders or not, now was when he would be living up to the billing. The manager had turned to him as his leader and it is in finals where we find out what players have the mettle to accept the pressure and deliver on what is being asked of them.

For Terry, victory was confirmation of everything Mourinho said he had with him. Chelsea did not waltz their way to the trophy; they had graft their way through the game and overcome a sense of adversity.

John Arne Riise had put the Reds ahead within the opening minute and it would not be until a Steven Gerrard own goal as the game was entering the final ten minutes that Chelsea would draw level.

It was all rather fortuitous as three Liverpool players attempted to defend a Paulo Ferrieria free-kick from deep, with Gerrard getting enough contact to divert the ball in off the post to leave Jerzy Dudek no chance.

Mourinho ran from the dugout, finger to his lips to silence the Liverpool supporters. There would be no such muzzling of his players from that point, though, as Chelsea squeezed the life out of Liverpool.

The game went to extra time and Didier Drogba put the Blues 2-1 up before Mateja Kezman made it 3-1 on 112 minutes. Antonio Nunez pulled one back for Benitez's side almost immediately, but Chelsea had enough to hold out and seal their first trophy under Roman Abramovich's ownership.

That was significant and so too was Terry's captaincy in the process of it all. The team had performed with the sort of spirit Mourinho craved and Terry was his mouthpiece on the pitch, driving the team forward to win the game.

'When the final whistle went, it was my best feeling in football. My first trophy. My first medal. Our first trophy as a group,' Terry reflected.

'We hoped it would be the first of many. The club's first trophy in five years and a trophy we hoped would usher in a glorious new era of domination for the club. All those thoughts were flooding through my head when that final whistle went.'

Chelsea: Cech; Ferreira, Carvalho, Terry, Gallas (Kezman, 74); Jarosik (Gudjohnsen, 46), Makelele, Lampard; Cole (Johnson, 81), Drogba, Duff.
Unused subs: Pidgley, Tiago.

Liverpool: Dudek; Finnan, Carragher, Hyypia, Traore (Biscan, 67); Gerrard, Hamann, Riise; Garcia, Morientes (Baros, 74), Kewell (Nunez, 56).
Unused subs: Carson, Pellegrino.

15

Chelsea 4-2 Barcelona
UEFA Champions League, Last 16
8 March 2005

The clock was ticking down and as things stood at 3-2 on the night, Chelsea were going out of the Champions League on away goals.

Barcelona had been blown away in the opening nineteen minutes of the game by some of the finest football Stamford Bridge had seen in its 100 years of hosting football matches. But through the brilliance of Ronaldhino, the visitors had got themselves back into the tie to make it 3-2, 4-4 on aggregate, and were just fifteen minutes away from progressing into the quarter-final.

Eidur Gudjohnsen, Frank Lampard and Damien Duff had put the Blues 3-0 ahead in those opening exchanges. It was football at its high-octane best. Chelsea were breathtaking, with the controversy leading into the game firing them up to blow the Catalans out of the stadium and seemingly back to Spain.

It had all started at the Nou Camp in the first leg when Jose Mourinho had suggested referee Anders Frisk had been compromised in his role that night. According to the Chelsea boss, Frisk had spoken to Barca manager Frank Rijkaard at half-time. When Didier Drogba was sent off soon after the interval, Mourinho was furious and spoke out against what he saw as an injustice against his side.

In the two weeks that separated both legs, Frisk had retired on account of the death threats he received on the back of the game. That added fuel to an already raging fire and led to Volker Roth labeling Mourinho and Chelsea as 'the enemy of football'.

According to reports at the time, referees were considering strike action against the perceived treatment of Frisk at the hands of Chelsea and Mourinho. 'It's the coaches who whip up the masses and actually make them threaten people with death,' the UEFA official Roth would later add.

So Barcelona's visit to London was highly anticipated, but it was not for the football. It was the controversy that inspired the night and Chelsea reacted in a way that nobody expected they would.

Far from cautious and tentative, Mourinho's side played with power and authority. They had the look of men who had been caged for the past fortnight and were finally being unleashed from their torment. The Chelsea name had been criticised and held up as something that did not represent the values of the game. The players had been forced to remain silent while the world poured scorn on them and their manager. They answered back with a display that would define that team for many years to come.

Even now Rijkaard must be attempting to fathom how it all happened. Chelsea were simply irresistible at first. And even when the momentum seemed to swing back in Barca's favour, they dug deep enough to claw their way back into contention.

When the skill and expertise seemed to fade, Chelsea's guts did not. Terry epitomised that with a fine performance at the back, proving to be Mourinho's dependable captain.

All the controversy aside, Terry knew something extra was on the line here. Mourinho had been a Barcelona employee under Sir Bobby Robson, working behind the scenes to complete his football apprenticeship. Mourinho had been a key figure alongside Sir Bobby, but now he was out on his own and attempting to prove himself. That it was Barcelona who would stand in his way of attempting to do that meant the manager desired the success all the more. He craved it like nothing else, if only to show the Catalans he was his own man and could do it against them.

'The manager had a sentimental attachment to them that must have made the prospect of playing against them all the more enticing,' Terry later reflected. ' He wanted to go back [to the Nou Camp] as the boss of one of the best club sides in the world.'

To do that, Mourinho's Chelsea needed to defeat Barcelona. He could not accept anything less as it was too important. The manager needed to cross off another achievement on his list to greatness and Barcelona were probably very high on that.

Mourinho needed his players to carry that desire over onto the pitch. As well as him, they needed to do it for themselves. For Chelsea to be a successful side in Mourinho's vision, it was moments such as this that would go on to form their identity in the modern game. It was the ultimate test and if they did not shirk it or shy away, it would be more than a game of football they would be winning. Would Chelsea remain as the nearly men? Or could they go out and not only just compete with the biggest clubs, but also beat them?

That is when any team makes the step over. The line is drawn; it is thick, bold and striking. It intimidates the masses, which is why it takes something unique to overcome it. It is in those moments when players begin to believe in the hype and belief that surrounds them.

Chelsea had to believe against the Barcelona name. It was a question of psychology. Chelsea had to accept they were Barca's equal and as Terry noted in his book *My Winning Season*, there were not many differences between both teams.

'There was a feeling that the energy was with them in the Spanish league just like the energy was with us in the Premiership,' the captain wrote. 'The torch was passing from Madrid to them, just like we were taking it from Arsenal and Manchester United in England. There was a youth and a purpose and a vibrancy about Barcelona that you had to admire and which I saw reflected in us.'

Indeed, they were both sides at a similar stage in their cycle, although with those red and blue striped jerseys, it was Barcelona who had the allure. They were the club with the rich history and prestige. Chelsea were still trying to get theirs.

While Ronaldhino, Deco and others were stars, Chelsea's youthful players were still making a name for themselves. They were not household names that would command attention across the continent whenever they came to town.

Mourinho had experienced it all from the inside and he was attempting to give Chelsea that same sense of romanticism. Chelsea had to beat Barcelona to get it and the moment was coming. The clock read seventy-six minutes; the scoreboard told us that Barcelona were going through.

'Damien Duff with the corner, in towards John Terry,' was how the game's decisive moment would start in commentary.

'It's there!' screams Clive Tyldesley, who has to take a moment to get his breath back as the net ripples. You can almost hear him drawing in a substantial intake of oxygen over the microphone, attempting to buy himself enough time to explain what Terry has just done. Eventually Tyldesley opts for the five words that define Terry's Chelsea career. 'Captain's goal from John Terry!'

The crowd is in a state of pandemonium. As the camera shakes briefly, we get a sense for the tremors that are rocking the foundations of Stamford Bridge.

'Chelsea have their noses in front again,' Tyldesley declares. 'Chelsea can sniff the quarter-finals again.'

The controversy was not over. From all that had happened in the Nou Camp – Drogba's red card, the allegations against Frisk – Barca would have complaints of their own against Ricardo Carvalho who upended Victor Valdes in goal, tugging him back as he dived to stop Terry's header.

The Chelsea captain did not see any of it, of course. He was running back to the half-way line, arm in the air, celebrating a fine moment in his career.

'It seemed too congested in the middle of the box, I knew Duffa's cross would be swinging out,' Terry added in *My Winning Season*. 'I gave my marker a little shove and tried to take him into the crowd and he got caught up in it a little bit. I was free of him, and I came back towards the near post and made contact with the ball. It wasn't a powerful header. Sometimes when you meet the ball with your head, you know it's in straight away, but it wasn't the case with that one.

'I didn't think there was enough on it. I thought I hadn't got enough power on it. But I kept watching it and no one got in the way of it. I saw [Mateja] Kezman trying to get a little toe on it so he could claim it, but he couldn't reach it either. And then it was in.'

Terry's later assessment is where he stands apart as a captain. He had just scored the biggest goal of his career, although he had other things on his mind.

'I just wheeled away towards [Joe] Coley and told the lads just to stay in the celebration for a minute so we had time to regroup ... I wish I had run to the fans and gone a little bit more mad.'

If Terry had done that, he would not be the captain he would become at Chelsea. When we discuss the qualities of a leader, the misconception is that the man who shouts loudest should be given the power to command. That is a part of it, but leadership comes by reminding those around you of what their duties are. It is about remaining rational when the mind wants to wander and, in this instance, get sucked into the melee a little more.

Terry resisted those urges. He was focused on managing the remaining fourteen minutes or so of a cup tie that had swung back and forth over the course of both legs. He did not want to be throwing this one away. The moment called for sound game management. It called for a captain and Chelsea had theirs.

Only when Pierluigi Collina blew the final whistle was there time for Terry's moment of catharsis. It was also the moment when Roman Abramovich's Chelsea was born in a very real sense.

Although the Russian had owned Chelsea for almost two years by this stage, it felt as though everything had been building to this. There were some watershed moments along the way, like defeating Arsenal in the quarter-finals the season previous, but to beat Barcelona the way they did told us Chelsea had finally arrived. A club was born.

Chelsea: Cech; Ferreira (Johnson, 51), Carvalho, Terry, Gallas; Cole, Makelele, Lampard; Gudjohnsen (Tiago, 79), Kezman, Duff (Huth, 86).
Unused subs: Cudicini, Smertin, Parker, Geremi.

Barcelona: Valdes; Van Bronckhorst (Sylvinho, 46), Oleguer, Puyol, Beletti (Giuly, 84); Deco, Gerard Lopez, Xavi; Ronaldinho, Eto'o, Iniesta (M. Lopez, 86).
Unused subs: Jorquera, Damia, Navarro, Albertini.

16

Chelsea 4-2 Bayern Munich
UEFA Champions League, Quarter-Final
6 April 2005

John Terry has spoken eloquently throughout his career about the demands of wearing the captain's armband at Chelsea.

For him, it was not merely about turning up on a Saturday and barking out orders on the pitch. Terry understood the position and level of duty that envelopes one in such a position of authority. The title is a small part of it.

'I was involved in the first team quite a bit when I was younger, even if I wasn't actually playing,' Terry once recalled. 'I used to sit back and just watch and listen. Before Marcel [Desailly], [Dennis] Wisey had the armband and he was a bit more of an in-your-face kind of captain, a ranter and a raver and typically English. He knew exactly how to get the lads going and get the best out of everyone. He recognised that some players might need an arm around them at half-time, whereas others he'd go absolutely mad at.

'I'd be thinking, "Why is he doing that?" But then you start to understand. Some players don't like to be told they're having a poor game. They know that already. But others do – they need geeing up. And it taught me how important it is for a captain to get to know the different personalities of the players in the team as soon as possible.

'Marcel was a bit quieter as a captain but he was very strong in what he said. When he spoke, everyone listened. He was one of those. But there's a lot of being a captain and I really learned from both of them. It's not just about the fun stuff everyone hears about like organising go-karting and paintballing. It's as much about things like looking out for the players who don't play every week, keeping them happy and focused in training.

'In those situations, sometimes a player's head can go. Sometimes they might not want to speak to the manager about their situation so it's my job to be a kind of liaison between the two.'

Terry also understood that as captain, he needed to play a similar role between the club and fans. He needed to be the figurehead, a voice to bond the boardroom with the terraces. That is done in many ways, whether it be by educating those in the dressing room of what it means to defeat a rival or, when winning the title, reminding the fans of who has helped the club reach the level it has, like he did when parading Roman Abramovich around the Stamford Bridge pitch at the end of 2004/05.

The burden of the captaincy often rested comfortably on Terry's shoulders. He embraced it and at times, exploited it to his benefit and others.

When Bayern Munich visited Stamford Bridge in 2005 for a Champions League quarter-final, the fallout from defeating Barcelona in the previous round was still lurking in the background. Jose Mourinho would soon receive a stadium ban for his accusations against referee Anders Frisk's conduct in the Nou camp, preventing him from attending the second leg against Bayern back in Germany.

The frenzy was being fed on a daily basis, although Terry looked unfazed by it all to the point where he was willing to follow Mourinho's lead in sticking it to the man. In this case, that man was very much UEFA.

When ten-year-old Joel Saunders arrived at Stamford Bridge for the game, he was supposed to be Chelsea's mascot for the night. It soon turned sour for him, though. UEFA's regulations at the time dictated that both clubs must have mascots to lead them out otherwise there would be none. With Bayern not bringing one themselves, officials from European football's governing body approached to tell Joel he would not be stepping out under the lights at Stamford Bridge after all.

'I was gutted, to be honest,' he remembers. 'It was something I had been excited – and nervous – about since I knew I was going to do it. With all that expectation of leading the team out, meeting John Terry and the players, it was heart breaking.'

Now, by this stage of his career, Terry had already carved out his reputation for arriving late to save the day for Chelsea. Lest we forget, he had done exactly that with his header against Barcelona to seal the 4-2 victory that had set up this tie with Bayern.

Walking through the East Stand reception as he made his way to the dressing room, Terry could not help but notice the distraught youngster all kitted out in his replica Chelsea strip.

'JT bent down and asked Joel how he was,' Andy Saunders, Joel's father explains. 'Then the lady who looks after the mascots explained the situation.'

Terry was unimpressed, gesturing to the UEFA official to come over and explain the situation. He did, before exiting with the outcome not changing things. Chelsea captain or not, UEFA weren't listening.

'I can't remember exactly what JT said, but it was along the lines of him pretty defiantly telling the officials that I would be coming on the pitch with him,' Joel continues.

'John told my dad to bring me to the tunnel entrance just before the teams were due to go out and he would bring me with him onto the pitch.'

Joel's father has been a Chelsea supporter for many years, so was not going to refuse the gesture from the club captain, regardless of the potential political implications with UEFA.

As kick-off approached, at the tunnel entrance the pair waited in hope that Terry would fulfil his promise. He did, taking Joel by the hand to walk out to in front of over 40,000 fans.

'To have him fight for me to be on the pitch was amazing,' says Joel. 'I remember him really taking the time to talk to me and make me feel important, even though it was clearly a huge match he was just about to go out and play.'

This was John Terry reinforcing the values he had been passed down by Dennis Wise and Marcel Desailly. He had observed their position as captains while he was coming through and he had understood the value in what they represented.

What Chelsea did out on the pitch that night made the headlines. They completely dominated Bayern and had it not been for a 90th-minute penalty from Michael Ballack – who would join the club on a free transfer twelve months later – would have recorded a more emphatic victory than the 4-2 result would suggest.

The final result still outlines Chelsea's superiority; although Bayern were never worth the two goals they did score. They were outclassed in every aspect of their performance – especially by Frank Lampard who scored a wonderful volley on the pivot that made it 3-1.

Scoring twice against the Germans – he scored Chelsea's second to cancel out Bastian Schweinsteiger's equaliser – Lampard stole the show that night, yet behind the scenes it was Terry pulling the strings. It always was.

We do not know what his team talk was before the game. Was he ranting and raving like his idol Wise would have been? Did he take the calm, considered approach more associated with Desailly? Either way, Terry was a big part of the victory for reasons that didn't just include football, like ensuring Joel Saunders did not miss out on being mascot for the night, regardless of what the regulations dictated.

'There was nothing UEFA could do,' says Andy. 'It was brilliant. I've always loved JT for doing that.'

The nature of events meant Joel would miss out on his chance to perform the traditional mascot duties such as rubbing shoulders with the players ahead of kick-off.

'Then JT invited me back, so I went to the Aston Villa game in September the following season,' Joel adds.

There was something about the ten-year-old being mascot that brought the best out in Lampard as Chelsea would win that game, too. This time it was 2-1, with the Blues' No. 8 bagging another brace. Famously, Luke Moore scored the first league goal against Chelsea that season to bring to an end a run of over ten hours for the Blues not conceding. That record dated back to the end of 2004/05 and resulted in much jubilation in the newspaper press who had been offering up incentives for any striker to breach Chelsea's backline.

'I met all the players before the game and it was incredible. Everyone was really nice and happy to take a picture and sign my autograph book.

'We had a hell of a team that day. There was Claude Makelele, Arjen Robben, Hernan Crespo, Michael Essien – it was legends everywhere!'

And Terry was their captain.

Chelsea: Cech; Johnson (Huth, 65), Carvalho, Terry, Gallas; Cole (Tiago, 82), Makelele, Lampard; Gudjohnsen, Drogba (Forssell, 89), Duff.
Unused subs: Cudicini, Morais, Smertin, Geremi.

Bayern Munich: Kahn; Sagnol, Lucio, Kovac, Lizarazu; Salihamidzic (Schweinsteiger, 46), Ballack, Hargreaves, Frings, Ze Roberto (Scholl, 73); Guerrero.
Unused subs: Rensing, Linke, Deisler, Jeremies, Hashemian.

17

Bolton Wanderers 0-2 Chelsea
Premier League
30 April 2005

Jose Mourinho had famously targeted Bolton Wanderers away as the game that would win Chelsea the 2004/05 Premier League title. He breezed into Stamford Bridge that season with a swagger English football had not seen since Brian Clough. This was all a part of the act.

Mourinho was not making that prediction late in the campaign, either. No, that has never been his style. Mourinho likes to do things with a sprinkling of panache to reinforce the things he says and does – he was predicting 30 April before the campaign had even started. He had that target in mind and it was now the duty of his players to deliver on that prediction.

Regardless of the resources at Mourinho's disposal, it was a big ask for a club that had not been champions in half a century to be so bullish in their pursuit. Not since Roy Bentley had Chelsea fans seen a captain in royal blue lift a top-flight league title. It happened in a time when television screens were still black and white, Chelsea winning the title in 1955 on just fifty-two points. That made them champions on the lowest-ever tally for winners.

Mourinho cared little for that vacuum in history. He had the arrogance and self-belief to want to change it for the better. He was not going to allow history to dictate how he conducted himself; he was not going wilt under the pressure and nor were his players. If anything, by predicting success to fall on a particular day, he was raising the stakes.

That plan nearly hit a bump in the road. Well, of sorts.

So dominant had Chelsea been in 2004/05, the 3-1 defeat of west London neighbours Fulham on 23 April could have seen them crowned as champions a week earlier than Mourinho had first imagined. Their closest challengers Arsenal had five games remaining, Chelsea four, so Arsene Wenger's side knew they had to pick up maximum points in their game in hand against Tottenham Hotspur to keep their faint hopes of the title alive.

The match was being played at Highbury on the Monday after Chelsea's victory over Fulham and the Blues players were not too far away from their television screens.

'We would have been champions without kicking another ball [had Arsenal not beaten Spurs 1-0],' John Terry wrote in his book *My Winning Season*.

'Some of the boys would have been quite happy for that to happen but I didn't really want the chase to end like that. I wanted to win it on the pitch and celebrate on the pitch. Not in a hotel room somewhere. I wanted to win it at Bolton the following Saturday. So I was pleased when Arsenal beat Spurs.'

Either Terry had an ill-judged fetish for anxiety or he was a player determined to do things completely on his terms. Looking at events throughout his career, it is probably the latter, which is what he was getting at with the Arsenal result. He did not want Spurs gifting Chelsea the title. Despite Chelsea enduring that fifty-year wait, he wanted to taste the glory himself to make it feel that bit sweeter.

Terry's sentiments were simple. It was not enough to be told he was a champion; he wanted to feel the emotion. It was only by going out on the pitch and taking three points off Bolton that Terry was going to satisfy that desire. He needed to feed it in order to make it feel worthwhile. Just finishing top of the pile was never going to cut it for him.

It was not just about winning the title at the Reebok Stadium that day; Terry had some demons to lay to rest in the process.

'It had become bit of a joke,' he recalled, talking of Chelsea's poor record in Lancashire. 'We had a team packed with amazing talents like Marcel Desailly, Gianluca Vialli and Gianfranco Zola, and yet we could never win at Bolton Wanderers. We had been bullied by them in the past.'

To put Terry's sense of foreboding into perspective, Chelsea had won just once in their previous six away visits to face the Trotters at their home. Their only win in that sequence had come in March 2004 when Terry himself scored the opening goal in a 2-0 victory.

That game was perhaps a sign of things changing for the better, although they were about to reach unprecedented levels for club and player.

'It didn't matter what Arsenal did anymore,' Terry continued. 'If we won, the title that was theirs would now be ours. We felt it was going to happen.'

So much so, the Chelsea players had come prepared. Alongside their football boots, they had packed video cameras into their bags for the game to record history being made. The moment was theirs and they were ready to seize it.

'You don't want to tempt fate ... but the manager had said it was going to happen and he was so confident, it spread to the rest of us.'

It was goalless at half-time, with Sam Allardyce's side doing a good job of keeping Chelsea at bay. They had enjoyed some good chances themselves, with Kevin Davies testing Petr Cech with a header from six yards out. El-Hadji Diouf looked to be in on goal at one point, only for Terry to get across in time to cover Ricardo Carvalho, preventing Diouf from squaring to the unmarked Stellios Giannakopoulos.

As Terry recalled, the story of the first half was mirrored in the team selection for the day. Chelsea were going for the title, yet we did not see much of the players who got them there. Arjen Robben and Damien Duff were both injured, while Joe Cole was also on the bench. Mourinho had gone for a different approach at the Reebok Stadium. He went for substance over style.

'[Mourinho] knew that it wasn't going to be pretty. He knew Bolton would throw everything at us, so he started with Geremi at right-back and Jiri Jarosik in midfield to give us a bit more height and muscle to cope with their tactics and bolster up at set-pieces ... He knew they would fight right until the bitter end and he wanted to pit our steel against theirs.'

Chelsea rode the storm, but Mourinho wasn't happy at half-time.

'I got back inside the changing rooms and walked straight into a bollocking from the manager,' Terry said. 'I don't think he had been that angry before in his time at Chelsea. Perhaps he sensed that we were starting to think the title was a formality ... He tore us apart, which had only happened once or twice through the rest of the season.'

Mourinho's rant worked. Chelsea looked a more formidable unit after the interval and it took just fifteen minutes for Frank Lampard to put them ahead.

The mettle Mourinho said he needed played its part as Jarosik won an aerial duel to give Didier Drogba the chance to flick on for Lampard.

Still, nothing seemed to be on. Lampard was moving away from goal just inside the area and in the direction of the corner flag, harassed and harried by Vincent Candela. He eventually shrugged him off to cut back inside, keeping his cool to give Jussi Jaaskelainen the eyes and send him the wrong way. Cue the wild celebrations with every outfield player swamping Lampard in front of the 3,000 or so Chelsea fans who had made the journey. There were still thirty minutes to play, but they knew this was it. The moment was not going to be thrown away.

'Bolton started to bombard us,' Terry continued. 'They poured so many men forward that we knew we had a chance of catching them on the break.' It's exactly what Chelsea did on seventy-six minutes.

Gary Speed's corner was knocked clear on the right. Eidur Gudjohnsen found Claude Makelele, whose pass infield for Lampard gave the midfielder nothing but space to run into from the centre-circle to the Bolton goal. Ricardo Carvalho was sprinting alongside him, desperate to receive the pass that would allow him to put the seal on the title. Lampard was having none of it, instead he rounded Jaaskelainen and fired into an empty net. 'Start carving their name on that trophy,' Andy Gray said ecstatically in commentary.

It was a surreal moment for any Chelsea supporter who had not witnessed glory of this kind at the club – and there were many. Even now Lampard's run from midfield seems to take an age and as the ball bobbles up in front of him, the logic of a football supporter says he is going to trip over it at any moment. The ball seems to be teasing him with every step, never allowing Lampard to have it fully under control until Jaaskelainen commits himself and he dinks to the goalkeeper's right to go beyond him before passing it into the net with his left foot.

Given the magnitude of what he has just achieved, Lampard looks completely calm. He runs behind the goal, patting the club crest on his shirt as he makes his way into the direction of the Chelsea fans where he performs an impromptu star jump to salute them.

His head drops for a second, perhaps a personal moment where he takes a breath to realise what that goal means, before every player, including the substitutes, pounce on him.

Bodies continue to pile in and when the bundle eventually breaks up, the last player to leave the embrace with Lampard is his captain, John Terry.

'When the final whistle went, I wanted to celebrate with Lamps first,' he said. 'He and I have been through a lot together … I knew what this day at the Reebok meant to him just as he surely knew what it meant to me.'

Chelsea were Premier League champions.

Bolton Wanderers: Jaaskelainen; Ben Haim, Candela (Jaidi, 77), N'Gotty, Gardner; Giannakopoulos (Nolan, 63), Okocha (Pedersen, 63), Hierro, Speed; Davies, Diouf.
Unused subs: Poole, Fadiga.

Chelsea: Cech; Geremi, Carvalho, Terry, Gallas; Tiago, Makelele (Smertin, 89), Lampard, Jarosik; Drogba (Huth, 65), Gudjohnsen (Cole, 85).
Unused subs: Cudicini, Kezman.

18

Liverpool 1-0 Chelsea
UEFA Champions League, Semi-Final
3 May 2005

Jose Mourinho was incensed. Four times Chelsea had played Liverpool that season and four times Chelsea had not suffered a defeat. Twice in the Premier League Mourinho's side had beaten Liverpool, as they had in the League Cup final before a goalless draw in the first leg of their Champions League semi-final. Chelsea were the superior team in every department, a fact reinforced by the thirty-seven-point gap that separated both sides in the league table come the end of the campaign.

The victory over Liverpool that mattered most to Mourinho would not be forthcoming, however. Chelsea were beaten 1-0 at Anfield, meaning it was Rafa Benitez who would be travelling to Istanbul with his players to face AC Milan for the 2005 Champions League final. Like his predecessor at Chelsea, Claudio Ranieri, Mourinho was failing at the exact same stage that the club had done a year earlier following that semi-final defeat to Monaco. Again, the stars appeared to be aligning for Chelsea; they were the favourites to be crowned European Champions for a first time and the feeling is that they should have been. Fate, bad luck – call it what you will – it did not work out that way. Chelsea were knocked out and they had to pick up the pieces, suffering heartache all over again.

It ruined Mourinho's dream of back-to-back European Cups with different clubs – a feat still to be achieved by any manager. More importantly, it crushed Chelsea's own European aspirations when, for the second season running, they appeared so close to realising them, only to fall at the last hurdle. Their European experiences were turning desperately sour.

Had Chelsea been beaten by the better side at Anfield, Mourinho would not have had any cause for complaint. That is a reality of elite sports. As simplistic as the notion is, sometimes you are just not good enough. However, Chelsea were good enough. It was only four days earlier that they had sealed the Premier League title against Bolton Wanderers, but at Anfield the match officials would decide their fate.

'I felt the power of Anfield, it was magnificent,' said the Chelsea boss at the end of the ninety minutes. 'I felt it didn't interfere with my players but maybe it interfered with other people and maybe it interfered with the result.'

Mourinho was referring to the only goal across both games. The 'ghost goal'. Luis Garcia scored it after just four minutes in the second leg, but even now it is a goal that is impossible to prove whether it was legitimate or not.

'You should ask the linesman why he gave a goal,' continued a visibly irate Mourinho. 'Because, to give a goal, the ball must be 100 per cent [over the line] and he must be 100 per cent sure that the ball is in.'

Behind the run of play and with his view blocked by William Gallas who was hooking the ball clear, it is difficult to judge how the linesman was so sure. Not even the television cameras could say for certain despite the thousands of hours that have been dedicated to replays since.

'We were the ones who had beaten Barcelona and Bayern Munich. We had knocked out the favourites,' John Terry wrote in *My Winning Season*. 'We were steaming along. We felt unstoppable. We had momentum. We had the best players. We had the best manager. It felt like it was our year to me. Not someone else's.'

Chelsea had not wanted to face Liverpool in the semi-final. By Terry's own admission, it was Juventus they thought would be the better opponents. It was not through fear of what Benitez's side could do, more with the fact that an all-English semi-final would blur the lines and make it about something more than football. Chelsea saw that as a dangerous and so it proved, with the hyperbole taking centre stage.

The game was not a Champions League semi-final anymore; it had become something much different. It was an English derby and that levelled the playing field somewhat.

Terry's belief was that Chelsea would have bullied Juventus and eventually outclassed them. They would have got the better of them over two legs and made their superiority count to book their ticket to Istanbul.

Neutrals relish derbies so late in major competitions as they throw up an extra narrative. The spectacle is inspired that bit more by a feeling of spite fuelled by nothing more than geography. That it was Chelsea and Liverpool coming to blows heightened it even more. Indeed, Chelsea had benefitted from it a year earlier against Arsenal.

'I think their league form lulled us a little bit. It conned us,' Terry reflected. 'I said to Lamps when we were in the dressing room an hour before the game that it felt too relaxed in there. It wasn't that people weren't pumped up. But we were all so confident, because we go to Anfield every season and because the Premier League table told us we were so much better than them. It didn't feel like the build-up to a Champions League semi-final.

'That's why we'd all wanted Juventus instead. We wouldn't have been relaxed if we'd been about to play them.'

Here were two clubs that were seemingly the antithesis of one another. Forgetting for a moment how the Moores family had bankrolled Liverpool's success in the 1970s and 1980s, the club was seen as a traditional powerhouse in the English game. Liverpool fans still sing their songs about 'King' Kenny Dalglish and his exploits down Anfield Road. It creates an air of mystique around the club, yet in more recent times all that history has stood for little in maintaining success on Merseyside.

Chelsea had just done what Liverpool had not since 1990, which was win English football's top-flight. Chelsea's two league titles at the time were no match to Liverpool's eighteen, although the momentum Terry spoke about did not relate to just one season. The pendulum had well and truly swung in Chelsea's favour when comparing the fortunes of the two clubs, with Roman Abramovich's investment a big part of that.

So it meant the sides meeting in a Champions League semi-final represented something different. It was established elite versus the young pretender and the latter doesn't always command the same level of romance.

For Liverpool fans, they had been forced to watch on as Chelsea overtook their club. Not only were Chelsea winning the title in 2004/05, the Reds had come nowhere near challenging them. They may have finished fifth, but the points difference between the clubs showed so much more. It was akin to them being separated by an entire division almost, the dearth in quality was that substantial.

Even before Jose Mourinho's reign, Chelsea had denied Liverpool Champions League football two years earlier when they reached fourth place in the league at their expense.

That final day showdown at Stamford Bridge had created the new Chelsea we were witnessing take shape. Without defeating Liverpool 2-1 that afternoon, we can only speculate as to whether or not Abramovich would have chosen another club in London to invest his wealth. It is the stuff of nightmares for Chelsea fans to consider where they would be without him given the financial collapse that was being tipped as being on the horizon.

It is not contrived to suggest Liverpool had contributed to the rise of this juggernaut. Through their own failings, bigger and more powerful clubs were being born in English football, of which Chelsea were very much one.

However, now a Liverpool side that had not influenced much in the season was being given a chance to roll back the years. The game meant something different to them than it did Chelsea. Even in commentary Clive Tyldesley had referred to the second leg as 'an Eighties revival night at Anfield'.

In truth, Chelsea had fluffed their lines a week earlier in west London. They were flat and did not dominate Liverpool enough as the game finished goalless. The only complaints they could have that night were with their own performance. They needed to punish their opponents and they did not, which meant it all came down to the second leg.

On Merseyside, a questionable decision on such a huge occasion is what proved the difference, which is why Chelsea, the manager and John Terry found it difficult to accept.

'It's all a blur to me and I haven't been able to bring myself to watch any of the game again,' Terry said. 'I know simulations suggest it wasn't a goal. I wish now that we had kicked up more of a fuss about it because there wasn't the kind of furious reaction you might have expected in that situation when there was a real doubt about whether the ball had crossed the line.

'It wouldn't have changed the decision but it might have encouraged the ref to right the wrong later in the game and give us the benefit of the doubt over another important decision.

'Perhaps it was because it was so early, but it all seemed a bit surreal.'

Those opening four minutes changed the game. It meant Liverpool could tighten their midfield to avoid Jamie Carragher and Sami Hyypia being exposed by Chelsea's dynamic front three of Joe Cole, Didier Drogba and Eidur Gudjohnsen. That trio had the ability to exploit a lack of pace at the back for Liverpool. Cole had the creativity, while Gudjohnsen and Drogba were the goal threats.

Liverpool cut the supply line, forcing Chelsea to play over the midfield from the back, which was suited to what Liverpool had defensively.

It was not until the 88th minute when Chelsea were gifted their best chance of the game. Frank Lampard floated a ball into the box for Terry, which he headed across goal. Jerzey Dudek collided with Hyypia in his attempts to punch clear, the ball landing at Gudjohnsen's feet.

'I thought, "Eidur, it's gone to Eidur. That's a fucking goal!" If it was going to fall to anyone, you would want him or Lamps on the end of it, especially that late on,' said Terry.

Gudjohnsen connected well with his shot, but it lacked precision and flew past Dudek's upright into the Kop's advertising hoardings.

'It was all gone in a split second. Eidur said it touched [Jamie] Carragher's leg and who knows what would have happened if we had been awarded a corner. But not for the first time in the competition, and not for the last, there was something about that game that felt, for Liverpool, it was just meant to be.'

Monaco a year earlier was more about Chelsea's own shortcomings. The Blues, then managed by Claudio Ranieri, had lost to a side that was better equipped. They managed both legs better than Chelsea, even with ten men at the Stade Louis II.

Under Mourinho, Chelsea had matured plenty in the twelve months that separated the games. They looked a side ripe and ready to become European champions. They looked ready to sustain it; winning the Champions League was not going to be a flash in the pan.

Whereas it was lack of nous that had let them down in 2004, this time it was a sense of fate – and it was certainly not looking favourably on them.

John Terry would have to get used to that when it came to the Champions League.

Liverpool: Dudek; Finnan, Carragher, Hyypia, Traore; Hamann (Kewell, 73), Biscan; Garcia (Nunez, 84), Gerrard, Riise; Baros (Cisse, 60).
Unused subs: Carson, Warnock, Welsh, Smicer.

Chelsea: Cech; Geremi (Huth, 76), Carvalho, Terry, Gallas; Tiago (Robben, 68), Makelele, Lampard; Cole (Kezman, 68), Drogba, Gudjohnsen.
Unusued subs: Cudicini, Johnson, Morais, Forssell.

19

Bolton Wanderers 0-2 Chelsea
Premier League
15 April 2006

Chelsea fans know only too well where they were on 30 April 2005. If they were not among the few thousand who had travelled to the Reebok Stadium that day, anecdotes invariably revolve around pubs and living rooms across London. It is a similar story for those fans overseas, many of which would have been following their weekly ritual of rising pre-dawn to watch Chelsea or staying up until the early hours to catch the Blues in action, depending on their hemisphere.

Whoever and wherever, Chelsea fans know exactly what they were doing the moment they witnessed the Blues win the title for the first time in fifty years. Some will even go into great detail about their breathing patterns when Frank Lampard rounded Jussi Jaaskelainen to make certain of a 2-0 win that rendered Jose Mourinho's men uncatchable.

Fast forward 350 days – so not a year exactly – and Chelsea found themselves in a similar position to where they had been in 2005. It was 2006 now and the Blues were on the verge of claiming back-to-back titles. As fate would have it, the fixture list had paired them with Bolton Wanderers.

So close were Chelsea to the title, the pressure of Manchester United attempting to reel them in did not seem to concern Mourinho that much. The manager was relaxed with the position of his team sitting seven points clear with five matches remaining in the season.

'For me, pressure is bird flu; I am feeling a lot of pressure with the swan in Scotland,' he told journalists in early April, two days before watching his team thrash West Ham United 4-1. The threat of a bird flu outbreak in Scotland was dominating the front pages and now Mourinho was attempting to get it in the sports section, too. Outside the Reebok Stadium later that month even a Chelsea fanzine was running with it thanks to the manager's comments.

The gathered reporters at Cobham were having none of it, though. They laughed and joined in the fun with Mourinho, but they wanted a real answer out of him on whether or not Sir Alex Ferguson was turning up the heat.

While Chelsea were apparently out of form – a crisis in 2006 was losing two Premier League games since the turn of the year – United had won nine league games on the bounce to put them right in the mix of a title shot. They were breathing down Chelsea's necks, but despite it all, Mourinho was claiming that he remained unmoved by it all.

'I am serious,' he continued, 'you are laughing, but I am serious. I am more scared of the bird flu than football. What is football compared with life? A swan with bird flu, for me, that is the drama of the last two days. I have to buy some masks and stuff. I am serious. Maybe for my team as well.'

The truth of it was that regardless of how well United were performing, they were running out of games to catch Chelsea. For that seven-point deficit to disappear, Chelsea would have to drop nine of their remaining fifteen. That would mean doubling the defeats they had suffered all season up to that point. It would have meant coming close to equaling the number of league defeats Chelsea had suffered in the two years Mourinho had been boss, which was just four in seventy-one matches at that stage.

'I think [Ferguson] has to be optimistic,' Mourinho added. 'If not, he's not in this job for so long. I'm not in the job for so long but I think I also have reasons to be optimistic.'

Of course Mourinho did. He would soon be back at the stadium where it had all happened for Chelsea in 2005. And the evening previous – aptly Good Friday – United had been held to a goalless draw by Sunderland at Old Trafford. It meant that a win against Sam Allardyce's men would all but gift wrap another league title for Chelsea. It would put them nine points clear with four games remaining and not even Kevin Keegan would be able to blow a lead like that, much to Fergie's annoyance.

Chelsea knew the task they had to complete. This time they did not keep the travelling supporters waiting as long, either.

A year earlier, it was not until the hour mark when Lampard had struck to send the away end at the Reebok into delirium. Chelsea circa 2006 did it just inside forty-five minutes as John Terry got in on the act on the stroke of half-time to put his side ahead.

Lampard's free-kick from deep had been a soaring one that caused confusion in the Bolton box. Nobody knew who they were picking up, which allowed Terry and Didier Drogba to steal a march on their markers. Such was the confusion that Drogba had even tried to claim the goal for himself, running off in celebration. As television replays would show, with players rising together, it was Terry who made the vital connection to divert the ball into the bottom corner of the net.

Football likes to throw up instances of déjà vu at times to get fans feeling mystical. It could be World Cup symmetry to suggest when a country will next be crowned world champions, or in Lampard's case, him scoring in the exact minute at the exact same stadium at the exact same end when he had first sealed Chelsea the title.

That happened in the second half as Lampard fired home Chelsea's second of the game on the hour to seal it. The significance of the moment was not lost on him either, running to the spot where he had celebrated in 2005, pointing to the Chelsea fans that it was there where history had been made. They did not need reminding of that fact.

At the final whistle, it was not Lampard who was in Mourinho's thoughts this time. It was Terry for the way he had not only scored the game's opener, but also proved his excellence at the back yet again.

Despite the scoreline, it had not been plain sailing for Chelsea again that afternoon. Ricardo Vaz Te had struck the post when the scores were level and Bolton threw wave after wave of attacks Chelsea's way. Terry was there repelling them and when his moment came in the opposition box, he did not turn it down.

Mourinho's words were simple for where his captain was concerned. 'John Terry is the best in the world in his position and he has a great attitude,' said the manager.

Two weeks later on 29 April, Chelsea entertained Manchester United at Stamford Bridge. They won 3-0. Chelsea were champions again.

Bolton Wanderers: Jaaskelainen; Ben Haim, Faye, N'Gotty, Gardner; Campo, Davies, Nolan, Speed (Nakata, 70) Vaz Te (Giannakoppoulos, 46); Borgetti (Pedersen, 46).
Unused subs: Walker, Okocha.

Chelsea: Cech; Geremi, Gallas, Terry, Del Horno; Makelele; Essien, Lampard, Cole (Ferreira, 82); Crespo (Robben, 60), Drogba (Huth, 86).
Unused subs: Cudicini, Wright-Phillips.

20

England 2-0 Trinidad & Tobago
FIFA World Cup 2006, Group B
15 June 2006

The Golden Generation was in a state of flux. We knew Sven-Goran Eriksson would be leaving his England post at the conclusion of the World Cup in Germany and it meant changes would be sweeping through the England camp.

Eriksson had been the custodian of England's brightest generation of players since they had last won the World Cup, but he had failed to get them beyond the quarter-final of any competition.

At the 2002 World Cup, England had fallen to Brazil at that stage, and at Euro 2004 it was a defeat on penalties that sealed their fate against hosts Portugal.

Germany was the end of the road for Eriksson and the hope was this talented group of players would finally gel enough to truly realise their potential.

The most famous face in the England squad was David Beckham. With his popstar wife and chiseled jawline, the midfielder had gone from villain to hero in the English footballing faculty.

It was at France '98 that he had seen red for kicking out at Diego Simeone and after a promising rise throughout the tournament, it was penalties that would again prove the Three Lions' downfall against Argentina. With Beckham dismissed to leave his country at a numerical disadvantage, the tabloids wasted little time in pointing the finger of blame in his direction.

Beckham had redeemed himself since then and was now the England captain. His captaincy was more about being a statesman than it was a leader, however. He did not exactly represent that bulldog English spirit that so many others before him had. Beckham went about his business with a more subtle tone, letting his performances do all the talking for him.

For a team given that Golden Generation tag, it was fitting he should be the superior figure of it. Beckham was symbolic for everything the modern footballer had become, no less the England team with the players' WAGs infamously following them throughout the 2006 World Cup with a slew of paparazzi photographers not too far behind.

With Eriksson soon departing, things would be changing for England, though. Incoming manager Steve McClaren wanted to appoint his own man to be at the forefront of his new era and it would be John Terry he would turn to.

As part of Eriksson's backroom team, McClaren would have seen enough of Terry behind the scenes to form an opinion of what he was all about. With or without the armband, McClaren would have heard Terry's voice in the England camp; it would have been a sound that carried authority despite the bigger names at the time that were playing alongside him.

Having his voice heard had long been Terry's desire. That need to leave his thumbprint on any team he represented is something he picked up from playing with Marcel Desailly at Chelsea. He was always the junior member of that particular partnership, but Desailly often encouraged Terry to be confident and assert himself.

It is a vital quality for any defender, let alone the captain. Centre-backs need to feel no fear in organising those in front of them, barking out the orders to keep the backline arranged and in shape.

Terry was proving himself the best in the business at doing that with Chelsea and despite Beckham's large shadow being cast over the England squad, McClaren wasted little time in ensuring Terry would usurp him.

Before he would, however, Terry was putting in a silent audition for a job he did not even know was available. Unknown to him at the time, his performances at the 2006 World Cup were going to be a big part of it.

As a spectacle, Germany 2006 is not one England fans will look back on fondly. It was underwhelming to say the least. Even down to England's Umbro kit, it all felt mediocre.

Umbro seemed to have a fascination at the time with including the St. George's cross in some form on England's shirts. It was akin to kit design by infants.

The World Cup 2006 number had a partial red cross on the corner of the right shoulder which, if anything, appeared more like a war wound picked up on the terraces than a reminder of the patriotism the England players should have been feeling when wearing the jersey.

It was all an anti-climax given the expectation ahead of the tournament and, with England being dumped out at the quarter-final stage yet again by Portugal on penalties, England's football went the same way.

One of the few positives to come out of the World Cup from an English perspective was the emergence of Terry, though. We started seeing the sort of performances from his Chelsea career crossover to those on the international stage. He was maturing, growing into the captaincy that was waiting just over the horizon for him.

They may have been minnows in every sense – Trinidad & Tobago were the smallest country to ever qualify for a World Cup at the time – yet the turning point for Terry's England career would come against the Soca Warriors.

The Chelsea man was an England regular; he had scored goals and won plenty of matches with his country. He had never performed a Terry-esque saviour act, though. Perhaps the time had never called for it, but then against Trinidad & Tobago it suddenly did with his acrobatic clearance right on half-time to keep the game goalless heading into the interval.

With names such as Dwight Yorke and Shaka Hislop playing against England, the game felt more like an English league derby than an international fixture, and that seemed to work to Trinidad's favour.

It was not so much a leveler, yet the familiarity took away from the spectacle for the Trinidadians. They were facing players they knew and it helped them shackle England's game plan. The Three Lions were being limited to half chances and when they did get an opportunity, they squandered it, Peter Crouch being the biggest culprit.

Then Stern John thought he had scored the game's opener. Quite where Paul Robinson had disappeared to, nobody knew, but a routine cross caused more problems in the England box than it should have when the goalkeeper decided to go AWOL. The ball ricocheted into the six-yard box leaving John and Rio Ferdinand in a two-horse race to get there first. John won his duel and just as he expected the net to bulge, a stretched leg appeared from nowhere to sweep the ball clear from danger. It was John Terry.

More impressive than the clearance and his ability to sniff out danger was that Terry came out unscathed from it all. He had crashed to the floor before his momentum took him into the net in the immediate aftermath of making the clearance, leaping into the air with his body out of control.

That one moment was a rite of passage for him in an England shirt. It was not about the fact England would go on to win the game 2-0 and that they would progress through their group. It was the way in which Terry was beginning to have an influence with his country in the same way he had done with Chelsea a few years previous.

The progress had been gradual and when Desailly departed, it meant the stage was there for Terry to make his stand.

With England he had been rotated at times by Eriksson, who was unsure of whether or not Sol Campbell was the better partner for Ferdinand at the heart of defence.

Terry had seen him off – helped by Campbell's ageing years – and now he had Beckham in his sights.

England: Robinson; Carragher (Lennon, 58), Ferdinand, Terry, A. Cole; Beckham, Gerrard, Lampard, J. Cole (Downing, 74); Owen (Rooney, 58), Crouch.
Unused subs: James, Carson, Campbell, Bridge, Neville, Jenas, Hargreaves, Carrick, Walcott.

Trinidad & Tobago: Hislop; Edwards, Sancho, Lawrence, Gray; Birchall, Yorke, Whitley, Theobald (Wise, 85); Jones (Glen, 70), John.
Unused subs: Jack, Cox, Andrews, Charles, Latapy, Wolfe, Scotland, Samuel.

21

England 4-0 Greece
International Friendly
16 August 2006

Steve McClaren had a grand plan for the England team under his guidance and he put John Terry right at the heart of it.

David Beckham was still only thirty-one years old and had some good years of service ahead of him regardless of his move to revolutionise Major League Soccer with LA Galaxy. That mattered little to McClaren, however, who had just taken over from Sven-Goran Eriksson.

He wanted to inject some new life into a team that was beginning to show signs of turning stale. England had just been knocked out of another major competition at the quarter-final stage and it was not just the manager who needed changing; the captain had to go also.

'I'm convinced he will prove to be one of the best captains England has ever had,' McClaren said confidently at the announcement of Terry inheriting Beckham's armband.

'John has all the attributes an international captain needs – leadership, authority, courage, ability, tactical awareness and a total refusal to accept second-best,' the new boss continued. 'He has been an inspiration for Chelsea and is at his best in adversity.'

Maybe McClaren was playing clairvoyant and could see the road ahead. Maybe what he lacked as a coach he made up with an ability for reading the stars as England and McClaren would need all of Terry's strength in adversity, plus a whole a lot more to get through the next couple of years.

From there being a clamour for Eriksson to depart when he did, England's fortunes under McClaren meant the Swede would have been welcomed back into English football with open arms. If only the FA knew what would follow upon his departure, they would have put up a bigger fight to keep him. Failing that, they would have cast their net much wider than a coach who had been part of Eriksson's underwhelming regime.

Things had been frustrating under the Swede, but with McClaren at the helm, that frustration would soon turn to a much different noun with far reaching consequences: failure.

All that was to come, of course. Before it did, McClaren's England would follow protocol and deliver that very English phenomena in football terms; we got a false dawn.

Only two years earlier Greece had been the surprise European champions when they upset the apple cart – and Cristiano Ronaldo – to win Euro 2004 in Portugal. They had done it with a reliance on defence coupled with an ability to prove devastatingly efficient in front of goal. Since their success at the Euros, their stock had fallen and World Cup qualification had eluded them. Then they arrived at Old Trafford in August 2006 and became England's whipping boys.

In terms of McClaren's reign as England boss, it felt like a significant moment. It was even more so for Terry.

Not only was he wearing the England armband for the first time as the bona fide leader of his country – he had worn the armband previously in October 2005, but only briefly when

Michael Owen was subbed off late on – but it was he who got this new era off to flying start. Not only was Terry skipper, he scored England's first goal of this new dawn.

'The whole night really could not have gone any better,' Terry said after his goal set England on their way after fourteen minutes. 'I've said it a hundred times, I couldn't feel any more proud than I do now. It was a great result and a great performance, but we have to make sure we carry it on in the same vein.'

That is where things get disappointing for Terry as England captain. McClaren spoke of him being a fine leader – which he has been in a Chelsea shirt – although defeating Greece on his debut as captain was one of the high notes in his international career.

There was the symbolism of his goal and what it meant to come while wearing the armband and it was also one of England's best performances in the following two years.

After the disappointment of Germany 2006, when England had never quite hit top gear despite the talent at their disposal, the immediate reaction to McClaren's England was that they looked threatening going forward again. One journalist went so far as to suggest that the manager had introduced a dynamism that had been lacking under the previous regime.

Gradually that good will eroded. England would not qualify for Euro 2008 under McClaren, leaving a black mark against Terry's captaincy. It was not down to his own failures, but as a leader in that side, Terry's name was being positioned alongside the manager's. He was just as much a part of where the Three Lions had failed.

By the time he would be afforded the opportunity to make amends for that in World Cup qualification, that campaign would also finish with a bittersweet tone.

It is not just Terry; the England captaincy has haunted many fine players in the history of football. Indeed, aside from Bobby Moore's exploits, it can be an arduous task to identify many others who have lived up to their billing. It is the failure that eventually comes to define them, whether that perspective is too harsh or not.

Despite being England's record goalscorer and also holding the record appearances for an outfield player, Wayne Rooney finds himself tarred with the same brush. England's abject showing at Euro 2016, where they were dumped out in the last sixteen by Iceland – a country boasting a population of just 330,000 – is something that will follow the striker around well beyond his retirement. We will talk of those records, but they will be laced with a sense of regret at potential never being fully realised on the international stage. It was on Rooney's watch, with him wearing the armband, that England suffered one of the biggest failures in a single match.

And so too it proved for Terry and that European Championships qualification campaign. It had all started so well with a friendly win over Greece to kick-start his captaincy, but not even Terry was immune from the poisoned chalice that continues to haunt every England captain since 1966.

England: Robinson (Kirkland, 45); G. Neville (Carragher, 78), Ferdinand, Terry, Cole (Bridge, 80); Gerrard (Richardson, 76), Hargreaves, Lampard, Downing (Lennon, 69); Crouch, Defoe (Bent, 79).
Unused subs: Foster, Young, P. Neville, Brown, Dawson, Jenas, Wright-Phillips.

Greece: Nikopolidis; Fyssas (Lagos, 29), Dellas (Anatolakis, 64), Katsouranis, Antzas (Kyrgiakos, 46); Vyntra, Zagorakis (Basinas, 46), Karagounis, Giannakopoulos (Salpigidis, 46); Samaras (Amanatidis, 46), Charisteas.
Unused subs: Chalkias, Kafes, Gekas, Papadopoulos, Georgeas.

22

Reading 0-1 Chelsea
Premier League
14 October 2006

Close to a decade on from the incident, Chelsea fans can look back at the club's 1-0 victory against Reading in October 2006 with a sense of humour more than heartache. Light-hearted memories do not detract from the injury Petr Cech suffered at the Madejski Stadium, but the way the game would eventually end was somewhat more jovial.

After Cech was carried off on a stretcher and subsequently sent to hospital when he collided with Stephen Hunt, his replacement Carlo Cudicini would have been expected to finish the game. He did not.

Like Cech, Cudicini was injured in battle – this time the culprit was Ibrahima Sonko, who smashed into him in midair to leave Cudicini out cold. Without another goalkeeper on the bench, Jose Mourinho had no choice but to put an outfield player in goal to see out the remaining few minutes of the game.

Up stepped John Terry, swapping his No. 26 jersey for Hilaro's goalkeeper strip. With the name on the back of the jersey, the sight of Terry in goal was a few letters short of being hilarious.

'I'd always gone in goal in training and joked with Jose that I was the No. 3 goalkeeper if someone got injured in a game,' Terry later remembered. 'To be fair, I'm all right in goal, so it was a natural choice for me to get called over and go into the nets when Pete and Carlo got injured at Reading.

'It was really nerve-wracking going in goal because they had a couple of long throw-ins late on and you can't prepare for that as an outfield player.'

Such was the attention on Terry's cameo as a goalkeeper that Umbro, his sponsor and boot supplier at the time, would later ensure he was well prepared for another stint between the sticks should Chelsea's situation ever get that drastic again.

'I put on a pair of gloves that weren't made by Umbro and afterwards they sent me a pair of their ones in case it happened again!'

Fortunately for Chelsea it would not and Terry could get back to focusing on his career as a defender. Losing two goalkeepers in a game is not only unfortunate, but rare. Especially when we consider the circumstances surrounding Cech and Cudicini being forced off.

Of the two, it was Cech's injury that dominated the headlines in the aftermath. Whereas Cudicini had been knocked out by Sonko's uncontrolled leap into the box, Cech suffered a fractured skull. The game was just fifteen seconds in when the goalkeeper got down low to intercept an early through-ball for Stephen Hunt, but got a lot more than he bargained for as the Irishman left a dangling leg to collide with his head.

It took five minutes before Cech was eventually removed from the pitch, although the impact would be everlasting. Now at Arsenal after spending eleven years as a Chelsea player, Cech has been forced to wear a protective helmet ever since the incident with Hunt. He was sidelined with his injury for over three months and the fallout continued for much longer as question marks over his future remained.

Never one to forget a perceived injustice, Cech's manager Mourinho did not flinch in his criticism of Hunt and the medical attention the goalkeeper received on the day. Mourinho labeled the Reading player's actions as a 'disgrace' and was similarly damning regarding the emergency services.

'The Cech one, the challenge is a disgrace. He is lucky to still be alive,' declared Mourinho at the final whistle. He was aghast at not only losing two goalkeepers to injury during the game, but also the events that had contributed to it. Both were heavy traumas to the head, although fortunately for Cudicini it was just a severe headache he would be nursing in the coming twenty-four hours, not a fear for his overall health despite it taking ten minutes before he was taken off the pitch wearing an oxygen mask having received treatment.

'Carlo I think was knocked out as a consequence of the way he hit the ground, but a knee coming at Petr like that, at such speed – the boy was even laughing afterwards,' Mourinho added to journalists.

'It was unbelievable and players should respect each other more than that.'

Indeed, Didier Drogba echoed Mourinho's sentiments on the incident in an interview with French sports paper *L'Equipe*.

'It's not an accident,' he was reported as saying. '[Hunt] saw he was going to hit Petr and he didn't try to avoid it. When Petr was carried out of the ground he was laughing.'

In the coming days, the debate switched from Hunt and whether or not he had deliberately hurt Cech to how long it had taken the goalkeeper to receive the care he required.

According to Mourinho, it had taken thirty minutes for an ambulance to arrive at the Madjeski Stadium. When it did, paramedics did not have access to the dressing room so Cech was forced to leave via a wheelchair in a small lift.

'If my goalkeeper dies in that dressing room or in the process, it is something English football has to think about,' said the Chelsea boss. 'This is much more important than football. I would like someone to tell me why my goalkeeper was left in this situation.'

The ambulance service hit back at Mourinho's claims, stating it was in fact Chelsea's own medical team who made the vital decisions on the day.

'They were offered two routes [out of the stadium]: one around the pitch on a stretcher or via a small lift in a wheelchair. Chelsea took the decision to go via a small lift in a wheelchair,' a spokesman said on behalf of South Central NHS Trust.

'Chelsea medical staff called the ambulance at 5.45 p.m., at seven minutes to six the ambulance arrived. At eleven minutes past six, [Cech] was in the hospital.' The whole saga was becoming a blame game, but in among it all it was Cech who was at risk.

Having been taken to hospital in Reading, the goalkeeper was later moved to John Radcliffe Hospital in Oxford, where he underwent an operation to insert two metal plates. So far as injuries go, it was one of the most severe to have been witnessed on the pitch.

Chelsea played Barcelona in the Champions League four days later and the good news for Cech was that he was well enough to watch the game on television from his hospital bed.

The better news that night in a footballing sense came from Drogba's boot as he scored the game's only goal immediately after the break to give Chelsea a 1-0 win.

Terry was not in goal against Barca. By this stage, he had given Hilario his goalkeeper shirt back and the Portuguese stopper made his Chelsea debut as Cudicini remained unavailable for selection.

Terry has also been a makeshift striker at times when Chelsea have been attempting to salvage something from matches. With the clock ticking down, and desperation the only tactic left, countless managers have thrown him forward in an attempt to get something unexpected.

He started out as a midfielder in Chelsea's youth team before his then coach Ted Dale dropped him further back into central defence. After the events at Reading in October 2006, he is one of the few players who can claim to have played everywhere for his club.

Reading: Hahnemann; Murty (Bikey, 36), Sonko, Ingimarsson, Shorey; Seol Ki-Hyeon, Harper, Sidwell, Hunt; Doyle, Lita (Long, 73).
Unused subs: Stack, Gunnarsson.

Chelsea: Cech (Cudicini, 5); Ferreira, Boulharouz, Terry, Bridge; Essien; Mikel, Lampard, Robben (Kalou, 82); Shevchenko (Cole, 63), Drogba.
Unused subs: Carvalho, Wright-Phillips.

23

Tottenham Hotspur 2-1 Chelsea
Premier League
5 November 2006

Alleged racism in any walk of life can prove just as detrimental to all involved as an actual act of discrimination that is carried out with racial motivations. For the accused, it is a strong allegation that is not easily forgotten, regardless of the outcome. For the victim, it brings an ugly side of society to the fore and puts them in the unenviable position of being reminded of prejudices that still exist.

For John Terry in November 2006, he had to deal with his character being judged on nothing more than hearsay; for Ledley King, the victim of an alleged racial slur from the Chelsea captain, it meant another black player in English football having to relive times past when it was difficult for players of colour to excel in the sport.

It is a part of the club's past that has left a regrettable stain on Chelsea's history, given the ordeal Paul Canoville was forced to endure during his time at Stamford Bridge in the 1980s. Discrimination is bad enough, but then when it is coming from your own supporters, it heightens the strength of the insults. Canoville was subjected to all sorts of racist behavior from Chelsea fans, even having bananas thrown at him while representing the club.

In the thirty or so years that have passed since then, Chelsea deserve much credit for how the club has driven that element of supporter away from west London. Now black players are celebrated without consideration for skin tone, treated as equals on the terraces by fans who rightly judge them more for what they achieve on the pitch than where they are from.

Canoville himself has helped that process, often speaking eloquently about his own experiences and playing a role in helping educate football supporters and wider society with an anti-discrimination message. His autobiography, *Black and Blue*, gives a particularly harrowing account of it all and the challenges that the former Chelsea winger had to overcome in life. The book is powerfully written, open and honest.

Racism was supposed to be a thing of the past, but then it bit back to shock Chelsea and Terry.

'I honestly don't know what happened,' Ledley King told *FourFourTwo* in a 2013 interview, recounting that day in November 2008 when rumours were suddenly rife that Terry had racially abused the Tottenham Hotspur defender before he was sent off.

'Me and JT were jostling in the box; I was defending a corner, he was trying to score. He ended up dragging me to the ground and he got up. I honestly can't remember what he said. I remember coming off the pitch and people saying it was something racist, but I didn't hear anything at the time so could never point the finger.'

Given the pair had been shoving each other just moments earlier, it is difficult to imagine King not acknowledging the exact contents of Terry's verbal tirade had they been as vicious as fans would later make out in internet chat rooms.

Words were definitely exchanged between the pair, but King's reaction was not that of a man who had been racially abused. It was only when Terry walked away from the incident that he got involved with other Spurs players and subsequently received a second yellow card and was sent off by Graham Poll.

'I'm still not actually sure what he was sent off for. I think he barged into Benoit Assou-Ekotto on the way back to his own end, and a couple of the other black French-speaking players – Pascal Chimbonda and Didier Zokora – went to defend their friend,' King added. 'Maybe some people jumped to conclusions because of that, but those players didn't hear anything either. It was only after the game that we were reading messages [suggesting it may have been racist], and we were surprised by that.'

What should have made the headlines coming out of White Hart Lane is that Chelsea had just lost their first league game against their London rivals at the thirty-third time of asking. Picking up three points from Chelsea had been a long time coming for Spurs indeed – so much so that a last league victory against the Blues pre-dated the Premier League. That came at Stamford Bridge in 1990; we had to go further back to 1987 for when Spurs had last won a league game on their home patch against Chelsea.

That would have frustrated Terry, along with the red card that came in the 72nd minute. He was and is a player who prides himself on maintaining records, so to be the Chelsea captain who lost that unbeaten run against such a staunch rival would have eaten away at him, especially as it meant a suspension to keep him out of action the following week.

The same could be said for Jose Mourinho. Like his captain, the Chelsea boss was in the business of making records, not conceding them. Since he had arrived in England, Mourinho had broken the Premier League's points record for a season, had not lost at home and was busy rewriting the annals of Chelsea and English football. Yet here he was, losing to Spurs, with nineteen years of history being wiped out on his watch in just ninety minutes.

That was the football side of things to get Mourinho and Terry frustrated. They would learn to live with that and with games on the horizon, it was not something that would come to define their season. Defeats happen, regardless of the opponents, meaning the frustration would have been a temporary one.

Allegations of racial abuse are much more far reaching, however. They are certainly not to be taken lightly and for Terry, it was something that refused to go away. The speculation would rumble on, with television replays being debated to clarify what Terry actually said to King. Still, nobody could make light of it and King would remain calm about the situation.

'It didn't affect my relationship with John,' he explained in that *FourFourTwo* interview. 'We played together when we were young [at Senrab], but we were never best buddies – we never spoke to each other off the pitch when we were younger, we just played in the same team. Obviously we've got a lot of respect for each other, and we've played for England together, but just because you play with somebody, that doesn't mean you speak off the pitch.'

The FA took no action against Terry over the alleged incident with King.

Tottenham Hotspur: Robinson; Chimbonda, Dawson, King, Assou-Ekotto; Ghaly, Zokora, Jenas, Lennon; Keane (Defoe, 85), Berbatov.
Unused subs: Cerny, Davids, Huddlestone, Mido.

Chelsea: Hilario; Ferreira (Boulahrouz, 46; Kalou, 68), Carvalho, Terry, A. Cole; Makelele (Wright-Phillips, 63); Essien, Ballack, Lampard; Robben, Drogba.
Unused subs: Cudicini, J. Cole.

24

Arsenal 1-2 Chelsea
League Cup Final
25 February 2007

Arjen Robben's corner was an in-swinger. Attacking the ball as it arrived in the Arsenal box were John Terry and Andriy Shevchenko. The Ukrainian would win his personal duel, but his header was a weak one and bounced off Abou Diaby. The ball span into the air, resting just inside the six-yard box for enough time to tempt Terry into having another bite at the cherry. The Chelsea captain charged it with his head at the same time Diaby was swinging a boot to punt it clear. Diaby made a clean connection, yet it was not the ball that cracked the leather of his boots; it was Terry's head.

Before the Chelsea defender had even hit the floor, the lights were out. Diaby had caught Terry flush on his jaw with a blunt force and the way his body contorted as he crashed to the floor, head first, all those inside the Millennium Stadium could see the danger the Chelsea captain was in. The cheers of the 70,000 fans inside the stadium fell silent almost in an instant. Breaths became gasps.

Terry had swallowed his tongue and stopped breathing, needing urgent medical attention to get him back to consciousness. The reaction of those around Terry would show the gravity of the situation. Both Chelsea and Arsenal players – Cesc Fabregas included – would proceed to wave frantically to the benches for the medics to come on while Arsenal physio Gary Lewin, who was fortunately close by, was quick to administer the first responder care. The players were all gathered around Terry, a look of shock and horror on their faces as they watched on, desperate for a sign of immediate recovery.

It would be five minutes before Terry was carried off the pitch on a stretcher. It was the 2007 League Cup final and after fifty-seven minutes of play, he would not feature again.

While Dider Drogba was scoring the winner late on in the game to complete his brace for the afternoon, Terry was in an ambulance and on his way to hospital.

'I remember walking out for the second half and nothing else until waking up in the ambulance on the way to the hospital,' Terry told reporters after.

What Terry could not forget was that eighteen-year-old Theo Walcott had put Arsenal ahead after twelve minutes before Drogba had got Chelsea level eight minutes later.

It was a London derby being played in Cardiff and Chelsea were set to reaffirm their dominance over Arsene Wenger's side.

Remember, prior to Jose Mourinho's arrival, the Gunners had long had the beating of Chelsea in this fixture. Then Mourinho came along and, almost overnight, things would swing in Chelsea's favour. League Cup final victory in February 2007 was a part of that as Mourinho extended his unbeaten run against Wenger's Arsenal to seven matches. For Chelsea, it was nine.

Terry would not be around to experience the winning feeling at the final whistle, but after the Chelsea players had finished up their celebrations on the pitch with the League Cup trophy – captain's duties had been left to Frank Lampard – it would not be long before Terry was back inside the dressing room holding it himself.

It was an extraordinary sight as all inside the Millennium Stadium an hour or so before had been concerned for Terry's health. Jose Mourinho was panicked on the sidelines, in deep discussion with the fourth official as he shook his head in disbelief. Was it all happening again for this Chelsea side? Only five months earlier Petr Cech had fractured his skull against Reading and that injury came close to ending his career. Now here was Terry, unconscious after a heavy strike to his head. Nobody knew what to expect; given Chelsea's recent past, those connected with the club were fearing the worst.

The captain had looked in a bad way, but then here he was, awake and back on his feet. He did not want to miss out on the fun and games with his teammates.

'I had the scan and they said it's OK. It was great to be back [with the lads], they were different class,' Terry added. 'I'm still feeling a bit groggy, though. It's thanks to the lads [that Chelsea won the game] as I didn't have much part to play in the second half. Throughout the competition they've been spot on.'

Terry's injury was much a sign of his commitment to winning as it was his bravery. It was that quality that English football has long since traded on; where players will throw their bodies in places others will not contemplate. The feeling is often that the technical ability may not always be there, but the desire to achieve something and risk plenty in the process, always is.

His diving header was the sort of action that makes a hero out of a man. Ask most football fans in England what qualities they associate with most in a player and it is those that Terry demonstrated at the Millennium Stadium. Fans want to see bravery from the players they are paying to watch. Most football supporters will talk of themselves in those terms, so when players are willing to put that moral code into action, their status is heightened. Flying boot in his face or not, there was little chance of Terry ducking out of the challenge. In the words of Atticus Finch from *To Kill a Mockingbird*, '[Courage is] when you know you're licked before you begin, but you begin anyway and see it through no matter what.'

In the modern game, those personalities are disappearing. The need for players to risk their health and general wellbeing is being replaced by those of technical supremacy, which has meant the focus has shifted. Warrior-like displays are taking on a new meaning.

In Terry's time, he would bridge the gap between the old and new. He had the same honesty that has long been marvelled, yet he would also prove to be a defender of some renown to succeed in changing times. Throwing himself into the boot of Diaby was a shocking symbol of all that. He saw his moment, his chance for glory and he could not refuse the bait.

Two years after taking the sort of hit that would floor even the meanest of heavyweight boxers, Terry reflected on that side of his game in an interview with *Chelsea* magazine.

'That's just how passionate I am about the game,' he said in May 2009. 'I think I've got an understanding with the Chelsea fans, which I have done ever since I came through the ranks at this club.

'For me, that understanding is knowing what it means to them. Also, for us players, it means knowing that we can make the fans' weekend great and make their lives great because they love the football club and follow us all over the world. So we owe them everything, every weekend and that's every time we pull on the shirt.'

It's that sense of duty that has often defined Terry. He has not been a player to speak confidently in the press and leave it there; his career has been about substance and that desire to deliver has been the essence of everything that he would become.

Him getting clattered, knocked unconscious and sent to hospital against Arsenal did not win Chelsea the League Cup. Didier Drogba did that, but Terry provided the spirit in the same way he always did.

Arsenal: Almunia; Hoyte, Toure, Senderos, Traore (Eboue, 66); Denilson, Diaby (Hleb, 68), Fabregas; Walcott, Aliadiere (Adebayor, 80), Baptista.
Unused subs: Poom, Djourou.

Chelsea: Cech; Essien, Carvalho, Terry (Mikel, 63), Bridge; Makelele (Robben, 46), Lampard, Diarra, Ballack; Shevchenko (Kalou, 89), Drogba.
Unused subs: Hilario, Cole.

25

Chelsea 1-0 Manchester United (AET)
FA Cup Final
19 May 2007

'When Wise went up to lift the FA Cup, we were there,' sing Chelsea fans. So too was John Terry.

Time and again the presence of Dennis Wise crops up in Terry's story. The former Blues captain has been such a big figure in his career, helping nurture Terry from the youth team through to playing with the seniors.

Wise won the FA Cup with Chelsea twice, first in 1997 before becoming the last captain at the old Wembley Stadium to be victorious there in 2000.

For a club that had never won a major piece of silverware at Wembley until 1997, it was a surprise that Chelsea should be the side to bring the curtain down on the famous venue. The romantic ideal would have placed one of the founding members of the Football League there instead, like a Preston North End, just for the thrill of seeing that tradition bask in the sun for one last time.

Wembley had been hosting FA Cup finals since 1923 after it was built as part of the British Empire Exhibition. Prior to that, Stamford Bridge had played host to English football's showpiece event for a period. Wembley was supposed to be a temporary structure, but Sir Arthur Elvin had seen the potential of it as a sporting venue. From selling cigarettes at the old Empire Stadium as it was known back then, he would eventually purchase it and transform Wembley into one of the most iconic venues in football.

Come 2000 however, Wembley was decrepit and old. It was a tired stadium and needed modernising, so seventy-seven years of history was ripped down and replaced with the stadium we know today.

Chelsea had beaten Aston Villa in the last FA Cup final there and John Terry was an unused substitute. It had been quite the season for the nineteen-year-old as a few weeks earlier he had been on loan at Nottingham Forest, busy helping David Platt's side pull clear of the relegation zone. Now he was picking up the first winners' medal of his career thanks to another Roberto Di Matteo goal in a Wembley final.

Fast-forward seven years and how times had changed for Terry. From the last to the first, Chelsea were back at Wembley for the great unveiling of the new structure that stood in the place of the old Empire Stadium.

Lord Foster had been responsible for its design, with the iconic towers now replaced by a domineering arch that supports much of the new stadium's roof. In time, Wembley's arch would come to be marvelled just as much as the towers, standing proud and high above the neighbouring roof tops, adding another site to London's expanding skyline.

Before Wembley had even been given time to establish itself in the modern age, Chelsea were writing their names in the history books there. In 2000, it had been Villa who succumbed to a 1-0 loss and now it was Manchester United's turn. And just like his idol Dennis Wise, Terry was wearing the armband as the captain who made the walk up to the Royal Box to collect the trophy.

This time, Chelsea would not have to wait seventy-four years to taste glory in this most special of arenas, as had been the case with the former Wembley Stadium. This time they were there from the very beginning. It was they who would be having their name set in stone for as long as the stadium stands. And among all of the celebrations, Terry is the man who features in all the pictures, his hands holding the FA Cup; the captain's armband donning his shirt sleeve. The legacy was being written.

It was a fitting way to bookend the history of each stadium; indeed, the symbolism was not lost. In one sense, Wise's Chelsea were passing the baton on to the next generation when Terry had been on the bench in May 2000. It was the baby steps of a player who was still learning his trade, but observing everything around him. Terry was able to survey the scene experience the feeling of success before he would go on to write his own narrative. Now the new stadium was finally complete and staging football matches, Terry was back there to confirm the journey he had made into greatness himself.

It was a rite of passage for him in many ways. By this time Terry had not so much emulated Wise's achievements in west London, but surpassed them. He was a two-time Premier League winner, an experienced and regular competitor in the Champions League. He had won the League Cup twice and was also England captain.

In every sense, the pupil had outdone his master, yet he needed to complete the journey by repeating Wise's success at Wembley. It was the final confirmation of all he had achieved since his time as a youngster. Wise had been a winning captain at Wembley and now Terry was. Not only that, he had helped repeat history in the same way Wise had by marking the official opening at Wembley and etching Chelsea's name into the stadium's folklore.

That's what the 2007 FA Cup final will always be remembered for. It was not great in any sense, but just by being the first, it stands apart from the others that have followed. It was the beginning of a new time and Chelsea was the club that would first taste success there.

'We have signed off the season on a high note and that makes me very proud,' Terry told BBC Sport at the final whistle. 'We kept going right until the end and this is what this team is all about.

'We're disappointed about the Premier League and the Champions League [where Chelsea had lost out], but we will come back even stronger next year.'

Given the connection with Wise's history at Wembley, winning the 2007 FA Cup would have ranked high for Terry, but as a club there were plenty of coincidences on that afternoon that would eventually play into a wider sense of destiny for superstitious Chelsea supporters.

The game had gone into extra time and right at the death, just before penalties, Didier Drogba had scored the winner. It was a cute bit of play that had set the Ivorian free to dink his touch over Edwin van der Sar after Frank Lampard's beautifully weighted pass on the volley.

'I love finals, you only reach them to win, and this was a very difficult game against a fantastic team,' said match-winner Drogba. 'I was looking for this first goal against Manchester United for two years and it happened today. Now we just want to celebrate.'

It was the start of Drogba's remarkable record in Wembley finals. In the five finals he played there, Drogba scored every time to win four FA Cups, although the 2008 League Cup final would end in defeat to Tottenham Hotspur.

It was the date more than anything that will relate to Chelsea fans most – Drogba and 19 May hold a special place in their calendars on the back of his exploits in Munich five years after Chelsea became the first club to lift the FA Cup at the new Wembley.

Before Drogba was marking the date in history for very different reasons, John Terry was marking another achievement on his list.

Chelsea: Cech; Ferreira, Essien, Terry, Bridge; Mikel, Makelele, Lampard; Wright-Phillips (Kalou, 93), Drogba, J. Cole (Robben, 46; A. Cole, 108).
Unused subs: Cudicini, Diarra.

Manchester United: Van der Sar; Brown, Ferdinand, Vidic, Heinze; Fletcher (Smith, 92), Carrick (O'Shea, 112), Scholes; Ronaldo, Rooney, Giggs (Solksjaer, 112).
Unused subs: Kuszczak, Evra.

26

England 1-1 Brazil
International Friendly
1 June 2007

Two weeks after lifting the FA Cup with Chelsea at the new Wembley Stadium, John Terry was back under the arch. This time it was with England and again he was making history. From being the first captain to win the FA Cup at the new venue, he became the first player to score in an international there.

It could have been very different had Gilberto Silva not seen a goal of his own ruled out for offside on nineteen minutes. That would have robbed Terry of his crowning glory, but he was eventually able to mark his name in the history books in the second half when he headed home from a David Beckham free-kick.

Having Beckham in the side to send over the sort of cross he did was ideal for Terry, although the wide man did steal some of the limelight from the England captain that night. It was his first game back in the England side since the 2006 World Cup, so the clamour to see him in action inevitably created a substantial sideshow. Beckham had been playing for LA Galaxy in Major League Soccer, so his inclusion in the side had proved somewhat of a shock. New manager Steve McClaren had made no secret of the fact Beckham was all but finished with England when he took over a year earlier, so bringing him back into the fold was a major U-turn on his part. Benefiting from his quality dead-balls, Terry was only too happy to welcome the former captain back into the England set-up.

'His delivery is superb,' said Terry of the cross that set up his goal. 'It was a great ball from Becks and it was about time I scored again.'

Despite the sense of occasion with Wembley staging its first ever England game since being rebuilt, McClaren's side were going through a tough spell. Appointing him as manager after Sven-Goran Eriksson's departure had not worked and England were struggling in their qualification group for Euro 2008. They had already lost to Croatia, which meant they were playing catch-up with Slaven Bilic's side as well as Russia. A goalless draw with Macedonia had not helped and of the nine games under McClaren's charge, England had won just four.

It was only a friendly, but they needed a win against Brazil to boost their spirits and get them back on track. That would not come as Diego equalised in the final stages to put a dent in England's confidence.

McClaren was doing the very thing so many England managers have in the past. A failure to take friendlies seriously was limiting his side and damaging their sense of morale. Too many changes throughout the game against Brazil unsettled the Three Lions to make them uneasy at the back, which allowed Diego to eventually sneak in and score when he did.

A trip to Estonia five days later – this time a European qualifier – saw England win 3-0, but it could not cover up the cracks. The fans were beginning to get on McClaren's back and with atmosphere surrounding the squad, it was no way to be unveiling a new, £700 million stadium.

Even players such as Frank Lampard were being turned on. Terry's Chelsea teammate, Lampard was booed during the game against Brazil and it continued when he was subbed off late on in the game.

'I'm disappointed. I don't like that for any player. But Frank is a tough kid and he has been through criticism before,' McClaren said in Lampard's defence. 'People doubted he and Steven Gerrard can play together but they proved against a world-class team that they can do their job and they did it very well.'

There it was again – the Lampard–Gerrard conundrum. Eriksson had tried and failed to make it work effectively and so too would McClaren. When Fabio Capello took over the reins, even he struggled to get the best out of them collectively.

The problem was always the system. A 4-4-2 was not working as it meant either one of the players had to restrict their game. Both got forward and made an impact in the final third, but were constantly looking over their shoulder to ensure the other was covering; it was never suitable. They could not play on instinct, instead being asked to sit too rigidly when they did not do that for their clubs. It was alien to them.

A Lampard–Gerrard midfield partnership needed another player in there with them and that would have meant sacrificing a striker. Given it was Alan Smith who played alongside Michael Owen against Brazil, on this occasion McClaren evidently lacked the conviction to even consider it, let alone attempt it.

Had Gerrard and Lampard repeated their goalscoring form from club football for England, the return would have been just as valuable as having another front man on the pitch. Lampard was a twenty-goals-a-season midfielder by this stage, but that sort of return was never going to happen in an England shirt. Fans saw that and it frustrated them; how could Lampard be so reliable for Chelsea, but then fail to produce consistently for his country?

That is where the boos were coming from, only they were directed at the wrong person. Without condoning that level of public humiliation, it should have been the manager who was failing to combine his team of undoubted talent into a winning force, who was feeling the brunt of it all.

Still, those problems for England, like Beckham's return, were the sideshow for the grand unveiling of the new Wembley on the international stage. The story was about how captain Terry had wasted little time to make his mark on a stadium that would become a home from home for him in the next few seasons.

Not only did Terry win the FA Cup in 2007 at Wembley, he was back there in 2009, 2010 and 2012 doing it all again.

There would not be any jeers for him, that was for certain. England were struggling to adjust to the new regime under McClaren and the best thing they had going for them was Terry.

England: Robinson; Carragher, King, Terry (Brown, 72), Shorey; Beckham (Jenas, 77), Gerrard, Lampard (Carrick, 88), Cole (Downing, 62); Owen (Crouch, 83), Smith (Dyer, 62). Unused subs: Green, Carson, Bridge, P. Neville, Bentley.

Brazil: Helton; D. Alves (Maicon, 65), Naldo, Juan, Gilberto; Kaka (A. Alves, 71), Mineiro (Edmilson, 63), Silva, Ronaldhino; Robinho (Diego, 74), Love. Unused subs: Doni, Alex Silva, Marcelo, Alex, Josue, Jo.

27

Manchester United 2-0 Chelsea
Premier League
23 September 2007

'A common goal' was the unfortunate headline to the picture caption in the October 2007 issue of *Chelsea* magazine.

It was referencing a shot of Jose Mourinho and Avram Grant together on the training pitches at Cobham, 'all smiles as they chatted'.

Within a few weeks of that picture being published, the only one with a grin would be Grant, who had replaced Mourinho as Chelsea manager before September was out.

The decision to sack Mourinho had struck a dagger to the heart of most Chelsea fans. Here he was, the manager who had delivered back-to-back Premier League titles and allowed Chelsea to dream of dominating English football, but the club were getting rid of him for political reasons. It was not because Mourinho was failing as a manager, but more because of how he conducted himself.

Now, it was on a smaller scale and with far less serious consequences, but to understand the shockwaves the decision to remove Mourinho caused in west London, we need only think of the 2016 European Union Referendum in the UK. When Britons voted to get out of the EU, such was the small majority in the exit camp that it all but divided the country. Politics started eating itself, with the shadow cabinet being depleted by resignations, while protests enveloped Parliament Square. Even Prime Minister David Cameron stepped down from his role as a result of the votes cast that changed the political landscape of Britain. At a time when the country needed it most, there was no leadership in power or opposition. It became a free-for-all.

In west London circa 2007, we saw Chelsea fans abandoning matches in the immediate aftermath of Mourinho's exit. 'Walk out for the Special One,' they sang. The campaign was not highly successful – nor well planned by those who took part. Much to the chagrin of the Sky Sports News cameras, the expected walkout for the first home game since Mourinho left was a low-key affair. With a reporter stood outside Stamford Bridge hoping to capture the moment thousands left in protest, it was barely in the hundreds. And of those who were leaving early, it was probably more to do with getting the tube home to avoid crowds after an uninspiring 0-0 draw with Fulham than it was to show their annoyance with Roman Abramovich.

As underwhelming as it was, the whole affair shone a light on the ill feeling at Stamford Bridge. There was divided opinion.

On one hand Chelsea fans did not want to see Mourinho go, but then there was a begrudging acceptance that it was Abramovich's vast fortune that was bankrolling the club's success and, ultimately, he called the shots. It was Abramovich's decision to sack Mourinho and Chelsea fans had little choice but to accept it and get behind the team. A protest en masse in Mourinho's honour was not going to bring him back, yet the divisions were clear from the supporters and the club.

Regardless of Grant being the shock appointment as manager – he had only recently been appointed Director of Football and was a relative unknown in England – Chelsea had an ace up their sleeve. While Chelsea fans would pine for Mourinho, they still had a figure to rally behind; they had John Terry. Grant was the manager, but Terry was very much the leader.

From a personal perspective, the departure of Mourinho only served to strengthen Terry's standing in west London. If Abramovich was going to replace his managers at a rate of one every fifteen months at Chelsea – that was the average life expectancy of a Chelsea manager employed by the Russian up to the summer of 2016 when Antonio Conte arrived – then the owner knew he needed to build some semblance of sustainability around the playing squad. With that in mind, Chelsea reinforced their support for the spine Mourinho had built and stuck with it. Terry was the strongest element.

The first game post-Mourinho came at Old Trafford just three days after he was relieved of his duties. That Chelsea would lose 2-0 was not the important thing – that it was Terry leading the team out was.

Grant was never a manager of Chelsea. Even from his opening press conference he had the look of a man who was there to do a job that satisfied others and not himself.

The contrast between him and Mourinho had been significant. Where Mourinho had shown himself to be his own man, addressing the press with confidence and a sense of arrogance that would serve him well in his three years, Grant appeared a lost man at his unveiling.

The Israeli was slumped in his chair, leaving the big questions to Chief Executive Peter Kenyon to answer. We can only speculate, but looking at how the remainder of the season would unfold, Grant seemed happy to leave the biggest decisions at the decisive moments up to his players.

The siege mentality Mourinho had thrived on remained strong in his squad. With Terry implementing that attitude, the Chelsea players came together and pulled the club through a season that had been wrecked so early on, but eventually salvaged something.

That Chelsea would go on to finish just two points behind eventual champions Manchester United and also reach the Champions League final that season says plenty about the power of those players to galvanise the feeling inside the squad and make it work to their benefit.

We are not talking in isolation, either. What Abramovich learned from 2007/08 about his Chelsea players – we must include Ashley Cole, Frank Lampard, Didier Drogba and Petr Cech in this, too – is that he could rely on them to keep Chelsea afloat in spite of the failures of managers he appointed.

Abramovich knew he could use his chequebook to make his problems go away. If a manager did not perform in the way the owner hoped, sacking him would not mean the end of Chelsea's season and their hopes of silverware. A pay-off would need to be negotiated, but that was all in the boardroom. Out on the pitch, with Terry leading the side as captain, backed up by those other leaders around him, the ship could be steadied and guided through troubled waters.

It started with Mourinho's departure and carried on at Chelsea when Luis Felipe Scolari was removed from his post in early 2009. After that, Abramovich would sack Andre Villas-Boas and Roberto Di Matteo mid-season, safe in the knowledge he had a character like Terry to safeguard the club's immediate future.

What Terry did for Chelsea in those times was very Mourinho-esque. Indeed, he and Lampard sustained that spirit that Mourinho had created. It did not matter who the manager was as, when their backs were thrust against a wall, it was those battling qualities that pulled them through. It was coursing through their veins, defining every part of their being and Abramovich relied upon it. If he knew he could not, perhaps the manager turnover would have been less in west London. Maybe he would have been more forgiving.

It was as that generations of player eventually started to depart Chelsea and suffer from their natural decline that the methods of old would no longer work.

When Mourinho was dismissed for a second time in December 2015 – just six months after winning his third Premier League title as Chelsea manager – the response was the same on the terraces.

Mourinho's name was chanted with passion and after newspaper reports suggested some players had turned their back on the manager, Diego Costa, Cesc Fabregas and Eden Hazard were all booed. The divisive nature of sacking Mourinho set in, only this time Abramovich could not call on that group of players as a collective. Only Terry remained at the club and those who had replaced his former teammates did not offer the same sort of mettle.

Guus Hiddink would prove a calming influence on the dressing room, yet Chelsea did not come close to salvaging their season in any sense. Performances under Hiddink were not too dissimilar from Mourinho and with a dressing room lacking the strength that had long been associated with Chelsea, not even Terry could inspire them to improve.

Almost a decade earlier, Terry was in his prime, however. When he stepped out on to the pitch at Old Trafford, he was doing it as much more than just a Chelsea captain. He was the figurehead for what the club represented. It was his time.

Manchester United: Van der Sar; Brown, Ferdinand, Vidic, Evra; Ronaldo, Carrick, Scholes, Giggs; Tevez (Saha, 79), Rooney.
Unused subs: Kuszczak, O'Shea, Pique, Nani.

Chelsea: Cech; Ferreira, Ben Haim, Terry, A. Cole; Mikel, Makelele, Essien; J. Cole (Pizarro, 76), Shevchenko (Kalou, 59), Malouda (Wright-Phillips, 69).
Unused subs: Cudicini, Alex.

28

Chelsea 3-2 Liverpool (AET)
UEFA Champions League, Semi-Final
30 April 2008

It was two weeks before Chelsea's Champions League semi-final with Liverpool would be decided, but Frank Lampard was in a rush to lay down a psychological marker for his teammates.

It would be the fourth time in as many seasons that the Blues and Reds had come to blows in Europe, with this latest installment the third semi-final. Chelsea had lost the two previous meetings at the same stage – first on account of Luis Garcia's 'ghost goal', the second on penalties – but things were about to change.

'We've had a bad experience twice in the semi-final against Liverpool, but those games count for nothing this year,' said Chelsea's vice-captain. 'We're just focused on reaching that final. We are determined to do it. We've failed at that hurdle a few times and it will be nice to finally get there and hopefully we can use the past experience from our other semi-finals to get through this year.'

Lampard's words were in an interview for the Chelsea matchday programme. The Blues had just beaten Fenerbahce in the Champions League, but rather than putting the focus back on the Premier League, Chelsea were happy to start the mind games well in advance of facing Liverpool. Even John Terry was getting in on it, using his pre-match programme notes ahead of the fixture with Wigan Athletic to drum home the desire from the dressing room to finally bury the ghost of Liverpool in Europe.

'Who knows what the balance will be when Liverpool come [to Stamford Bridge] for the second leg,' Terry wrote. 'What I do know is that in the two second legs at Anfield, their players have gone on about what a difference their crowd made. Now it's our turn to say that.'

It was a bold move for a club that was still in the throes of a title race with Manchester United. Within twelve days of facing Wigan, Chelsea would defeat Sir Alex Ferguson's side 2-1 at Stamford Bridge to leave nothing but goal difference separating them at the top of the table with just two games remaining. That fixture led into the second leg with Liverpool.

In the modern game, with sanitised communication strategies and an approach all about damage limitation in the media, clubs seldom use an official publication to fuel the spectacle of what is on the horizon. It is often quite the opposite, with the official word attempting to play down the drama and not strengthen the spotlight on players. It was especially the case for Chelsea whenever it involved Liverpool, yet here they were feeding the rivalry with a hefty portion of pre-match jesting.

For Chelsea to be talking the game up so early outlined just how deep the feeling of resentment ran from them to the Anfield club. This latest Champions League clash was a final shot at redemption to put things right after the heartache they had suffered. The communication strategy outlined it and the policy was being implemented by the two leaders of the camp – Terry and Lampard.

For all the talk, by the time the second leg came around, the landscape had shifted dramatically. In the two weeks since Lampard and Terry had rallied the troops, calling on Chelsea fans to get ready for a fight, the sense of occasion came with a deluge of sub-plots. Right at the forefront was the death of Lampard's mother, Pat. She had passed away after a battle with pneumonia and her death had brought a cloud over Stamford Bridge as the club and fans mourned with the midfielder.

Before the Manchester United league clash, Terry had addressed supporters with words of condolence for Lampard.

'Myself, the players and everyone here, send our condolences to Frank, his dad and to his sisters Natalie and Claire,' he said, again in his pre-match programme notes. 'We're all deeply sorry for the loss of his mum. All our thoughts and feelings are with him and his family ... It's difficult for me to follow on from that now, but we are at such a crucial stage of the season.'

That was it. Here Chelsea were at such a vital period in not just the campaign, but the club's history, and it was tragedy away from the pitch dictating it. As professionals, the players had to tell us they were focused and Lampard's loss was not going to impact them; yet there was a strange feeling around Stamford Bridge. Terry was embodying that, having a moment of reflection to put everything into context. How would he continue to put so much effort and focus into his game when one of his closest friends and allies was suffering so much?

Lampard missed the United game and it was up to Michael Ballack to score twice to give Chelsea the victory that levelled them with United at the top of the table. For Lampard to be missing because of such personal grief was a big factor for Chelsea. While Terry was the overall leader of the side, Lampard was a key instigator in it all. He scored the goals and made things happen from midfield; as Terry pushed them on from the back, Lampard translated it into something tangible in the opposition half.

The pair were a duo, a partnership that was not officially labeled through their positions on the pitch. They worked as sole influencers, yet it was together when they were at their devastating best. Terry and Lampard had the sort of chemistry that builds dynasties and here they were, acting it out at Stamford Bridge.

Lampard had missed the biggest game of the season against United, though, and with the second leg against Liverpool coming just four days later, even the Chelsea players were unsure if he would be featuring in the Champions League. Avram Grant had refused to pressure him into playing, explaining the decision would be Lampard's alone.

It had been a John Arne Riise own goal in the 90th minute that put Chelsea in control of the tie. Dirk Kuyt had put Liverpool ahead in the first half, but Riise would head in a Salomon Kalou cross into his goal to put the Blues in the ascendancy.

For once Chelsea held their luck at Anfield, having Petr Cech to thank for some fine saves that kept them in the game before Riise's gaff. Finally Chelsea had got the rub of the green.

Now at Stamford Bridge the emotions would be high, especially as Lampard had put the loss of his mother to one side to step back into the line-up. It was a brave move from a player who had been on the receiving end of some tortuous moments that had involved Liverpool in the Champions League. With everything going on in his personal life, did he need to put himself through it all again?

With all that emotion, Chelsea needed a leader with a calm head and Terry showed he was the man most capable.

The talk of Liverpool was being deflected now; the focus had become about the challenge Chelsea faced and not who their opponents were. Chelsea had been willing to whet their appetite long before, although now it was business. Terry's voice had a different tone; he was expressing a desire to take opportunities, 'owing it to ourselves to make the next step in the Champions League'.

Didier Drogba scored twice on the night. His first was cancelled out by Fernando Torres, taking the tie into extra time with both sides locked at 2-2 on aggregate and with an away goal each. Then Ballack was upended by Sami Hyypia inside the box and Lampard stepped up.

The entire stadium was with him and he did not buckle, marching forward to slip the ball to Pepe Reina's left and put Chelsea back in front. Then came Drogba's second (Chelsea's third) in the 105th minute that killed it, although a late Ryan Babel goal made for a tense closing few minutes.

When the final whistle went, Grant fell to his knees pitchside; his arms in the air, praising a divine influence. He would have done better to focus on Terry and Lampard, who by this stage were embracing to mark a special moment in their lives.

Chelsea were going to Moscow.

Chelsea: Cech; Essien, Carvalho, Terry, A. Cole; Ballack, Makelele, Lampard (Shevchenko, 119); J. Cole (Anelka, 91), Drogba, Kalou (Malouda, 70).
Unused subs: Cudicini, Belletti, Alex, Mikel.

Liverpool: Reina; Arbeloa, Carragher, Skrtel (Hyypia, 22), Riise; Alonso, Mascherano; Kuyt, Gerrard, Benayoun (Pennant, 78); Torres (Babel, 99).
Unused subs: Itandje, Finnan, Lucas, Crouch.

29

Manchester United 1-1 Chelsea
(AET, United Win 6-5 on Penalties)
UEFA Champions League Final
21 May 2008

'I was in Moscow, stood behind the goal and I just thought it was a moment he would never get over,' remembers Chelsea legend Pat Nevin.

The moment the Scot is referring to is one that should have marked John Terry's career apart from everybody else's in a Chelsea shirt, but for all the right reasons. Only it is with sad eyes and heavy hearts that Blues fans will recall Moscow 2008.

Terry had been given his Didier Drogba moment before the Didier Drogba moment had ever been imagined. The Chelsea captain was ahead of his time, ready to write history and steal a glory that his teammate did not know would ever exist. Terry was about to step up and score the winning penalty in a shoot-out that would win Chelsea the Champions League for the very first time.

He looked confident, too, striding up to face Manchester United goalkeeper Edwin van der Sar, pulling down on his captain's armband as if to reinforce the point of who he is and the lofty position he dictates at Stamford Bridge.

Terry had the look of a man who had been dealt a date with destiny that he was not going to turn his back on. He knew what it all meant.

'He has felt the pain of semi-final defeats in the Champions League for Chelsea,' Martin Tyler commented in the commentary box, just as the referee blew his whistle to action Terry forward.

Up he stepped. One step, two step, three step, shot. Van der Sar was helpless, already diving to his right, in the opposite direction to where Terry had placed his spot kick. The ball seemed to move in slow motion through the air, breaking through each rain drop that fell to the floor. A stadium held its breath; west London fell silent with the expectation. Fists were clenched in hope; cheers were about to engulf the night air. Were we about to have a new European champion?

Well-beaten, the goalkeeper had to look over his shoulder in fear the ball was about cross the line and deliver Chelsea the cup. But it did not. The net did not ripple; the Chelsea fans did not enter a stage of delirium that only winning a trophy for the first time can deliver. No, it was the sound of leather on steel that van der Sar heard as Terry's shot struck the post before ricocheting off into the gathered pool of photographers. Then time sped up.

Terry's left foot had gone from under him in the Moscow rain, causing him to slip and deflect the ball off the target as he struck it with his right.

Van der Sar could not believe his luck. While Terry was sat there, his head in his lap, the Dutchman's celebration was one of a man who knew all too well that he had been given a major lifeline. Van der Sar's face said it all – a look of shock that Manchester United were still in with a shot of winning the European Cup.

The game would go to sudden death and after Ryan Giggs bagged United's seventh penalty, it was Nicolas Anelka's miss that would eventually see Chelsea lose out.

Terry's tears would tell us what it all meant to him. He felt it more than any other Chelsea player that night as it was he who had missed the biggest penalty of the game. He was not trying to keep Chelsea in it – it was his penalty that would have sealed the sweetest victory of them all in his career and Chelsea's long history. The ghosts of Anfield would have been laid to rest; a huge part of his career would have been fulfilled.

Of course, it should not have been like that. Had Drogba not been sent off deep into stoppage time for a petulant slap on Nemanja Vidic, it would have been him stepping up to take the spot kick. And we would see in Munich four years later just how clinical the Ivorian was from twelve yards.

Terry had not taken a penalty for Chelsea in a competitive fixture before Moscow, and he did not after. The fact he was so willing to make that walk and shoulder the burden was the sort of decision that endeared him to Chelsea fans. Knowing success was that close, he could not shirk his duty and allow another player to inherit the burden. Drogba was unavailable, so the captain had to do it for him.

'Because it was against Manchester United, it was a weird day,' Joe Cole remembered. 'We were playing against our mates at the end of the day, so we didn't want to lose.

'I wouldn't say it was a classic final. It was fearful, trepid; there was no flowing football. But I felt with the balance of play over the 120 minutes, we were the better side.

'I came off the pitch with about 20 minutes to go because [Nicolas] Anelka was the penalty taker. I remember sitting there and when JT's gone to take the penalty, I was confident as I'd never seen him miss one [in training]. Technically he was very good, but the gods weren't with us that night.

'It's staggering we didn't win the Champions League. I think we should've won it once or twice, but it just wasn't meant to be.'

Chelsea would continue to win things domestically, though. After losing to Manchester United in the Champions League final of 2008, the Blues almost got back there for a rematch only to suffer an away goals defeat to Barcelona at the death in the 2009 semi-final. That season still ended in glory with the FA Cup to cap off Guus Hiddink's spell as interim manager with a valuable piece of silverware.

A year after defeating Portsmouth at Wembley, Terry was leading Chelsea to a Premier League and FA Cup double – the one and only time Chelsea have achieved that feat.

The heartbreak of Moscow still lingers, though. It's a moment that haunts Terry, although as Nevin explained, it is what adds to his legend at Chelsea. That night may have impacted him, but then the trophies never dried up. He went on to enjoy more success with the Blues in the face of his own adversity.

'A few years down the line he was still lifting trophies and was still a big figure at the club,' Nevin added. 'He wasn't broken by what happened in Moscow. He was still the same player and it takes a lot of mental strength to not allow things like that to affect you. A lesser player would have struggled to overcome it, but not John.

'Nobody was annoyed with John for missing that night because he showed the heart to step up and take a penalty kick.'

Terry called four of United's Champions League winners that season his international teammates. Just seven days after watching them parade around the Luzhniki Stadium, singing in the rain as though they were Gene Kelly and Debbie Reynolds, Terry was lining up with them for England. Alongside Rio Ferdinand, Wes Brown, Wayne Rooney and Owen Hargreaves, Terry was singing the national anthem with his usual gusto at Wembley.

USA were the opponents and as if to make a point about his state of mind, Terry scored the opening goal of the game. England won 2-0.

Manchester United: Van der Sar; Brown (Anderson, 119), Ferdinand, Vidic, Evra; Hargreaves, Carrick, Scholes (Giggs, 87); Rooney (Nani, 101), Tevez, Ronaldo.
Unused subs: Kuszczak, O'Shea, Silvestre, Fletcher.

Chelsea: Cech; Essien, Carvalho, Terry, A. Cole; Ballack, Makelele (Belletti, 119), Lampard; J. Cole (Anelka, 99), Drogba, Malouda (Kalou, 92).
Unused subs: Cudicini, Alex, Mikel, Shevchenko.

30

Germany 1-2 England
International Friendly
19 November 2008

England were still in their honeymoon period under Fabio Capello when they travelled to Germany for a friendly in November 2008.

It was the early stages of a relationship that any manager who takes on the role as the Three Lions boss finds himself. Capello's track record alone had seen his appointment being described as a coup for the FA; the fact that the Italian was not Steve McClaren made things even rosier.

Capello was coming in on a mandate to shake up the England squad. Where McClaren had gone wrong was that he attempted to be too friendly with the players. He had been close to them under Sven-Goran Eriksson's reign and after being put in charge, had not distanced himself from the dressing room enough. He wanted to be among the players, yet be the boss all at the same time. Those sorts of conflicts never mix well in a dressing room. There has to be a distance and it is that sort of mistake the best managers often avoid making.

As a coach under Eriksson, McClaren had been the buffer, so becoming manager proved a culture shock. The relationships had to be different.

If only that was the reason for his failure, McClaren and England may have stood a chance. Throw inept tactical decisions and systems that did not suit certain players into the mix and McClaren's shortcomings were plentiful.

His appointment and subsequent fifteen-month reign were a disaster, so Capello had the look of a knight in shining armour as he rode down Olympic Way to take up residence at Wembley. He was so far removed from his predecessor that his divinity was granted before a ball had even been kicked under his guidance.

The same problems that plagued McClaren would eventually prove Capello's downfall, too, however. Eventually his stardust ran out; he was stripped back by the media to reveal the same drawback every England manager had suffered before him: he was human and by default that meant he would fall into the trappings of his character. For an England manager, that most human of qualities is never a positive thing.

The problem for the Italian was that rather than being too friendly with the players he coached, the same qualities that got him the job were to his detriment. Capello cracked the whip too much and it did not create a balance in the dressing room.

He desired a team of John Terry clones who were battle-hardened and ready to do the hard yards. His management required players of a certain mentality who could handle the intensity and revel in it.

That was the character the Chelsea and England captain had traded on throughout his career before he met Capello and it was why the Italian kept him on as skipper when he was made England boss.

Capello believed in Terry for the same reasons Jose Mourinho had four years earlier. When he looked into the defender's eyes, Mourinho saw a winner and he worked to build Chelsea around him. Working every day on the training ground, Mourinho had a player who was the counterpoint for his Chelsea.

International management is different. Coaches have limited exposure to their players, so the job is not about making them improve the technical side of their game. The focus shifts to discovering formulas that work best and how to bring players together. It is for that reason an emphasis on the captaincy becomes so vital; managers need every ally they can get and the captain comes top of that list. He needs to embody the manager's philosophy in the dressing room and on the pitch.

Indeed, for a manager such as Sven-Goran Eriksson, having David Beckham around was all rather handy. He revelled in the limelight and did not mind appearing on the front pages of tabloids. Beckham was never that much different. Capello was a no-nonsense manager and in Terry he had his no-nonsense captain.

Coming inside the first year of his reign, England defeating Germany in their own backyard only served to feed the belief in Terry from Capello. It was not just the victory, but the fact Terry had scored the game's winning goal with just six minutes remaining. It was leadership of the highest order; the captain arriving to do the captain's job.

When we look at the team that night, it hardly inspires either. Capello had taken a strike force of Gabby Agbonlahor, Darren Bent and Jermain Defoe to Germany. Aside from Defoe, it was a front line made for the lower reaches of the Premier League. It was far from international quality.

That was the reality of the England team Terry was leading at the time, though, so to come away with a victory over a significant foe was all the more remarkable. An experimental squad or not, England were getting results.

Terry was helping Capello's stock rise all the more in the first year of him taking the England job. It was when Terry eventually lost the captaincy due to his alleged indiscretions off the pitch when Capello's regime would gradually unravel.

At the 2010 World Cup when Terry's now infamous press conference ahead of the final group game against Slovenia was seen as an attempt to undermine Capello's power, Terry was on the other side of the divide and that did not help heal the wounds that were gradually being exposed in South Africa.

When the pair worked in unison, however, England were never stronger in Capello's period of management. The England side was difficult to beat and were certainly not the same team that had underperformed with McClaren at the helm. From not reaching Euro 2008, England made it to the World Cup two years later, but it was without Terry wearing the armband. That same sense of determination had gone, the momentum lost.

From beating Germany in Germany, 'Die Mannschaft' would send England home early from South Africa with a 4-1 victory in the last sixteen. Both countries were fielding their strongest eleven at this stage, but regardless, England were missing something more vital. The entire tournament had seen them lack any real leadership and without his captain, Capello was not as effective.

Had Terry worn the armband, it probably would not have worked out any better for the Three Lions, such were their problems. It was England in tournament mode and as we have so often seen, it does not matter who wears the jersey as the outcome is often the same.

The feeling with Capello's England was the unity he built with Terry in those early games had dissipated. Things had taken a different path and it limited the team's ability to grind out results in tougher moments.

They had that quality in Berlin's Olympic Stadium.

Germany: Adler (Wiese, 46); Friedrich (Tasci, 68), Mertesacker, Westermann, Compper (Schafer, 77); Schweinsteiger, Jones (Marin, 46), Rolfes, Trochowski; Klose (Helmes, 46), Gomez (Podolski, 57).
Unused subs: Hinkel, Hitzlsperger.

England: James (Carson, 46); Johnson, Terry, Upson, Bridge; Wright-Phillips (Crouch, 90), Barry, Carrick, Downing; Defoe (Bent, 46), Agbonlahor (Young, 77).
Unused subs: Robinson, Richards, Lescott, Mancienne, Davies, Parker.

31

Chelsea 1-1 Barcelona
UEFA Champions League, Semi-Final
6 May 2009

Two weeks after the event and John Terry was still talking about it. The heartache and sense of injustice that had long defined Chelsea's forays in the Champions League had haunted them once again when Barcelona snatched a dramatically late 1-1 draw at Stamford Bridge to win the tie on away goals.

Andres Iniesta's last-minute strike took the Catalans to the final to face Manchester United. It should have been Chelsea; it should have been a rematch from twelve months earlier; John Terry should have got his chance of redemption in Rome after the misery of Moscow.

It was Tom Henning Ovrebo who had ensured none of that would happen. A fortnight on the wounds remained raw.

'The Champions League ... well, I still find it hard to say anything that won't get misinterpreted or get me into trouble,' Terry wrote in the Chelsea programme for the Blues' last home game of the season.

A huge sigh of regret leapt from the page. The use of an ellipsis was the symbol of choice to fill the space for the words Terry really wanted to say, but could not.

'One year we'll win [the Champions League] and when we do I think we'll be the most deserving of teams ever, just because of the long wait and semi-final hardships we have endured.'

Barcelona had topped them all. The 'ghost goal' four years previous with Liverpool was suffering enough, although this was on another level. It is not often we can say it with total conviction in sport, but Chelsea were robbed against Barcelona. There was nothing subjective about it like in 2005 – the facts were clear that the referee had had a howler and it was Chelsea paying the price.

It was not the fault of Pep Guardiola's side or any shenanigans on their part, either. It was the luck of the draw and Chelsea had to face the harsh reality of Ovrebo being the man who would decide their fate in such ridiculous circumstances.

Indeed, the referee got few things right on the night and even Barca themselves could feel aggrieved when Eric Abidal was sent off in the second half for tripping Nicolas Anelka.

Chelsea's French striker had clipped his own heels when running through on goal, but the referee adjudged that Abidal had been the guilty party and upended him.

The score was 1-0 in Chelsea's favour by then and it meant Barca's task was going to be ever more difficult, playing with ten men with twenty-five minutes left on the clock.

Michael Essien had fired Chelsea in front with a spectacular volley after nine minutes, but the cushion should have been more. While Barca were left feeling aggrieved for Abidal receiving his marching orders, the decision should have actually come forty minutes earlier when he fouled Didier Drogba in the box. Chelsea's Ivorian was all set to pull the trigger when one-on-one with Victor Vadles, only for Abidal to bring him down. It was a penalty and as the last man denying a goalscoring opportunity, Abidal should have been taking an early bath.

Ovrebo did not see it that way, instead keeping his whistle at his side as Valdes smothered the loose ball, allowing play to go on. Drogba was left to punch the floor in disgust.

So perhaps the Norwegian was attempting to make up for his earlier error where Abidal was concerned. It was harsh on Barcelona, but then they did have previous in the game where the left-back was concerned. The balancing act was in play.

That sort of explanation goes a long way in football. Even retired referees will concede there are moments in matches that have played on their mind and influenced them at a later stage.

Ovrebo made up for it in that instance, but Chelsea would still end the game in credit with the referee; they should have been awarded at least three other penalties. On the balance of play, just one of them would have taken the game away from the visitors, who despite their vastly talented line-up, only managed one shot on target all night.

The first penalty shout was for a foul on Florent Malouda that appeared to be inside the box, but Ovrebo gave a free-kick instead, from which Drogba almost scored.

With the clock ticking down, though, Barcelona should have never been in with a chance come the 90th minute when Iniesta struck gold with the flick of his right boot.

As their backline became stretched, holes were appearing at the back and Anelka seemed ready to exploit that fact when he exposed Gerard Pique. Brushing the ball beyond the defender, he was through on goal, ready to kill the game off and end Barcelona's European hopes. Only Anelka could not latch on to his own pass as Pique had raised an arm to deny him and despite the linesman and referee being well placed, nothing was given.

'It was clear as day,' Frank Lampard told journalists after. 'There were three [penalties] that were clear and I can't understand why they weren't given. That's the most disappointing thing.

'We could have killed them off tonight. We had chances and decisions that went against us, but we're not going to cry about it in terms of Barcelona. They're a great team and are deservedly in the final. The way we played, the way the game developed and the decisions that were blatant for everyone to see, that's a very frustrating thing.'

The third penalty Lampard claimed was for a block by Samuel Eto'o with his arm to deny a Michael Ballack shot. Chelsea had thrown men forward after Iniesta's equaliser and even Petr Cech was in the Barcelona box attempting to grab the winning goal. When the ball fell to Ballack, his shot was goal-bound, but a raised arm from Eto'o kept it out. Stood in line of the flight of the ball, Ovrebo turned his back and chased the run of play as Barca cleared their lines.

Ballack and Chelsea were livid, chasing Ovrebo across the pitch. Ballack's fury was animated with his expression, his face contorted in utter disgust at Ovrebo's refusal to award a spot-kick.

'I'm still full of adrenaline and I have to try to calm down to give a right analysis of what has happened,' said Blues boss Guus Hiddink. 'You have to sometimes give the benefit of the doubt to the referee ... but if you have three or four situations in a sequence, then I can fully understand [why the Chelsea players were frustrated with not being awarded a penalty].'

That is where the heartache came. Chelsea had been forced to dig in and combat the tiki-taka style incorporated by Barcelona, yet they had done enough to overcome it. Or at least they thought. Had the referee performed, the story would have been a different one as Chelsea had not just lived with Guardiola's side, they had shown themselves to be their equal.

That is why Lampard was so disappointed after; it was why Terry could not bring himself to fully articulate his regret even a fortnight after the event.

Whereas Chelsea were on the cusp of a repeat Champions League final with Manchester United, Barca themselves were close to realising something spectacular. Champions League winners for second time in 2006, it was their 2009 success that would cement Guardiola's place in modern football history.

He had set about changing football with his principles based on possession and a complete fascination with not conceding it. Barcelona were becoming one of the greatest sides ever in club football and being crowned as kings of Europe was the moment they would realise it.

Chelsea would have stopped them in their tracks had it not been for Ovrebo. Their journey may have taken another course, but history tells us where that great side was officially born.

The last word would fall to Drogba at the final whistle. 'Hey, hey,' he shouts, spotting the television camera just outside the Stamford Bridge tunnel. 'It's a disgrace. It's a disgrace. It's a fucking disgrace.'

The outburst was unpalatable, yet equally summed up what every Chelsea fan was feeling.

Chelsea: Cech; Bosingwa, Alex, Terry, Cole; Essien, Ballack; Anelka, Lampard, Malouda; Drogba (Belletti, 72).
Unused subs: Hilario, Ivanovic, Mancienne, Mikel, Di Santo, Kalou.

Barcelona: Valdes; Alves, Pique, Toure, Abidal; Xavi, Busquets (Bojan, 85), Keita; Messi, Eto'o (Sylvinho, 90+7), Iniesta (Gudjohnsen, 90+6).
Unused subs: Pinto, Caceres, Hleb, Pedro.

32

Burnley 1-2 Chelsea
Premier League
30 January 2010

How do you turn negative headlines into something positive? Well, the best place to start is by changing the subject. It is a skill that politicians have long since mastered – they call it spin.

John Terry found himself neck-deep in hot water in January 2010 when news of an apparent extramarital affair broke. It was not any ordinary affair, either. According to widespread tabloid reports – first in the now defunct *News of the World* – the Chelsea and England captain had been romantically involved with Vanessa Perroncel, who was the ex-girlfriend of Terry's long-time friend Wayne Bridge. To add fuel to the fire, Terry had attempted to put an injunction in place to prevent news of the alleged affair being made public.

By this stage, Bridge was no longer sharing a dressing room with Terry at Stamford Bridge after leaving Chelsea to join Manchester City in 2009. They were England teammates, though, and the assumed affair subsequently ended Bridge's international career as he refused to play on the same team as Terry. It also meant Terry would be stripped of the England captaincy by manager Fabio Capello, denying him the chance of leading his country out at that summer's World Cup in South Africa.

All that was to come and before it did, Terry was busy attempting to weather the storm the newspapers had been whipping up.

The *Mail on Sunday* published what it described as an exclusive that Terry had reportedly arranged for Perroncel to have an abortion during their affair. 'The pregnancy and termination are thought to have been the "consequences" referred to by the High Court judge who threw out the £170,000-a-week footballer's bid to seek a draconian gagging order to keep his affair secret,' the paper wrote.

Rival tabloid the *Mirror* ran an interview with two of Perroncel's supposed close friends. According to the red top, Terry had attempted to 'play Cupid' when Perroncel and Bridge had initially split the previous July. 'And it wasn't long before Terry had seduced lonely Vanessa and began a passionate four-month relationship with the woman who until so recently had been his best friend's partner,' the report added.

Everywhere Terry turned, the headlines were coming at him. The daggers were well and truly out and the British media was wasting little time in sticking them in.

Such was the frenzy, it led to Terry being booed on the terraces; not by his own fans, but anywhere Chelsea would travel. It all started away to Burnley, the very weekend when it was being reported across the press that Terry had allegedly been unfaithful to his wife.

Turf Moor is a football stadium from a bygone age where the fans sit on top of the pitch and can create a raucous welcome for visiting teams if they feel up to it. Just ask Manchester United, who had fallen victim to the hostilities earlier that season.

It had been Burnley's first-ever home match in the Premier League and the midweek setting made for the perfect environment to welcome the reigning champions so soon in the campaign. The lights were on, the volume turned up and the fans packed inside Turf Moor to play their part as the fabled twelfth man. It worked, too, as Robbie Blake scored the game's only goal to record a historic win for the Clarets.

When the Chelsea team bus pulled into town, however, the inspiration was very different, but the desired outcome all the same. Burnley wanted to get one over one of the big boys again.

This time it was not about a David and Goliath battle; it was more about good versus evil. Here was John Terry, the England captain who had apparently just committed adultery with his friend's ex-partner. And not only that, he played for Chelsea, who were owned by an oligarch; the club who had 'bought' their way to success and titles.

For a club of Burnley's size and history, Chelsea were everything that football should not represent. The town is just as traditional as the football club and the fans hold the same values that tradition dictates. They do not like change, least of all when it is inspired by foreign influence. Chelsea were a symbol of a changing world and like every traditionalist, the Clarets needed to stand up against it for the greater good.

How much all of that is actually true is subjective. Chelsea fans will tell you that, if anything, the club represents progress and that should be seen as a positive thing regardless of how their change of fortune has come about. What defines Chelsea now is success and since the first rules of the game were published by the Football Association in 1851, it has been that fundamental spirit that has taken football forward to become the global game. What can be more traditional than that? As they are wont to do, opposition fans will hardly agree.

Still, Roman Abramovich or not, the news surrounding Terry's private life had amplified the desire of those inside Turf Moor for their club to get one over Chelsea. It was a time when the Blues and their captain needed to change the conversation; it was a time when they needed their own spin doctor (ironic given that Alastair Campbell, the man famed for his manipulation of the press under Tony Blair's New Labour government was and is a staunch Burnley supporter).

Terry served up the sort of answer that would have had even Campbell impressed. Not only was Terry on the winning side, it was he who would score the winning goal in the 82nd minute. There was no surprise about who would claim the assist either – it was Frank Lampard.

For all that was going on in his personal life, Terry was ending the debate about football right there. The media and the wider football public could pass judgment on the rumours about him, but on the pitch he would remain unfazed, as that header would prove. The hyperbole was not going to get the better of him. If there was any question about his suitability to remain as Chelsea and England captain, he had just shown his club and international managers that it should not be considered.

The issue Terry faced with England and Capello was that football rarely decides those things at international level. It becomes a moral judgment and no matter what he did on the pitch, the pressure for him to be stripped of the captaincy was always going to prove too much. Had Capello wanted to, not even the England manager could save him from his fate.

Chelsea manager at the time, Carlo Ancelotti, had no doubts where he stood in the debate. 'There has been no discussion about [Terry] not being captain of Chelsea,' he would tell reporters. Ancelotti seemed genuinely disturbed by it all, unable to comprehend the interest in whether or not Terry should be Chelsea's captain. This was his club and his team, so why should he be held to ransom and forced to make a moral decision about one of his players? Ancelotti had grown up in Italy where sportsmen and women are judged more for what they do in the sporting arena and not outside of it. He could not understand the culture.

'I don't know why you are asking me this question,' he would add. 'I need only worry about [Terry's] professional life and he has done well in every game for me. I am not worried. On Friday, he had an excellent training session so it was not necessary to speak with him.'

The Perroncel stories would rumble on although later in 2010, Bridge's former partner and Terry's rumoured sordid love interest would give an interview to the *Observer*, where she offered her side of events.

'It was a friendship,' she said. '[But] I suppose they wanted a "John Terry in kinky sex" story.'

Whatever story the media wanted, Terry was continuing to write his own when it came to football. Defeating Burnley had kept Chelsea above Manchester United by a single point at the top of the table, also keeping Arsenal at bay, who were a further four points back in third.

That was all Chelsea fans were concerned with. They wanted to win the title again and Terry was fulfilling his professional duties.

Burnley: Jensen; Mears, Cort, Carlisle, Kalvenes (Edgar, 35); Eagles, Elliott, Bikey, McDonald (Paterson, 60) Blake (Thompson, 72); Fletcher.
Unused subs: Weaver, Duff, Gudjonsson, Nimani.

Chelsea: Cech; Ivanovic, Alex, Terry, A. Cole (Deco, 76); Lampard, Ballack, Zhirkov; J. Cole (Sturridge, 72), Anelka, Malouda.
Unused subs: Turnbull, Carvalho, Ferreira, Matic, Borini.

33

Chelsea 8-0 Wigan Athletic
Premier League
9 May 2010

Chelsea's task was a simple one. They led Manchester United by a single point in the title race, so they had to match their result on the final day of the season in order to be crowned Premier League champions for the third time in six years.

Carlo Ancelotti's side would face Wigan Athletic at home, while the Red Devils entertained Stoke City at Old Trafford.

Mid-table and their top-flight status long since secured, Tony Pulis' side had won just one game since early April. In that run, Chelsea had beaten them 7-0 to record an emphatic win at Stamford Bridge. If there was a hypothetical beach somewhere in warmer climes, the players were most certainly on it. Wigan themselves were not that much better off in the form guide, narrowly avoiding relegation despite just four victories since the turn of the year.

It was not that record that made John Terry nervous ahead of kick-off, though. It was more that Wigan had a tendency to turn up against some the Premier League's so-called bigger sides. Less than a month before this title decider, Roberto Martinez's side had beaten Arsenal 3-2. They had come back from 2-0 down with ten minutes remaining to pull off a shock victory – one that all but ended the Gunners' faint hopes they may be able to challenge Chelsea and United right to the final weekend of action.

Liverpool had also been on Wigan's list of big scalps, as had Chelsea way back in September when Ancelotti's side succumbed to a surprise 3-1 loss at the DW Stadium.

The Latics may have struggled for much of the season, yet when they faced teams more willing to play football rather than scrap it out for points, we would see some of their better performances.

That made sense since Martinez had built his reputation in management on a willingness for his teams to play at all times. Well, try to at least.

When a manager persists with that policy at a club of Wigan's size and with their resources, it is perhaps naive. Wigan needed a bit more substance to withstand the battles they would face against sides struggling with them in the bottom half of the table, whereas Martinez had built them with the idea they would play like a side challenging for the European spots. It was a commendable approach, but without attracting players of a calibre good enough to implement his ideas, Wigan were always destined to find times tough in the top flight.

Regardless of their toil, it still meant they had the potential to cause an upset at times, as we had seen. Terry knew it himself, too.

'That was the most nervous I have ever been before a game,' he would later explain, expressing the mood in the Chelsea dressing room as the Blues' day with destiny approached.

'I thought we'd win, but I didn't sleep the night before, I was really nervous, and that kind of stands out in my memory.'

That loss in September earlier in the campaign would have played its part. Indeed, losing at the DW Stadium was a massive shock to the system for Chelsea, who under new boss Ancelotti had won all eight of their opening fixtures in all competitions. They had also sealed the Community Shield with a 4-1 penalties win against Manchester United having drawn the game 2-2.

After the problems under Luis Felipe Scolari, this was a different Chelsea side we were seeing. Guus Hiddink had helped restore their confidence by bridging the gap between Scolari's departure and Ancelotti's arrival, so things were looking up until Wigan put a dent in Chelsea's armour.

Chelsea had not just lost that day – Wigan were deserved victors, with Petr Cech's dismissal early after the interval adding to Chelsea's frustrations.

So here were Wigan once again, facing Chelsea and ready to cause an upset in the title race. But then something unexpected happened: they completely collapsed and Chelsea took advantage to romp home.

'We went and smashed them 8-0,' Terry remembered, questioning the wisdom of his pre-match angst. 'What a way to do it. The nerves and the excitement before those big, important, decisive games, was really important to me.'

It was a spectacular way to become champions; not just because of the scoreline, but as it meant Chelsea broke a few records along the way, namely becoming the first Premier League side to score 100 goals or more in a season. Didier Drogba's hat-trick also saw him pip Wayne Rooney to the Golden Boot award to make him the league's top goalscorer with twenty-nine for the season.

On the pitch afterwards, Ancelotti was understandably in celebratory mood.

'I'm very proud to train this club,' he told BBC Sport. 'I feel well in this club. I have a very good relationship with everyone and think that we worked very hard this season as a group and we deserve to win.'

Ancelotti was then asked if recent victories against Manchester Unitied and Liverpool had boosted the title push. 'It was about continuity,' he answered.

That continuity came in the form of the manager relying on certain players over the course of the season, of which John Terry had been one. A 2-1 win at Old Trafford in early April may have seen the pendulum swing back in Chelsea's favour, but if it was decisive games that journalists were looking for, they had to go back further to November.

Sir Alex Ferguson's side were the opponents again and Chelsea won the game 1-0. The goalscorer? John Terry.

His header came in the 76th minute from a Frank Lampard free-kick to maintain Chelsea's position of strength in the title race when they were racking up points. The momentum was being maintained, taking points from their main rival to keep their run of form going.

Over the course of a thirty-eight-game season, it is rare for one game to prove pivotal in ultimate glory. However, defeating United was, given that Chelsea would win the title by a single point. It was the difference that separated them.

It had been a frustrating afternoon for Chelsea back in November until Terry's goal. The front men were struggling to break down a stubborn United rearguard, so up stepped Terry to seize the initiative. He was Chelsea's game changer when all else failed.

It would take another seven months for him to fully appreciate the achievement that afternoon, but he got it with an 8-0 thumping of Wigan.

It was the game that sealed Chelsea the title, but defeating United thanks to Terry all those weeks before is what in effect won it.

He was not done there, of course. A week later, he had an FA Cup win to make history again as the first Chelsea captain to win the league and cup double.

'Amazing,' Terry said when the BBC reporter mentioned a potential Double, scenes of celebration going on all around him as Chelsea players saluted the tens of thousands in the crowd that had remained inside Stamford Bridge to see them lift the Premier League trophy.

'It's the first time a few of the lads have won the Premier League here. It's been three years since I've won it and it's not a nice feeling. Today, this is what I remember, this is the feeling. This is what I want more of, year after year now.

'We'll enjoy tonight, but we'll be back in training next week and ready to go down in the club's history. We're all looking forward to it.'

So on to Wembley Terry and Chelsea went.

Chelsea: Cech; Ivanovic (Belletti, 59), Alex, Terry, A. Cole; Lampard, Ballack (Matic, 70), Malouda; Kalou (J. Cole, 59), Drogba, Anelka.
Unused subs: Hilario, Ferreira, Zhirkov, Sturridge.

Wigan Athletic: Pollitt; Boyce, Caldwell, Gohouri; Melchiot, Diame (Scharner, 72), McCarthy, Watson (Thomas, 61), Figueroa; N'Zogbia, Rodallega (Moses, 82).
Unused subs: Stojkovic, Scotland, Cywka, Mostoe.

34

Chelsea 1-0 Portsmouth
FA Cup Final
15 May 2010

There is a song they sing down the King's Road about John Terry. 'Double, double, double, John Terry's won the Double,' it goes. For reasons of decency and the sanity of Tottenham Hotspur fans, we will have to end it there.

The sentiment is very much about the success the captain has enjoyed during his career, while said other club has failed to match his individual accomplishments in that time. It is because of the 2010 FA Cup final against Portsmouth that Chelsea fans are able to sing it at all, though.

Even in these times of rich owners creating super-clubs that seemingly have bottomless pits of funds to finance their success, winning the Double is no mean feat. Just six clubs had won English football's top flight and the FA Cup in the same season before Chelsea were presented with the chance of doing it themselves in 2010.

Preston North End had been the first when they secured the Double in 1889. That was the first-ever season of the Football League competition and as if to reaffirm their dominance of the English game, William Sudell's side had remained undefeated all season. Aston Villa would repeat Preston's league and cup success in 1897, but it would then be over sixty years before another club would do it.

While Chelsea fans like to remind their arch-rivals Spurs about Terry's success, it was their London neighbours who were double champions in 1961. Arsenal (1971, 1998 and 2002) and Manchester United (1994, 1996 and 1999) are England's most successful clubs when it comes to the Double, winning it three times.

Speaking of songs, Liverpool fans are often heard singing about Chelsea's history and a perceived lack of success in west London. Well, despite their own triumphs down the years, the Reds have only won the Double once themselves when they were Division One champions and FA Cup winners in 1986. Chelsea would equal that record in 2010 with a 1-0 defeat of Portsmouth at the new Wembley.

Victory beneath the famous arch meant John Terry became just the ninth captain in 121 years to do it, and as it stands at the beginning of the 2016/17 season, no other skipper has since had the honour.

Chelsea were fresh from thrashing Wigan Athletic 8-0 in the Premier League a week earlier when they arrived at the home of English football. That emphatic victory over Roberto Martinez's side had crowned Chelsea as champions by a single point advantage against Manchester United. It was the finest of margins in a league campaign; for it to come down to just one point out of a potential 114 for the season outlined just how close the title race had been.

A single point won Chelsea their fourth League title and so a single goal would deliver them their sixth FA Cup – incredibly their third in four seasons since the new Wembley had been opened in 2007.

The stadium was becoming a home from home for Chelsea as they had also featured in a League Cup final there in 2008, not to mention the Community Shield twice. Of the ten games they could have featured in up to the end of the 2009/10 season, Chelsea had played in six and won five.

On every occasion, Terry had been the captain and despite the Blues being overwhelming favourites, facing Portsmouth came with a few sub-plots that added to the sense of occasion.

If Terry had been nervous the weekend previous when he was preparing to line up against Wigan, he may well have been feeling the weight of circumstance bearing a heavy load on his shoulders at Wembley.

He was familiar with the surroundings; not only were Chelsea regular visitors, but Terry was often leading England out at the national stadium. In the opposition dugout, however, was Avram Grant.

The Pompey manager had been in charge of Chelsea in the immediate aftermath of Jose Mourinho's sacking in September 2007 and it was the Israeli who would have the honour of being the first manager to lead the Blues out in a Champions League final come the end of 2007/08.

That night still torments Terry. His missed penalty would have crowned Chelsea as European champions for the first time in the club's history, but instead he was forced to watch Manchester United parade the trophy around Moscow's Luzhniki Stadium.

How much of an influence did Grant have on Terry's slip that night? Very little, if any, yet coming up against him in a final still represented a psychological barrier for the Chelsea captain to overcome. Grant was a reminder of how Terry's place in history had been ripped away from him. Now, here he was, hoping to be the first player in Chelsea history to lift the FA Cup in the same season the club was champions of England and it was Grant who stood in his way. It was as though he were a timely reminder delivered by fate to show Terry that guarantees are hardly a bankable commodity in sport.

Even though Portsmouth had finished rock-bottom of the table that season – they were relegated after entering administration and suffering a nine-point deduction – the presence of Grant would have brought about a sense of unease in Terry. Footballers do not like to be reminded of their vulnerabilities and here Terry was having to face his own failures in a final. Again.

Frank Lampard and Nicolas Anelka had both gone close in the first half; the former had struck the upright from all of 30 yards with a swerving effort. Salomon Kalou had even fluffed his lines when gifted with an open goal after Ashley Cole found him unmarked on the edge of the six-yard box. The Ivorian struck the crossbar instead when it was harder to miss than score.

As the game dragged on and Chelsea seemed intent on making things more difficult than they needed to be, the feeling grew that Portsmouth would eventually get their chance if Chelsea were not taking theirs.

There was more frustration as Terry looped a header off the woodwork. Pompey should have scored themselves when Frederic Piquionne missed an open goal of his own, firing against a grateful Petr Cech. It was Cech who would keep the scores level shortly after the interval, too, when he denied Kevin Prince-Boateng from 12 yards.

Aruna Dindane had been chopped down by Juliano Belletti, giving away a penalty. It was a lazy tackle from the Brazilian as he stuck out his leg, inviting Dindane to make contact and tumble.

With all that had passed between Terry and Grant two years ago in Moscow, it was going a to be spot-kick that would be prove decisive for one of them again. It was Grant ruing his luck however, with Boateng's penalty down the middle a poor one that allowed Cech to hook it clear with his legs having already dived right.

The game swung on that moment. Pompey's belief had been growing, but now it was visibly sucked from them. Boateng was collapsed on the floor in the Chelsea box, inconsolable as his teammates gathered around to pick him up. His very literal collapse would prove symbolic for what was to come. Within three minutes, Didier Drogba was scoring the free-kick that would win the FA Cup for Chelsea.

In typical fashion for how the game had gone that afternoon, Drogba's effort crashed off the woodwork before resting in the back of David James's net.

Drogba had earlier stuck the bar from a set-piece, claiming the ball had crossed the line when it bounced free. There was no doubting this one, though, as he bent it around the wall and into the bottom corner to fool James, who had expected his shot to loop over the wall. It was Drogba's third goal in an FA Cup final; he would finish his career with four in four.

That personal bit of history for Drogba outlined how influential he had been in English football. For strikers, it is a numbers game with goals scored proving the ultimate decider in success or failure. Where he's concerned, there has not been a more prolific player in cup finals.

So it proves for captains. How do we judge their tenure at a club? Performances remain subjective; fans can debate how a captain displayed certain qualities, but those sorts of observations are limited to those with the privilege of being in attendance. It is trophies in the cabinet that are the ultimate factor and in 2010 Terry did what no other captain at Chelsea ever had. Double, double, double, John Terry won the Double.

Chelsea: Cech; Ivanovic, Alex, Terry, A. Cole; Lampard, Ballack (Belletti, 44), Malouda; Kalou (J. Cole, 71), Drogba, Anelka (Sturridge, 90).
Unused subs: Hilario, Ferreira, Zhirkov, Matic.

Portsmouth: James; Finnan, Mokoena, Rocha, Mullins (Belhadj, 81); Dindane, Diop (Kanu, 81), Brown, Boatend (Utaka, 73); O'Hara; Piquionne.
Unused subs: Ashdown, Ben Haim, Borre, Hughes.

35

Slovenia 0-1 England
FIFA World Cup, Group C
23 June 2010

On the eve of kick-off between England and Russia at Euro 2016, John Terry was sat in front of a television reminiscing about his international career.

The Chelsea captain had been four years retired from England duty, but it did not mean his desire to follow the Three Lions and watch them succeed had weakened. The popular view was that he should have been in the England squad for the tournament regardless of his age as he remained his country's best defender.

As if to remind the world of why those views remained so strong among some sections of the media and England supporters, his message of goodwill to Roy Hodgson and his players came with a picture attached.

'Good luck to Roy and all the boys tonight. Come on England,' Terry wrote on Instagram. Beneath his post sat one of his most celebrated moments in an England shirt; it was the penguin dive against Slovenia from the 2010 World Cup in South Africa.

Guy Mowbray's reaction in the commentary box summed up the feeling of the millions watching back home in England when the replays outlined just how far Terry was willing to go to avoid his team conceding that night.

England were playing with the usual sense of trepidation that follows them in tournament football. After a 1-1 draw with USA in their opening game, failure to score past Algeria a week later meant they had just two points from their opening two games. If Fabio Capello's side were to progress, they had to beat Slovenia in their third and final group game. Anything but victory and they would be on an early flight back to London.

Jermain Defoe had scored after twenty-three minutes to settle the nerves against the Slovenians, but without another goal following, England retreated more and more until they were all but defending on their own goal line. They were nervous, the anxiety spreading across the team as the thoughts of a goal and the repercussions it would bring took hold. They were the superior side, but with fear controlling them, they did not look it. Things were beginning to get frantic. With just under twenty-five minutes remaining, Slovenia looked certain to score.

In came a cross from deep to the edge of the box, which Zlatko Dedic headed into the path of teammate Milivoje Novakovic. The English defence seemed to part like a tale of biblical proportions – all rather apt given their red kits – but Terry managed to stick with his man to block Novakovic's shot. Still, with three other defenders rushing to the ball, it was Terry who made the tackle from the floor to dispossess Novakovic from the rebound, spilling the ball free for Dedic to have a shot himself, which Glen Johnson blocked. Eventually Valter Birsa shot wide and the danger was over.

Then the replay analysis came and we saw Terry's act of, well, near insanity. As Dedic lined up his shot with Terry struggling to get to his feet, the defender knew he was not going to make the block if he relied on more conventional methods. Rather than accept his fate, Terry launched himself head first at Dedic's feet instead, ready to take the ball flush on his face from close-range in the name of preventing a Slovenia goal.

The sight of Johnson stood behind Terry, anticipating an altogether different pain as he clutches his nether regions, makes Terry's actions all the more striking. It shows the margins that separate Terry from his peers.

'And look at John Terry,' Mowbray says, 'that is real commitment to the cause.'

The chuckle that precedes the commentator's words articulates the astonishment at what he has just witnessed. Head first, Terry is seen throwing himself into the action at a split second. For a player who had been knocked unconscious in the League Cup final three years earlier when colliding with Arsenal's Abou Diaby, swallowing his tongue in the process, Terry was living up to that warrior tag he had long since adopted.

Prior to the game Terry had given an extraordinary press conference where he had attempted to rally the troops. He had spoken about being put in front of the press that afternoon in order to represent the players and England. He was talking like a captain and when the game came, he would play like one.

'One hundred per cent,' Terry had responded when one journalist asked if he was going to be the 'big leader' against Slovenia. The problem was that Terry was no longer the England captain. He had lost that duty a few months previous when news of his alleged indiscretions with Wayne Bridge's ex-girlfriend had made the headlines. It was not for him to be talking in such terms, yet it mattered little. He was not backing down.

'I've said since I lost the armband that nothing has ever changed for me,' he continued. 'Whether it be on the training field, in the camp, in the dressing room; I'll still be the same. No one will ever take that away from me. I was born to do stuff like that and I'll continue to do that in the dressing room and on the training field.'

He was talking with the look of man determined to be heard. It was clear he saw himself as England's leader regardless of the reality and now he was stepping up, taking his moment in the spotlight to remind the gathered media and football fans who he was and what he saw himself as representing.

Given how England's first two games had gone in South Africa, the travelling fans had been heard booing them after the goalless draw with Algeria and Terry had a message.

'I wouldn't have booed [had I been a fan on the terraces],' he said. 'I'm sitting here today on behalf of the team asking the fans to get behind us again because when they do we have the best fans in the world.'

There it was again. The phrase Terry would continue to revert back to: he was there on behalf of the players. He was there to be the leader and now he was calling for a unified front to get England through their group.

He received much criticism for that. With Steven Gerrard the England captain in his place, speaking for the players and management was his job, not Terry's. So why was he doing it? Was he attempting to lead a mutiny and shift the axis of power back in his favour or was it a more selfless act than that? Had Terry seen what England needed and gone out to address the media in attempt to help them get it?

Regardless of how we interpret the politics, the truth came with that flopped dive in the 67th minute in Port Elizabeth as Terry attempted to stop Dedic in his tracks. Rallying cry, captain or not, he was putting everything on the line for his country. His words from the press conference a couple of days previous were being delivered upon.

It was the sort of moment even his strongest detractors could not deny summed up the spirit Terry brought to Chelsea and England. It was total commitment, regardless of how impressive his overall display was in any given game. You knew what you got from Terry. This was it.

That Terry reminded England of what they were missing shortly before kick-off against Russia in their opening game of the 2016 European Championships made the result all the more frustrating.

Like the match against Slovenia, it was a cross from deep that had caused problems in the backline. There were just 90 seconds left on the clock and the Russians were desperate to draw level, throwing whatever they could at the English defence.

As the ball came in, England looked disorganised. Gary Cahill and Chris Smalling were out of position and Danny Rose, one of the smallest players on the pitch, was isolated. Vasili Berezutski planted himself on the left-back to exploit every bit of his six-inch height advantage to beat him in the air and loop his header over Joe Hart. The game would finish 1-1 to the disappointment of an England side that had dominated from start to finish.

It would be folly to suggest Berezutski would not have had the opportunity to score had Terry been there for England. What grated on the minds of many, though, is that he was not.

Slovenia: S. Handanovic; Brecko, Suler, Cesar, Jokic; Birsa, Radosavljevic, Koren, Kirm (Matavz, 79); Ljubijankic (Dedic, 62), Novakovic.
Unused subs: J. Handanovic, Seliga, Dzinic, Ilic, Filekovic, Mavric, Krhin, Komac, Stevanovic.

England: James; Johnson, Terry, Upson, A. Cole; Milner, Lampard, Barry, Gerrard; Rooney (J. Cole, 72), Defoe (Heskey, 86).
Unused subs: Green, Hart, Dawson, Warnock, King, Lennon, Wright-Phillips, Carrick, Crouch.

36

QPR 1-0 Chelsea
Premier League
23 October 2011

t was ninety minutes to forget, only John Terry would never be able to. The repercussions of losing a derby with west London rivals QPR would drag on for close to a year and by he end of it, Terry's reputation would be in pieces. He would be stripped of the England aptaincy for a second time – meaning he would not lead England out at Euro 2012 – while is international career would also come to a premature end.

With Jose Bosingwa and Didier Drogba both sent off before half time at Loftus Road, Chelsea would have been forgiven for thinking things could not get any worse. They were lready trailing 1-0 by that time and the afternoon felt like one of *those* days. Nothing was going right for Andre Villas-Boas's men, then Terry clashed with Anton Ferdinand during . set-piece in the 85th minute and everything snowballed. There were the handbags on the itch in the immediate aftermath, but it was the verbals as Terry walked away that would hape his next eleven months. Come the final whistle, Terry was being accused of racially busing Ferdinand in the melee of their confrontation.

The pair had reportedly spoken amicably after the game in the dressing room about the ncident and Terry released a statement in a bid to put an end to the allegations being made gainst him.

'I thought Anton was accusing me of using a racist slur,' he said. 'I responded aggressively, aying that I never used that term.'

Such was the furore, Terry was hoping it would put an end to the incident. Unlike the revious allegations against him following a similar clash with Ledley King in 2006, that vas not going to happen. Within twenty-four hours, the Metropolitan Police had received an nonymous complaint from a member of the public so had opened up an investigation into vhat happened at Loftus Road. From an argument on the football pitch, things had suddenly aken a heightened focus.

'Anton was present in our dressing room [after the game],' Villas-Boas would reveal later hat week. 'For us, [the players' conversation] was the end of the story and it still is. It's just a nisunderstanding and something blown out of all proportion.'

The police did not think so and shortly before Christmas, the Crown Prosecution Service nnounced that Terry would be formally charged for racist offences, with a date set for the Magistrates Court on 1 February 2012.

All the while, the FA were conducting an investigation of their own, which was then held p because of the legal proceedings against Terry, who had remained available for England uty at the insistence of manager Fabio Capello.

'I think [John Terry] is innocent until proved guilty,' the manager had commented in November ahead of a friendly with Sweden at Wembley. 'For this reason I selected him.'

So strong was Capello's support of Terry, the Italian would eventually resign from his job as England manager in February in protest at the FA's insistence Terry lose the England captaincy while his court case was ongoing. Terry's date with the magistrates had seen the case passed up Westminster Magistrates Court, which meant the case not being heard until 9 July, after the European Championships in Poland and Ukraine that summer.

Capello did not give his official view on things at the time, but in 2015 he eventually gave some insight to the in-fighting that took place at FA headquarters over the situation surrounding Terry.

'You know what happened with me, they decided [Terry] could not play with the national team and I didn't understand because he was not guilty,' said the former Three Lions boss. 'When it happened I said to the President [David Bernstein] "You decided he's guilty?" No, he's not guilty, it's good you can play with the national team and I don't understand why you don't play.'

Capello's views were not in keeping with those above him. The FA's policy was to take the captaincy from Terry and that was that. The manager was powerless and equally unhappy with the ruling, so walked out.

As the case dragged on, it was impacting all sorts of decisions around the England team. Rio Ferdinand – Anton's brother – was no longer a part of the setup and as Euro 2012 approached, new boss Roy Hodgson was tasked with a conundrum. Would he bring Terry and risk potential factions in the England camp? Or would he leave his best defender at home? That alone divided opinion, although Hodgson eventually decided to name Terry in his squad.

That summer would prove bittersweet for Terry. He would have wanted to feature for England regardless, yet here he was again at a major championship and Steven Gerrard was wearing his armband.

That had happened in 2010 when alleged indiscretions in his private life had seen Terry lose the captaincy ahead of the World Cup. Two years on to the month, Terry was being told he would not be England captain for the Euros.

A man of his stature would have wanted to lead England out in Poland and Ukraine. That was the whole purpose of his captaincy, yet despite leading England through their qualification campaign, Terry had to settle for being just a member of the playing squad. It would have eaten away at him.

Having suffered the heartache and frustration of walking out behind Gerrard for England's four matches before Italy eliminated them, Terry had his court case to contend with.

It lasted four days before he was cleared of any wrongdoing and found not guilty of making a racist insult directed at Ferdinand during the QPR defeat.

That was not the end of it for Terry, however. Two weeks after the courts had handed out their verdict, the FA charged Terry based on their own investigation.

The charge was for using abusive and/or insulting words and/or behaviour towards Ferdinand. Further allegations suggested that this included a reference to the ethnic origin and/or colour and/or race of Ferdinand.

Requesting a personal hearing to defend himself, it would not be until September 2012 – almost a year since the incident – that the FA's independent regulatory commission hearing would hand the Chelsea defender a four-game ban and £220,000 fine.

Only a year earlier, Liverpool striker Luis Suarez had been found guilty of racially abusing Patrice Evra. The Uruguayan had been given an eight-game ban for that, although no legal case had been brought against him.

Despite Terry being cleared by the legal courts, the sports authorities still had a case as they only needed to prove certain words were used in the incident with Ferdinand, not the intent of them.

As Terry had always admitted he had used the word 'black' while repeating what he thought Ferdinand had accused him of saying, the ban and fine were soon forthcoming.

The Suarez–Evra incident also played a key part in the process according to former FA officials.

'I'm really sad that it's come to this. I can't say that it's a huge surprise because of the precedent of the Suarez case and I suspect it's not a huge surprise to those around John Terry as well,' commented former FA Chief Executive David Davies.

Shortly before the FA made public their verdict, Terry retired from international duty at the age of thirty-one.

A spokesman for Terry expressed his 'disappointment' that the FA had reached a 'different conclusion [to the] not guilty verdict of a court of law'.

QPR: Kenny; Young, Hall, Ferdinand, Hill; Barton, Derry (Mackie, 82), Faurlin, Wright-Phillips; Taarabt (Smith, 62), Helguson.
Unused subs: Murphy, Orr, Buzsaky, Puncheon, Bothroyd.

Chelsea: Cech; Bosingwa, Luiz, Terry, Cole; Mikel, Sturridge (Ivanovic, 36), Meireles (Malouda, 72), Lampard, Mata (Anelka, 46); Drogba.
Unused subs: Turnbull, Romeu, McEachran.

37

Chelsea 4-1 Napoli (AET)
UEFA Champions League, Last 16
12 March 2012

Was it a crisis?

Chelsea had just lost 3-1 away to Napoli in the last sixteen of the Champions League to leave their European hopes hanging by a thread. Not only that, just one win in the last five Premier League games since mid-January meant qualification for Europe's prime cup competition the following season was just as much in question.

The big stars were reportedly unsettled by Andre Villas-Boas's methods, which had been reinforced by the Blues sitting some twenty points off the pace behind Premier League leaders Manchester City. Performances were not in the line with the multimillion pound roster the Blues could boast.

Only two years earlier, Chelsea were winning the title with a record goals haul under Carlo Ancelotti. They had been the first Premier League side to score 100 goals or more in a single season and while the following campaign had finished trophy-less, they were still runners-up to Manchester United. Now they were nowhere even near challenging for the title again and the atmosphere around the club was turning sour. So yes, Chelsea were in the mire. They had reached the crossroads the club so often has in the past decade or so – the manager had been long walking the plank and Roman Abramovich would have to push him now or take a risk with the club's long-term ambitions in mind.

Would it be Villas-Boas that Abramovich put his faith in? Or would the owner give his trusted lieutenants from seasons gone by his backing by getting rid of the man who was attempting to move the club on without them in the picture?

It was an uneasy position to be in. From Villas-Boas' corner, he was attempting to bring about some major changes in west London. He had arrived much like Mourinho had in 2004 as European football's rising star in management – he was very much flavour of the month. He did not have a Champions League winners' medal draped around his neck, but spending the season unbeaten in Portugal, he had done enough to earn his reputation. He had also guided his former side to the Europa League to reaffirm his rising status.

It was a fine record for a manager who was just thirty-three years old. He would have still been playing football professionally had he boasted the talents. Villas-Boas was a different breed altogether, though. He was from the new school, a great football mind trained with an emphasis on analysis and statistics. Rather than play his way to the top, he had studied his way there.

Indeed, Villas-Boas had been no stranger to the Chelsea dressing room as he had worked under Mourinho in his previous life as an opposition scout. Remember those detailed opposition reports that were leaked during Mourinho's time as boss? They were the work of Villas-Boas who had meticulously studied Chelsea's Premier League rivals to arm the Blues players with everything they needed to take them down.

He knew what made John Terry and Frank Lampard tick as players, but as people, Villas-Boas didn't quite grasp it enough. When players who have delivered unprecedented success to a club and remain in their prime are being phased out, there are few who would take it easy.

The likes of Terry, Lampard and Didier Drogba were supreme competitors, with huge egos fed by the success they had achieved throughout their careers. If there were any players in the dressing room deserving of better treatment from the manager, it was that trio.

Villas-Boas was in a rush, though. His press conferences and interviews were complete with quotes about his project and where he was taking Chelsea. He had the biggest plans and when he looked to the future, the age of Terry et al. dictated they would not be able to sustain what he had in mind. He needed a different breed of player.

By employing Villas-Boas in the summer of 2011, paying Porto a handsome compensation package for their young manager in the process, Abramovich had bought into that ideal. Perhaps he did so with a blinkered view and did not realise the strife Villas-Boas's appointment would bring about, though. Perhaps he did not realise the lengths that Villas-Boas was willing to go to in order to achieve his goal of emulating the success of his mentor Mourinho.

Come March 2012, Chelsea were locked in a civil war. The reports across the media were of factions in the dressing room; battle lines were being drawn and you were either on the manager's side or the players'.

When Chelsea lost 1-0 to West Bromwich Albion on the opening weekend of March, Abramovich made his decision. He did not make a public statement to declare allegiance to one side or the other, just a decision that told us where he stood. Begrudgingly or not, he sacked Villas-Boas and that five-year project he often spoke of was over within eight months.

It seemed Chelsea's season was, too. By this stage they were fifth, three points behind Tottenham Hotspur, who occupied the fourth and final Champions League spot. Harry Redknapp's side had the momentum with them as well, riding the crest of a wave without the pressure of being an established European giant. Reaching the Champions League was going to be a bonus for them whereas Chelsea *had* to.

With Roberto Di Matteo installed as interim manager, he had to change things rapidly if the season was to be salvaged.

A former Chelsea player himself, Di Matteo had been on Villas-Boas' coaching staff, so had seen the turmoil first hand. His approach to making the switch from assistant to manager was a simple one.

'He was very smart,' says Frank Lampard. 'He just took all the individuals aside. A few of us were disgruntled at the time. I was out of the team a lot; AVB had dropped me for the Napoli away game and a lot of other games. Ashley [Cole] had come out at times and Didier [Drogba].

'We had always been big characters there and felt we had a lot to give. Robbie just came in, called us all in separately and said "I need you. I need you for these big games coming up. I want everything from you." We just said, "No problem boss, we're in," and individually he got so much out of the team. The big players in the team produced.'

It started when Napoli came to Stamford Bridge for what was supposed to be a dead-rubber. Two goals to the good from the first leg and Edinson Cavani leading the attack, the Italians were expected to be too powerful to overcome Di Matteo's revitalised team.

From facing a broken side a few weeks earlier, this would prove an altogether different challenge, however. Having a sense of the occasion and that it could be their last journey together as one on the big stage, those big players Lampard spoke of came into their own. Led by John Terry, Chelsea pummelled their opponents into submission.

Just look at the scoresheet that night at Stamford Bridge and it tells us everything about how the game was won and why it was won.

Drogba scored the first, an exquisite header that he powered beyond Morgan De Sanctis. That got Chelsea back into the game before Terry arrived to score a header of his own just two minutes after the interval. As if to drum home the old guard renaissance theme, it was Lampard who delivered the corner for his teammate to direct across the goalkeeper and into the back of the net.

Chelsea were going through at that stage, but then Gokhan Inler scored to make it 4-3 on aggregate. The pendulum had swung and Chelsea needed to equalise just to force extra time, let alone win overall.

Having seen Drogba and Terry score, Lampard was not going to be outdone and drew the tie level on aggregate to make it 3-1 on the night with a spot-kick. He blasted it home.

The anxiety inside Stamford Bridge was incredible. An unpredictable season had made those on the terraces unsure of what to expect. Whereas Chelsea had been reliable for so long, the nature of Villas-Boas' reign had made the fans uneasy; they were caught up in a whirlwind of emotion. They had been let down all season by indifferent performances that had meant Chelsea's campaign had become an unnecessary struggle. But then here they were, the heroes of the past dragging them back from the dead. Drogba, Terry and Lampard – the players Chelsea had been built around, delivering on their reputations.

When extra time came, the feeling was growing that Chelsea had enough about them to strike the final blow against Napoli. They just had that look of winners, the aura that followed them around the pitch told us it; the belief was beginning to return and the fans were sensing victory. Terry was barking out his orders from the sidelines with Di Matteo, having been substituted, organising and bossing everyone around him. Chests were being pumped, bodies put on the line and then Drogba's cross found Branislav Ivanovic, who fired home into the roof of the net in front of the Shed End to cue wild celebrations right on half time of extra time.

There was still a half of football remaining, yet the slumped shoulders of those in the grey shirts dictated where the game was headed. The comeback was complete and Napoli were beaten. They just had fifteen minutes before it would become official.

Di Matteo's request was being honoured. He wanted everything from his big players – he needed John Terry to be the leader, for Drogba and Lampard to inspire with goals at the big moments. They were doing it.

The only concern now was how long they would be able to sustain it. How wrong would Villas-Boas prove to have been by turning his back on them?

Chelsea: Cech; Ivanovic, David Luiz, Terry (Bosingwa, 98), Cole; Lampard, Essien; Sturridge (Torres, 63), Mata (Malouda, 95), Ramires; Drogba.
Unused subs: Turnbull, Cahill, Mikel, Kalou.

Napoli: De Sanctis; Campagnaro, Cannavaro, Aronica (Vargas, 111); Maggio (Dossena, 37), Inler, Gargano, Zuniga; Hamsik (Pandev, 106), Lavezzi; Cavani.
Unused subs: Roasati, Fernandez, Britos, Dzemalli.

38

Bayern Munich 1-1 Chelsea
(AET, Chelsea Win 4-3 on Penalties)
UEFA Champions League Final
19 May 2012

Watch the video replay closely and the expression on John Terry's face can be made out. It is only slight, but the eyes give him away. The referee has not been alerted to the knee in the back of Alexis Sanchez yet, although the thought is running through Terry's mind that he is in for it if another official has spotted his shenanigans.

Terry is fifty-three minutes away from reaching the second Champions League final of his career. Lord knows he has featured in enough semi-finals in that time – five in fact before facing Barcelona in 2011/12 – but this year it would not be a penalty shoot-out or defeat that will bring the heartache. It is a self-inflicted pain.

When there is a break in play, the referee rushes back to the edge of the Chelsea box and shows no hesitation in brandishing Terry a red card. That rules him out of Chelsea's trip to Munich for the Champions League final if the Blues can overcome Barcelona at the Nou Camp.

Terry's expression after his collision with Sanchez meant that this time there is no need for forensic analysis. The gravity of his fate is clear. Terry is crestfallen. He cannot believe it.

Chelsea were leading 1-0 from the first leg thanks to Didier Drogba's goal, yet travelling to Catalonia was different. It was in this stadium the whole of Europe had witnessed Lionel Messi and his colleagues embarrass the meanest of sides. Getting a result in the Nou Camp when both sides are sporting eleven men is a trophy in itself, so when the home side has a numerical advantage, the task is that bit harder. In fact, it is not. It is actually impossible. Statistics tell us it is not the done thing.

Terry had committed the cardinal sin that night. From being Chelsea's saviour and leader in years gone by, he had regressed to become the villain.

For all he had achieved in a Chelsea shirt, Blues fans were rightly easy on him. They were disappointed, but then this was John Terry – it was difficult to be angry with a man who had made a rare mistake while donning the club colours. It was completely out of character and he did not deserve a lynching. Even the pundits in the Sky Sports studio were not willing to go that far.

'You have to feel for him,' said Graeme Souness. 'He is such a leader; he's been such a stalwart for Chelsea. He's their main man and he's going to miss the biggest game you can play in if you're playing for your club and they don't come along every year.'

As Souness alluded to, it was more a personal bereavement for Terry than club-wide grieving. Even with ten men, Chelsea were able to get the result they needed against Barcelona, with the game finishing 2-2 on the night to send them through to the final against Bayern Munich.

With Terry's red card, what followed next made it seem all over, though. Sergio Busquets had levelled the tie on aggregate just two minutes before Terry's moment of madness and soon after, Andres Iniesta made it 2-0 to put Barcelona firmly in control.

Barcelona were in the ascendancy and when teams are a man down, that wide-open pitch at the Nou Camp becomes even more so. The likes of Messi float into space without effort, using their instinct to pick off opponents around them. Gaps appear and the Barcelona midfielders are intelligent enough to not only spot them, but exploit them.

Even before Barcelona were Europe's biggest force, Chelsea had felt the effects of that. It was in 1999/2000 when the Blues had blown them away in west London with a 3-1 victory to put them in a promising position before travelling to Catalonia.

It was the Champions League quarter-final and Chelsea had done the unthinkable to get so far in their debut season in the competition. Facing Barcelona was supposed to be where their journey ended, but after that first leg display, they had every reason to think a semi-final place was a reality.

They came so close. They were within seven minutes of going through until Dani scored to make it 3-1 on the night in Barcelona, which levelled the scores on aggregate. With an away goal apiece, parity was well and truly restored and it went to extra time. Having stayed in the tie for ninety minutes, the extra half hour proved too much for Chelsea. Celestine Babayaro was sent off and Barcelona would eventually win 5-1, 6-4 on aggregate.

It was the numerical advantage that had eventually proved the difference. Chelsea could not cope after that.

Roberto Di Matteo was in the Blues' line-up that night and here he was, this time as manager, watching something similar happen to Chelsea again. Terry was sent off and Barcelona were taking charge. (If we're talking Chelsea–Barcelona coincidences, Anders Frisk was the referee that night back in April 2000, too. Remember him?)

Terry must have felt the weight on his shoulders of all 95,845 fans inside the stadium. Sat in the dressing room, hearing the cheers for Iniesta's goal as they rushed through the tunnel, his heart would have sank. The Nou Camp's foundations would have been shaking as Barcelona celebrated. Maybe he was hoping they would not withstand the pressure so everything could collapse around him. His world would have felt like it was doing just the same.

Two minutes later, though, a teasing through-ball from Frank Lampard to send Ramires in on goal changed the mood. The Brazilian, for once, did the Brazilian thing and chipped Victor Valdes with aplomb to make it 2-1. It was as much out of character as Terry's earlier indiscretion. A rare moment of skill that Ramires was hardly known for. He was supposed to be the running man in midfield, not the scorer of exquisite goals.

The heart was beating again, the corpse of Chelsea's Champions League hopes drawing breath. The Blues were back in control, their away goal the security blanket for the next forty-five minutes. Now all they had to do was dig in deep and stop Barca from scoring.

It was one of the few moments in Terry's Chelsea career that the club would achieve something without him. Lionel Messi hit the bar from a penalty in the second half and when Fernando Torres made it 2-2 on ninety minutes with a breakaway goal – cue *that* Gary Neville co-commentary – the game was up for Barcelona. Chelsea's remarkable Champions League run was getting one last chapter. Only Terry was not going to be part of it in Munich.

'It does look bad on the replay,' Terry told Sky Sports when he discussed his red card at the end of the game. 'I raised my knee but hopefully the people out there who know me, know I'm not that kind of player.

'At the time I was bewildered, but looking at the replay it looks a red card. On a personal note, of course [it hurts to miss the final]. But we deserve to be in the Champions League final. I really hope [the red card] doesn't take away from this win.'

It did not, but what it did do was make the task of winning the competition that bit harder. Chelsea's defensive strength was being diluted, as Branislav Ivanovic would miss the final through suspension also.

The pair would not be on the pitch at the Allianz Arena. They were instead forced to bite their nails pitchside with the rest of the Chelsea fans who had made the journey to Bavaria. They were powerless watching on, unable to influence proceedings in the slightest.

If Terry was not playing, his imprint was certainly felt on the team, though. In some ways, so too was the influence of Jose Mourinho. That's not to suggest Di Matteo was not vital as manager, of course he was, but Chelsea would eventually win the greatest prize in club football by relying on the foundations that had been laid years before.

Not just in Munich, but throughout the entire Champions League campaign, it was those players from Mourinho's era who were delivering for Chelsea when it mattered most. The likes of Juan Mata were sprinkling some stardust along the way, although the biggest characters were those from a time that was becoming Chelsea's history.

Terry, Lampard, Ashley Cole, Didier Drogba and Petr Cech were clinging on for dear life to remain relevant in the present like they had been in the past. The same winds of change that had brought about their generation at Stamford Bridge were beginning to sweep in now and it meant their time was drawing to a close. Two seasons after winning in Munich, only Terry and Cech would remain Chelsea players, with the latter as Thibaut Courtois' understudy. That's how close they were to their dream never being realised.

Andre Villas-Boas's reign as manager was a failure. Di Matteo had replaced him and returned to the principles of old to get the best out of the team and it worked. But the principles Villas-Boas had preached had sown the seed, even if Di Matteo was yet to nurture it.

The old guard had resuscitated Chelsea against Napoli in the Champions League last sixteen and they continued doing it for the rest of the season. Lampard would score a big penalty against Benfica in the quarter-final, while it was Drogba's goal in the first leg against Barcelona that had set things up at the Nou Camp.

Then came the final, when Chelsea seemed to be down and out yet again in the Champions League, the Ivorian's bullet header clawed them back from the brink to cancel out Thomas Muller's goal with just two minutes remaining of the game. That meant extra time and, with the scores remaining 1-1, penalties.

Even before the drama of spot-kicks, it had been left up to Cech to stop Arjen Robben from 12 yards after Drogba had upended Franck Ribery.

It was the way the narrative was going; it was how the story had always been written. From hero to villain, there was always another Chelsea player to cover up the mistakes of the last. It was teamwork, which had started with Terry.

He did not kick a ball in Munich, but winning the Champions League remains a justification for all that Terry had represented in his time as Chelsea captain up to that point. It is why the pictures of him in full kit and on the pitch celebrating at the end with his teammates provide a light-hearted moment. Those moments should not be mocked, rather celebrated. Terry was as much a part of the success as Drogba, who scored the decisive penalty in the shoot-out. It was Terry who had helped put the club in this position. And even though he did not play, he still lived the moment like he had.

'The Champions League, all day long [was the biggest buzz I felt after a game],' he would tell *Chelsea* magazine. 'To go and win it after Moscow – that was by far the best. It was a funny one for a lot of the lads, actually. Big Pete [Cech] missed out on all the dressing room celebrations because he was getting drug tested. He was unbelievable in the game, the semi-final and for the whole build-up, but he's not in any of the photos of that night. He's nowhere to be seen.

'It was just the emotion of the whole day and the build-up to it. We got back to the hotel and six or seven of us were in bed by midnight – we were exhausted. It drains you mentally. These are great experiences that will live with me forever.'

Bayern Munich: Neuer; Lahm, Tymoschuk, Boateng, Contento; Schweinsteiger, Kroos; Robben, Muller (van Buyten, 87), Ribery (Olic, 97); Gomez.
Unused subs: Butt, Rafinha, Usami, Pranjic, Petersen.

Chelsea: Cech; Bosingwa, Cahill, David Luiz, Cole; Mikel, Lampard, Kalou (Torres, 84), Mata, Bertrand (Malouda, 73); Drogba.
Unused subs: Turnbull, Ferreira, Romeu, Essien, Sturridge.

39

Moldova 0-5 England
FIFA World Cup 2014 Qualifier
7 September 2012

For a football player who has won every major honour in the game, John Terry's career should not come laced with a sense that it has been unfulfilled. His individual and collective success is a fact Chelsea supporters take great delight in reminding opposition fans about.

'John Terry, he's won more than you,' they will sing. Quite often, the achievements of a single player will outstrip considerably what a club accomplished in a century of competition.

It puts things into perspective. Here is a player coming from the ranks of an unfancied club who has gone on to emulate so many major names before him.

When Terry was coming through at Chelsea, success was defined more by the cups and the Blues getting some sort of moral victory over teams whose resources could outdo theirs. A fruitful campaign would be marked by defeating a few of the big boys and enjoying a cup run in the process.

That perspective started to shift as the twentieth century drew to a close. Dennis Wise lifting the FA Cup in 1997 and repeating the feat three years later inspired that. Yet expecting Chelsea to start the season as favourites to lift the title? Expecting Chelsea to deliver on that expectation? That reality was always supposed to be a dream.

The club had been the great underachievers of English football. Chelsea were knocking on the door, but the best that would happen is their efforts forcing it open just a fraction – enough for them to taste a title race, but not to the point they could actually experience that feeling of dominance.

It is with that in mind that we can surmise Terry was not supposed to win four Premier Leagues. He was not supposed to be winning the Double; he was not supposed to be the pre-eminent defender of his generation by remaining a Chelsea player. To do any of that, he would have to leave Chelsea.

West Ham United have taken great pride in labeling themselves the Academy of Football, although only it has been by going elsewhere at the end of their apprenticeships that many of the best players to come through at Chadwell Heath have achieved their acclaim, Chelsea's very own Frank Lampard being a fitting example.

Terry came through at Chelsea. This was the club that had long hinted at greatness but had always found some way of bringing the curtain down prematurely on their hopes.

When Ted Drake's team won the title for the first time in Chelsea's history in 1955, they did not capitalise on the momentum that level of triumph brings. The next season, they would finish in sixteenth place, just four points above relegated Huddersfield Town.

Subsequent seasons would see the Blues finish thirteenth (1956/57), eleventh (1957/58), fourteenth (1958/59), eighteenth (1959/60) and twelfth (1960/61) before eventually propping up the table in 1961/62, when they were relegated from Division One.

The point is that, from a position of strength as champions, Chelsea did not build on it. Drake's success was a one-off and despite some false dawns in the fifty years that separated their first and second title victories, Chelsea had not been a club to sustain their dominance. Their history was more about sporadic periods of excellence. There was never a dynasty.

So for Terry to come through and achieve what he has, there should not be any sense of him looking back and feeling his career could have had something more – perhaps that there were elements missing. He did the unexpected and gave a generation of Chelsea fans the sort of stories their elders had passed to them from the 'Kings of the King's Road' age.

Despite this, Terry has regrets, notably with how his international career ended on a sour note. 'I loved [playing for England] up until a certain point when everything went on,' he would later tell Jamie Carragher, his former international teammate, in an interview for the *Daily Mail*.

'It disappointed me, more than anything. I look back on my 78 caps and I am unbelievably proud. I was captain for two spells. It is the biggest honour you can have in football. As a kid, it is the thing that everyone wants. I am just disappointed with how it ended, really.'

It ended in victory over Moldova on 7 September 2012, yet somehow the game feels like a defeat for Terry's England legacy. When the whistle blew time on that game, not even Terry knew that would be it for him, that his time was up.

He had restored his position in Roy Hodgson's side and at thirty-one still had much to offer his country. England's golden generation was gradually disappearing, yet the expectation was that Terry would be last to go.

Even at the conclusion of 2015/16, close to four years after the event, Terry was being mentioned as England's best defender. His impact on the international stage has been so significant that the Three Lions have yet to sufficiently replace him.

Had it been footballing reasons that stopped Terry from reaching 100 caps for his country, it would have been easier for him to swallow. It was not. Instead, politics would play their part as the FA pursued charges of racism against him. Terry had already been found not guilty of racially abusing Anton Ferdinand in a court of law, although under the FA's jurisdiction, they found cause to continue their own case against the Chelsea captain.

'I never saw myself walking away,' he continued with Carragher. 'It took something that big to say "enough is enough". Once you get to 50 caps, then 60, then 70 – I had a target of 100 caps. That is all I ever wanted to do.

'Number one was to play for England, second was to be captain and third was to get 100 caps. I will watch games now and it kills me. I watch England games and think "I could have been playing there."'

It is not that Terry could have been; he should have been. Five days after helping his country record another clean sheet on his watch, Terry would be rubbed out of the international picture for good. It killed off his chances of carving out one of the greatest legacies in English football.

'I had one more cap than [Wayne Rooney] when I retired,' Terry recalled. 'I would have been there or thereabouts [for 100 caps], so that kind of eats away.'

It could have been better. In the days, weeks and months between when Terry played his last England game and the end of the 2015/16 season, England played forty-one times.

Assuming Terry was fit for those games – which he often was in Chelsea colours – he would have reached 119 England caps. That is more than David Beckham's 115, which is a record for an outfield player.

If we consider England's Euro 2016 campaign and the friendly matches that built up to it, it is feasible Terry could have surpassed Peter Shilton's overall England caps record of 125.

Of course, it is all hypothetical. We will never know what number of caps Terry would have reached in an England shirt; all we can say for certainty is that seventy-eight was not enough. It was not enough for the player who proved himself to be his country's finest defender of his generation.

Terry continues to lament his international career ending prematurely, although he would admit to Carragher that he has been tempted to return to the England fold if the chance was presented to him.

'In the back of my mind, something was saying "come back, get to 100 caps – show a bit back at them",' he said. 'When you have gone through everything as a player, you have been away with them, played with injections to get through games and to get turned over, it really saddens you [for things to end the way they did].

'The fight inside me wanted to go back and play. I wanted to get to 100 caps because I would have been captain. They told me that I would never be captain again but if I got to 100 caps, you are captain. That was the mentality I had in every game I watched.'

Terry should never have been watching England for all those years. He should have been playing; he should have been going out on better terms that more accurately reflected his standing in the England game.

Moldova: Namasco; Bulgaru, Epureanu, Armas, Golovatenko; Onica; Suvoov (Dedov, 46) Covalciuc, Gatcan, Patras; Picusciac (Sidorenco, 76, Ovsianicov, 85).
Unused subs: Negai, Racu, Cebotaru, Paseciniuc, Bordiyan, Pascenco, Ivanov, Doros, Alexeev.

England: Hart; Johnson, Lescott, Terry, Baines; Milner, Gerrard (Carrick, 46), Lampard, Oxlade-Chamberlain (Walcott, 58); Cleverley; Defoe (Welbeck, 68).
Unused subs: Ruddy, Butland, Walker, Bertrand, Cahill, Jagielka, Sturridge.

40

Aston Villa 1-2 Chelsea
Premier League
11 May 2013

European football has never been kind to John Terry. He may have two winners' medals in his trophy cabinet somewhere for the Champions League and Europa League, but the truth is that the biggest moments of his career have been ruined by bad luck or in the case of that Barcelona semi-final in 2012, a moment of personal madness.

Straight from the off in his Champions League career, Terry was to experience the heartache of it all. Against Monaco in the 2003/04 campaign, Chelsea were beaten 3-1 by ten men inside the Stade Louis II before a 2-2 draw at Stamford Bridge prevented them from reaching the final.

That was the first season of Roman Abramovich's new era as owner. The Blues had just dumped Arsenal out of the quarter-finals in dramatic fashion and given the other sides that were left – Porto and Deportivo La Coruna – Clauio Ranieri's team looked a good bet to go all the way.

The curse would set in when Chelsea actually started to believe they could achieve something. When that belief and sense of expectation took hold of the players, suddenly their hopes and dreams would crumble around them. It happened in 2004 and would be repeated at the same stage of the 2004/05 season with the 'ghost goal' loss to Liverpool.

The trend continued. In 2007, Chelsea lost to Liverpool in the Champions League semi-final at Anfield again. This time it was penalties that did it for them. Then in 2008 when Chelsea eventually reached the final, it was John Terry's slip for his penalty in the shoot-out that prevented his side from winning the trophy. Had he not hit the post, the European champions would have come from London for the first time.

When Chelsea looked to be on the brink of a reaching the final for successive seasons against United in 2009, Andres Iniesta's equaliser for Barcelona was a cruel blow that saw the Catalan side go through on away goals. That game would also be defined by a number of seemingly legitimate penalty appeals being denied by referee Tom Henning Ovrebo.

Chelsea reached their second Champions League final in 2012, but Terry missed that game through suspension as he was sent off in the second leg of the semi-final against Barcelona.

Given all the near misses Chelsea had suffered in Europe, Joe Cole once noted how the 'gods not being with Chelsea' at times. In 2013, like at any other time in Europe, it seemed they were not with Terry, either.

This time, Chelsea had reached the Europa League final and despite Rafa Benitez's insistence on rotating Terry's position in the Chelsea line-up, it was difficult to imagine the interim manager would not be starting him against Benfica at the Amsterdam Arena. For all the differences between the pair, there would surely have been a begrudging acceptance from Benitez that Terry was the sort of figure most managers would want in a major European final. Benitez had experienced what the presence of leaders can do in those circumstances when he guided Liverpool to Champions League success in 2005. At the heart of his defence that season was Jamie Carragher and as time has shown us, Terry was the Liverpool man's superior in every department.

Surely Benitez would have to play Terry despite a hint that it would not be the case just four days before the Europa League final.

Chelsea were playing Aston Villa in the Premier League, with David Luiz and Branislav Ivanovic both rested ahead of the midweek trip to Amsterdam.

Having been injured in the first half of the season, Terry had only returned to action in late January after being missing since early November's 1-1 draw with Liverpool. Plenty had happened in that time, notably Benitez replacing Roberto Di Matteo as manager.

Chelsea had become the first side to win the Champions League only to get knocked out in the group stages the following season. In terms of their defence of the title, statistics would tell us it was the most feeble in history.

With Terry missing for long spells, Di Matteo had not been in a position to call on the same lieutenants he had en route to victory in Munich. Didier Drogba's last contribution had been to send Manuel Neuer the wrong way with his spot kick that won the cup, while Terry's absence was proving vital.

With a new-look team, Chelsea were struggling to establish themselves again and it meant the manager would have to fall on his sword.

By the time Terry was fit and playing, Benitez had been at Chelsea for two months. He clearly had different ideas, despite the captain's desire to prove him wrong.

So would he have played him in Amsterdam? Terry's Chelsea past and reputation suggests yes, but then his rotation in and out of the squad leading up to the game raises a significant question mark.

None of the speculation mattered as Terry would make the decision an easy one for Benitez. Against Aston Villa he got injured and would miss what remained of the season, including that trip to the Netherlands for the Europa League final.

There it was again; the European curse was back to haunt Terry. Somewhere along the line, fate was dealing him an unfortunate hand. There was no conversation he could have with the manager to convince him otherwise, not even an injury to a fellow teammate could give him the chance of playing against Benfica. Terry was out and the third European final of his time at Chelsea was going to be played out before a backdrop of bitterness and regret.

Like the Champions League final a year earlier when Terry was suspended, Chelsea stood on the brink of a unique place in history. They were the first London club to win European club football's greatest prize and twelve months later were afforded the chance to carve out another story. No other team in the history of football has won the Europa League the season after lifting the Champions League – not currently or in their previous guise as the UEFA Cup and European Cup.

Not only that, if Chelsea could claim the Europa League it would complete a clean sweep of every European trophy possible given Chelsea's previous success in the European Cup Winners' Cup and Super Cup. Not Liverpool or Manchester United with their decorated histories could compete with that achievement; nor London rivals Tottenham Hotspur and Arsenal.

Chelsea would go on to beat Benfica 2-1 and they did it in just as dramatic fashion as they had won the Champions League. History was made by Branislav Ivanovic's 90th-minute header that looped over Artur Moraes in goal to win the game at the death.

Like in Munich, Terry had been forced to watch on from the sidelines and experience it all as though he were a supporter on the terraces. That can be seen as a good enough substitute for some, but not for a player who had given Chelsea so much. For successive years he was not part of the club making European history.

If Terry remembers a 2-1 victory over Aston Villa in May 2013 with a hint of sadness given what it meant for his Europa League final hopes, it is much different for Frank Lampard.

Terry's long-time friend and teammate had been waiting quite some time to break Bobby Tambling's goalscoring record of 202 for Chelsea. He had famously netted his 200th against former club West Ham United on 17 March but had sufffered a goal drought as the season drew to a close.

Seven games passed before he made it 201 against Swansea City in late April and as we entered May, it seemed he was running out of games.

Like Terry, Lampard had suffered under Benitez's reign. He was not used to being in and out of the side and Chelsea fans were worried they could be witnessing his last year with the club. Would the record ever be broken?

Well, they got the answers to some of those questions at Villa Park on 11 May when Lampard scored twice to put him on 203 Chelsea goals, surpassing Tambling and putting himself in the record books in the process.

It was a wonderful moment for a player who ranks alongside Terry as one of Chelsea's all-time greatest players; the new record was testament to everything he had achieved while donning the No. 8 jersey.

Lampard was held aloft by Petr Cech at the final whistle, sitting on the goalkeeper's shoulders to soak up the adulation of the Blues supporters who had made the journey from London to Birmingham.

The contrast in Terry's fortunes was stark as just fifteen minutes earlier the defender was himself being lifted off the pitch, but on a stretcher and by paramedics, not his teammates.

Aston Villa: Guzan; Lichaj, Vlaar, Baker, Bennett; Sylla, Westwood, Delph; Agbonlahor, Benteke, Weimann.
Unused subs: Given, Williams, N'Zogbia, Holman, Gardner, Bent, Bowery.

Chelsea: Cech; Azpilicueta, Cahill, Terry (Ivanovic, 77), Cole; Ramires, Lampard; Moses (David Luiz, 46), Mata, Hazard; Ba (Torres, 88).
Unused subs: Turnbull, Ake, Oscar, Benayoun.

John Terry and Frank Lampard with the Premier League trophy. (© Tom Hevezi/Press Association Images)

Previous: John Terry, Frank Lampard and Florent Malouda during a training session while on a pre-season tour of the US. (© Owen Humphreys/PA Archive/ Press Association Images)

Above: John Terry and Frank Lampard sign autographs for fans. (© Darren Walsh/Chelsea FC/Press Association Images)

Opposite: John Terry is challenged by PSG's Zlatan Ibrahimovic during a pre-season friendly in August 2015. (© Darren Walsh/Chelsea FC/Press Association Images)

Previous: Terry attempts to block a shot by Slovenia's Zlatko Dedic during the 2010 World Cup. (© Martin Rickett/PA Archive/Press Association Images)

Above: John Terry celebrates victory over Dynamo Kiev at the end of a match at Stamford Bridge in the 2015/16 Champions League. (© Andrew Matthews/ PA Archive/Press Association Images)

41

Chelsea 2-0 Hull City
Premier League
18 August 2013

Nine years earlier, Jose Mourinho's Stamford Bridge arrival had been about something different. We know the quote, we know the impact he made in west London and on the Premier League in general. Times had changed, though. Mourinho had moved on from 2004 and so had Chelsea. The manager was a bigger personality than he had ever been; Chelsea were a fully fledged member of the elite. The focus now would be about something different.

Mourinho was not coming to Chelsea to tell the world how special he was. If anything, his opening press conference was more about his satisfaction at being back. 'I'm the Happy One,' he joked to the media when he was asked if he remained special.

Of course, Mourinho had to say that. He was returning to Stamford Bridge on the back of a turbulent three years with Real Madrid where he had not enjoyed the experience in the way he would have hoped. There was a hint of success when he won the title with Real to dent Barcelona's dominance in Spain, yet he would have left the Spanish capital with a sense of not fully delivering on his mandate.

A serial winner, Mourinho is supposed to offer a virtual guarantee of titles and the delivery of hordes of other trophies. The 2010/11 Copa del Rey and 2011/12 La Liga title were part of that with Real, but then for a manager of Mourinho's billing, there was an expectation that three years would have delivered plenty more to the Bernabeu. Even in Europe, Mourinho could only get his side as far as the Champions League semi-finals where they would lose to Barcelona (2011), Bayern Munich (2012) and Borussia Dortmund (2013). For any other club, three successive semis would be a sign of progress and sustained success, but for a club like Real Madrid, it is far from being on-message. The club is obsessed with the European Cup and were even more so at the time as they were chasing their tenth victory in the competition – *la decima*. The whole point of Mourinho's arrival was to speed up that process of winning it again.

Missing out for a third season running, Mourinho would depart Madrid and head back to England. He left a broken dressing room in his wake, too. Reports of his relationship breaking down with key players were rife and it was all very different from what we had seen in the past. It was a subject well documented by Spanish journalist Diego Torres in his book *The Special One: The Secret World of Jose Mourinho* that painted the picture of a Machiavellian figure obsessed with control and his image.

When Mourinho had departed Porto, Chelsea and Inter Milan before, it had always been with a sense of regret, that he was leaving a bit too early. The manager was leaving because he wanted to, not because the dressing room or the fans were calling for it.

At Chelsea in 2007 Mourinho had been sacked, but it was still a difficult position for all involved. From the boardroom to the players and fans along Fulham Road, it left a feeling there was unfinished business. Mourinho was adored at Stamford Bridge and it had meant there was always a feeling he would be back. That was not the case at the Bernabeu; he was glad to depart and the feeling from the Real hierarchy was mutual.

Mourinho got his Chelsea return in the summer of 2013 and after his Madrid nightmare he needed to regroup and surround himself with players he could trust. It said plenty that at the top of the list of his allies would again be John Terry, the player who had served him so valiantly in the past.

Mourinho had made Terry his captain nine years earlier when he first arrived and despite the Chelsea defender being at a far more advanced stage in his career, it was the No. 26 to whom Mourinho was turning to again to build his new Chelsea.

It had been far from plain sailing for Terry. Just weeks before Mourinho had been confirmed as the club's new manager, Terry's Chelsea future was being questioned. Rafa Benitez's spell as interim boss had seen him cast aside for long spells, used in a rotation system that did not benefit him in the slightest. It seemed David Luiz and Gary Cahill were emerging as the preferred central defensive partnership, with Terry being phased out. His power and influence, captain or not, was on the wane.

Andre Villas-Boas had made that same mistake as Benitez a couple years earlier and he had ended up losing his job on the back of the failures it brought about. The manager had underestimated Terry and without him in the side, Chelsea struggled. Benitez did something similar, which contributed to him losing the political war on the terraces and made his job untenable. Mourinho was not about to start those games. He knew what Terry was all about and if he was to get this Chelsea side back to where they wanted to be, he needed the captain at his side for every step along the way.

First things first, though; Terry would have to prove he was not just a figurehead. If Mourinho was asking Terry to lead his side into battle just like the old days, he needed to be just as capable as he was in the old days.

'A couple of years ago, he disappeared,' Mourinho later said of Terry, explaining that he was not sure of the player he was inheriting for the second time.

'A couple of injuries, one or two managers that stopped believing in him at the club bringing in other defenders that they thought would be John's replacement. And especially in the season before I came, which was Rafael Benitez's season, I thought "this guy's finished" because he's not playing finals, he's not playing in big matches. I thought he was in trouble.

'When I came, I came with that question mark: "Which John am I going to find? What can he do? Can he improve? Can he become close to the John I know?"

'John was 23, 24-years-old [when I first met him], I thought he had fantastic potential and just needed the next step in terms of quality and qualities around him, the way we organised the team, not only as an individual but as a team.

'We built a fantastic team in 2004, defensively we were very strong. So John reached the top. He won everything with Chelsea, he was the captain of England. John reached the top.'

Now Mourinho needed him to do it all again. The Special One, the Happy One; call him what you will, Mourinho was talking about emulating his great idol Sir Alex Ferguson at Manchester United. He was no longer a man on a mission to win things across Europe in a bid to prove his greatness to the footballing faculty; the focus had shifted. He had done all that; now he wanted to create his dynasty at Stamford Bridge.

The first step in that process was to test Terry's resolve to see if he could be the player that everything revolved around once more. The manager was not worried about age, it was character and ability that was top of his list of requirements. Terry was now thirty-two years old and different questions were being asked of him now.

As the 2013/14 season dawned with a home fixture against newly promoted Hull City, Terry had to show his manager that he could be relied upon. Terry had to secure his Chelsea future to ensure he was a part of the changes that were about to come at Stamford Bridge.

Chelsea: Cech; Ivanovic, Cahill, Terry, Cole; Ramires, Lampard, De Bruyne (Schurrle, 67), Oscar (van Ginkel, 85), Hazard; Torres (Lukaku, 75).
Unused subs: Schwarzer, Essien, Mata, Ba.

Hull City: McGregor; El-Mohamadi, Chester, Davies, Figueroa; Meyler (Huddlestone, 59); Aluko (Boyd, 79), Koren, Brady; Graham (Livermore, 59), Sagbo.
Unused subs: Harper, Rosenior, Bruce, McShane.

42

Crystal Palace 1-2 Chelsea
Premier League
18 October 2014

Jose Mourinho had taken his Chelsea side to Selhurst Park in the latter stages of the 2013/14 season knowing that a victory would put them right at the heart of the Premier League title race. If Chelsea could defeat their London rivals, who themselves were fighting to pull away from the relegation zone, they would arguably be favourites to win the title with six games remaining.

It went the other way. Chelsea lost 1-0 and their title bid all but went with it, with Mourinho telling reporters that his team had lacked the 'balls' to win the game.

It was a moment that confirmed his belief that Chelsea were the little horse among the clubs going for the championship that season. They may have had the name and reputation, but there was something lacking.

To top it all off, the defeat at Palace came courtesy of an own goal from John Terry. It was a collector's item, just as three points for Palace against Chelsea in the Premier League have proved down the years.

When Chelsea returned to south London six months later in October 2014, there was a different swagger about the club. They had acted with rapid precision in the transfer market that summer to snap up Cesc Fabregas and Diego Costa, leaving Mourinho's squad to have a different sheen to it. Far from the little horse, Chelsea were looking like a side that was maturing into a rampaging stallion.

Despite the season being just seven games old, Chelsea were already five points clear of their main challengers Manchester City at the top of the table. Beating the Eagles would cement their dominance further. And Mourinho's comments this time on his players? They had 'big balls' according to the boss.

The outing was significant for many reasons in Chelsea's season. Not only was it another three points en route to running away with the title, the team had lived up to the manager's desire to scrap for victory. They had learned from the mistakes in the previous season and they earned the right to leave with the win this time. The game was also Terry's 500th as Chelsea captain.

'To be able to do it once was my dream as a 16-year-old, but to do it as many times as I have done and to have the success I've had at this football club, I'm unbelievably proud of that,' he said at the time.

We hear it said so often about players in the modern era that it has entered the realms of cliché now; players are just passing through, so it's rare to expect them to withstand multiple regimes and remain loyal.

Football is a sport that is dictated by change. Owners, managers, players – they all disappear at some point. So it's rare for one player to make 500 appearances at one club, let alone do it as captain. When a player does it at a club like Chelsea, where money was no object throughout the majority of Terry's time at Stamford Bridge, it makes the feat all the more impressive.

'I had to prove myself time after time, when new managers were coming in and the club had money to spend on the best players,' Terry added. 'I had to be up for the fight and say. "OK, let's go again," and not just accept the level and think I'd made it. I always wanted to improve and that goes back to the supporters and them believing in me.'

It said plenty about Terry that he was able to arrive at Selhurst Park and play a big part in changing the narrative from what we had seen in March. Back then it was Tony Pulis in charge and the performance that day was very much about disrupting Chelsea and stopping them play.

It worked as Pulis's side frustrated the Blues in the way we have seen his teams do to others throughout his managerial career. It was Neil Warnock this time out, another traditionally British manager whose teams are about 'putting it up 'em' in an attempt to level the playing field, bridging the gap in quality with graft and commitment.

Whenever the so-called bigger sides face teams of that ilk, there is a requirement that they mix it just as much themselves, which is why Terry had proved so valuable to Chelsea throughout the previous 499 games he had captained them.

It was not by accident that Mourinho had turned to him to be his captain when he first arrived in English football. The manager knew what he was getting; he needed to build his team around a granite base and Terry offered it. And here he was, now the wrong side of thirty but still playing to those same principles and doing it more effectively than any other player could. That was the key to his longevity and Mourinho knew it.

The newspapers did not miss out on the significance of Terry's 500th appearance as Chelsea captain, either. The *Daily Mail* wrote of Terry being his 'usual influence fearless self'.

As Matt Barlow wrote in the same report, 'Terry was bang in the middle of the chaos which erupted when Cesar Azpilicueta was sent off, offering advice to referee Craig Pawson while avoiding trouble.'

His tenure with the armband was 500 games old, but it was the same Terry we were seeing. His influence on the Chelsea side had hardly waned; if anything it was stronger than ever as the transition from one generation to the next needed a man of his repertoire to help oversee it on the pitch.

Terry signed off the day on Instagram with an image of a bottle of Sassicaia champagne draped in his armband that had '500' written on it in felt tip pen. He wrote:

Today was my 500th game as Chelsea captain. I had the pleasure of playing and learning from the best with Dennis Wise and Marcel Desailly two heroes and great captains who always had time for me as a young boy. A glass of SASSICAIA to celebrate. Thanks for your unbelievable support. JT

Crystal Palace: Speroni; Kelly, Hangeland, Delaney, Ward; McArthur (Guedioura, 69), Jedinak, Ledley (Mariappa, 58); Puncheon (Zaha, 69), Bolasie; Campbell.
Unused subs: Hennessey, Doyle, Gayle, Chamakh.

Chelsea: Courtois; Ivanovic, Cahill, Terry, Azpilicueta; Matic, Fabregas; Willian (Luis, 42), Oscar, Hazard (Salah, 86); Remy (Drogba, 90+1).
Unused subs: Cech, Zouma, Mikel, Solanke.

43

Chelsea 2-0 Tottenham Hotspur
League Cup Final
1 March 2015

It was New Year's Day 2015 and Chelsea were being ripped apart by Mauricio Pochettino's Tottenham Hotspur side.

As empathic as it was, the result and performance had been as unexpected as, say, Leicester City being crowned 2015/16 champions. But that happened and thrash Chelsea 5-3 Spurs did.

The Blues had been top of the table from the opening weekend right through to the Christmas period. They had endured some shaky performances in the intervening games, like a goalless draw away to Sunderland before losing to Newcastle United at St James's Park a few weeks later in December. They were the Premier League's dominant side, though, and were cruising their way to the title.

Just prior to that first defeat of the season in all competitions – a run that lasted twenty-one games – Chelsea had put three goals past Spurs without reply. Eden Hazard, Didier Drogba and Loic Remy had all scored to continue that oldest Premier League tradition of them all that sees Chelsea taking all three points off Spurs whenever the sides meet.

Indeed, Chelsea victories against Spurs are as much a feature of the calendar as the festive season. There may not be a specific date etched into a specific month, but when the fixture list is published, Chelsea fans invariably mark the weekends where six points can be guaranteed. That is the punchline to the joke at least.

So Chelsea being well and truly humbled at White Hart Lane was a major shock, ensuring that normal service did not resume.

Inspired by a rampant Harry Kane, Spurs tore through Chelsea to leave them feeling battered and bruised. So much so that Chelsea's reliable form before the New Year's Day encounter changed significantly on the back of it.

In the six games leading up to the 5-3 defeat, Chelsea had won five and drawn one. In the six games that followed, the Blues won three, drew twice and lost to League 1 Bradford City 4-2 at home in the FA Cup.

It was hardly a crisis, but the sheen had been taken off the season. There was a sense of Chelsea suffering from an episode of post-traumatic stress. It meant they faced the ultimate test to overcome that when, two months to the day since Spurs so heavily beat them, Chelsea would face their old foe again in the League Cup final at Wembley.

By this stage, Chelsea were getting caught up in all sorts of problems on and off the pitch. During the away leg of their Champions League tie with Paris Saint-Germain that preceded the final, a small group of Blues fans had racially abused a black Parisian on the city's Metro network. As Souleymane Sylla attempted to board a train, Chelsea fans pushed him off before targeting him with racially themed songs.

Chelsea's response was exemplary, dealing with the issue head-on to disassociate the club from those involved in the incident, working with police to ensure the fans in question were not only identified, but banned from Stamford Bridge. At the club's next home game against Burnley, supporters also played their part as they rallied with anti-racism placards.

That Burnley game was to impact the League Cup significantly. Nemanja Matic was sent off for retaliating against Ashley Barnes, whose high tackle should have seen him also dismissed and receive a lengthy ban. Neither followed with the FA claiming they wanted to avoid re-refereeing every incident, so chose not to pursue charges against Barnes.

It meant that Matic – the player on the receiving end of the horror tackle – would miss the League Cup final, severely denting Chelsea's preparations as they attempted to contain Kane and Christian Eriksen, who were proving Spurs' best performers of the season.

Psychologically, Spurs had the edge. But then Chelsea had John Terry to help calm their nerves. The Blues captain had been in positions like this throughout his career, putting in backs-to-the-wall displays on more than one occasion. Before the game had even started, the expectation was that Chelsea would have to dig deep in the same way to overcome Spurs.

They needed a platform to achieve that. With no Matic, Chelsea had to adapt. Kurt Zouma was drafted into the defensive midfield – a position where he had never played before in a Chelsea shirt.

Come full time, his performance would draw comparisons with Chelsea legend Marcel Desailly, yet it was Terry's captain's display that would prove most vital in winning another cup with him as the leader.

He wore the armband and Terry took on the responsibility yet again to put Chelsea where they needed to be, scoring the game's opening goal right on half time.

It was a strike scored with all the instinct we should expect from a striker. In the Spurs box to attack Willian's free-kick, Terry had a late change of approach as he dropped off his marker in between the penalty spot and six-yard box to pick up any scraps. His gamble paid off, as Danny Rose's near-post header ricocheted off Eric Dier and fell into Terry's path. All the captain had to do was fire home from eight yards, leaving Hugo Lloris no chance in goal.

Putting Chelsea ahead was important for plenty of reasons, least of all the Blues had drawn first blood against Spurs to turn the tables on them after the events of New Year's Day. Had it gone the other way, quite how Chelsea would have reacted not even Mourinho can confidently say. Would the seeds of doubt have been sown? Would Chelsea have collapsed like they had done two months earlier? One thing is for certain and that is Spurs would have been energised, using their previous victory as inspiration.

Terry killed that off with one strike of his boot. He stepped up to declare enough was enough, that the façade was over. Chelsea were the dominant side in this fixture and he was not going to allow Spurs fans to think otherwise.

It is moments like the League Cup final when talk of power shifts can feel very real. Had Chelsea lost it would have been the first time since 1971 that Spurs had secured back-to-back wins against Chelsea in the same season. It had been more than forty years.

It takes much more than those sorts of milestones to erode away at years of being dominated. Equally, though, it would have felt significant given the occasion and the circumstances in which it came. Mourinho was supposed to be creating his Chelsea dynasty and winning the League

Cup was a big part of that. When he was first in charge, he had targeted League Cup success to give his players that winning feeling and was repeating the same methods in his second stint.

The Chelsea squad was at a similar stage to 2004/05. The talent was there, but they had not won things consistently as a group. Mourinho needed to foster that feeling among the players so they could carry it over into lifting the Premier League come May.

Had Spurs thrown a spanner in the works, it would have meant Mourinho's plans being severely dented. Chelsea had to win simply because they had invested so much in ensuring they did.

That is where the psychological edge is formed in derby matches. When one team wants it that much, when one team needs it to validate their progress, defeat can be futile. The opportunity was there for Spurs to strike the blow, but they missed it. Instead Terry made the most of what fell his way and Chelsea won the fifth League Cup in their history, fifty years on from their inaugural success in the competition.

Chelsea: Cech; Ivanovic, Cahill, Terry, Azpilicueta; Ramires, Zouma; Willian (Cuadrado, 76), Fabregas (Oscar, 88), Hazard; Diego Costa.
Unused subs: Courtois, Luis, Ake, Drogba, Remy.

Tottenham Hotspur: Lloris; Walker, Dier, Vertonghen, Rose; Bentaleb, Mason (Lamela, 71); Townsend (Dembele, 62), Eriksen, Chadli (Soldado, 80); Kane.
Unused subs: Vorm, Fazio, Davies, Stambouli.

44

Leicester City 1-3 Chelsea
Premier League
29 April 2015

There are moments in a season that symbolically seal trophies before the time comes to step over the line and actually win them for real.

In the cups it could be a dramatic late winner in extra time that breeds an unshakeable sense of belief, like Chelsea experienced themselves en route to the Champions League final in 2012. It was Branislav Ivanovic who scored the goal that defeated Napoli in the last sixteen, firing in Chelsea's fourth on the night at Stamford Bridge to complete one of the competition's most memorable comebacks. That was the moment when the tide turned for their European campaign.

In a league season it could be a run of victories that open up a gap at the top. Or in Chelsea's case in 2015, it could be a single game that would crush the hopes of their rivals who were hinting at picking up some momentum at a vital time. Just when Arsenal and Manchester City thought they may have an outside chance of snagging Chelsea before reeling them in, their hopes were dashed.

Chelsea would win their fifth league title – their fourth of the Premier League era – against Crystal Palace on 3 May 2015. They did so in the way every romantic desires, playing in front of their own fans so they could enjoy a party after. Chelsea were not relying on others to win in their absence so they could be gathered around a television screen hugging each other in a kitchen; they were sharing the moment with those who followed them every week.

When Eden Hazard scored that only goal against Palace, he mimicked wiping the sweat from his brow to express relief that he had eventually hit the back of the net. Just seconds before his header, the Belgian had stepped up to take a penalty and was outwitted by Julian Speroni, who got down low to his left to save his effort. The ball spilled up into the air, right in Hazard's path and this time, with the goalkeeper committed right, Hazard knocked it the opposite side of him to eventually score.

Satirising his nervous state, Hazard was inadvertently referencing the fact the job was finally done. Chelsea would be champions and everyone else could go home. It was not that Palace game that got them there, though. That game had come four days earlier away to Leicester City.

Two clubs at opposite ends of the spectrum, Chelsea were going for the title while Leicester were busy pulling off the great escape to beat relegation. Rock-bottom as the season entered April, something magical happened. Seemingly with nothing left to lose in the season, Nigel Pearson and his players put the house on red and came up trumps – suddenly they started winning games with a swashbuckling brand of attacking football that took the Premier League by storm.

It had started against West Ham United where a 2-1 victory saw the Foxes start to tug on the coat-tails of the teams above them. At the time it seemed nothing more than a consolation as they were still four points from safety, propping up the table and had won just one other league game since the turn of the year.

Defeating the Hammers gave them confidence, though, and by the time Chelsea arrived at the King Power Stadium at the end of the month, Leicester had won a further three games on the bounce. Taking maximum points throughout April, the Foxes were now a point outside the drop zone. It was a turnaround of epic proportions.

Chelsea themselves were edging toward the title. They were striking off the games, one by one as they approached the finishing line. It was not with the same conviction as we had seen in the earlier stages of the season. They appeared leggy at the very time title-chasing teams should not be. Mourinho had not rotated his squad effectively and some poor business in the January transfer window had unsettled the side, not strengthened it.

Andre Schurrle had been sold to Wolfsburg for a tidy profit and in his place Juan Cuadrado was brought in. The Colombian was largely ineffective and struggled to adapt to English football. So much so, it meant Hazard, Oscar, Willian and Fabregas playing for every minute Mourinho could squeeze out of them. He had little choice as the alternative was a player who could barely trap a ball. So effective for Fiorentina and Columbia, Cuadrado had seemingly forgotten the fundamentals of being a footballer.

It was the sort of headache managers do not want to be dealing with during the run-in; the focus should be on winning games and not worrying about the implications of whether or not a player could get injured.

In hindsight, the results throughout the closing stages of 2014/15 look healthy on paper at least. The New Year's Day loss to Spurs aside, Chelsea would not suffer another defeat in the league until the title was already wrapped up. The circumstances of those wins were not quite as straightforward as the fixtures and results matrix would have us think, however.

Away to struggling Hull City in March, Chelsea almost threw three points away. They were 2-0 up within nine minutes but somehow allowed Steve Bruce's side back into it. By the half-hour mark it was bizarrely 2-2 after some woeful defending. It took a late goal from substitute Loic Remy to ease Chelsea's nerves as the game ended 3-2.

In the following outing against Stoke City, Charlie Adam scored from inside his own half to peg Chelsea back to 1-1 before Remy again proved the saviour with the winner after the interval.

When the Blues travelled to meet west London rivals QPR they had been frustrated for long meet spells. Attempting to avoid relegation, Rangers had made it a scrappy affair and Chelsea just could not get a grip on the game. Cesc Fabregas would score in the 88th minute to win it 1-0.

We were seeing a team grinding out results like champions are celebrated for, yet they had been doing it against teams who were moving in the wrong direction. Facing Leicester would be different as they were a side with the sort of motivation that allows for the unpredictable. It was a Leicester side in the beginning stages of the form that would eventually make them Premier League champions themselves the following year.

Travelling to the Midlands was dangerous territory and Marc Albrighton's opening goal right on half time was proof of the theory. Leicester had Chelsea rattled and despite the gap at the top being ten points, Manchester City and Arsenal were revelling in it. Chelsea's performances leading into the game had caused Manuel Pellegrini and Arsene Wenger to sit up and take a little more notice. Perhaps the title was not a foregone conclusion; perhaps Chelsea were running out of steam and Leicester were about to confirm it. Perhaps they could capitalise on a late season collapse.

Had it come about, it would have been catastrophic – the mother of all shocks of any top-flight campaign. No team had been this dominant in English football for a generation. Leading from the opening weekend and never off the top spot, Chelsea were going to be the English champions in every sense. None of their so-called rivals had done enough to seriously challenge them and Mourinho's men had made a mockery of the title race in the process.

But was the little horse returning? Were Chelsea beginning to feel the weight of expectation that has engulfed many teams before them? Could the title race go the same way it had the year previous when Liverpool fans had lined the streets to welcome their team into Anfield as if the Premier League was already wrapped up only for Demba Ba and Chelsea to spoil the party?

It was not just the Liverpool players who knew the impact of that game; the rest of the world had witnessed their collapse with three games to go that allowed Manchester City to sneak in and steal the title from under their noses.

The circumstances were much different, yet 1-0 down at the interval against a resurgent Leicester side, Chelsea were flirting with the idea at least.

The ace up Mourinho's sleeve was the players who had done it all before for him. Within three minutes of the restart, Didier Drogba had pulled Chelsea level to calm their nerves. It was the sort of instant reply any side needs to silence the buoyant home crowd. Leicester had given their fans paper clappers before the game and they made a piercing snap as 60,000 pairs of hands whacked them together. For an opposition player, it must have felt as nauseating as it was wretched.

Those clappers soon faded with Drogba's strike and they went for good after seventy-eight minutes when Chelsea scored their second of the game. Hazard would score the goal that won the title against Palace, but it was Terry's fumbled effort at the King Power that had effectively sealed it.

'That could be one of his biggest-ever goals for Chelsea,' was Gary Neville's assessment from the Sky Sports commentary position.

Kasper Schmeichel had made a good save from Gary Cahill's header and as Neville would point out over the television replay, when the ball bounced free in the box it was then about who was most alive to it, who had the anticipation to follow up and get there first. It was John Terry.

'He's alive, makes the movement in behind his man and while [the Leicester players] all stop, he's on the move,' Neville continued. 'He's alive and slices it off his shin pad.'

The camera immediately switches to Mourinho who is stood on the sidelines and his fist pump says it all. He knows what it all means. Chelsea did not need the third that Ramires would score four minutes later.

'To be losing at half-time is not boring, it's pressure,' the manager would say at the final whistle. 'The way we played in the second half, probably against the best team in the last month, was magnificent.

'The April month, the month when everybody was expecting Chelsea to drop points ... was exactly the month where we destroyed opponents.'

Chelsea had not just done that in April. It was how their entire season had shaped up. Arsenal, City, Manchester United – they were nowhere. They were the also-rans, merely there to make up the numbers. Chelsea were the heavyweights.

The title was going back to Stamford Bridge.

Leicester City: Schmeichel; Wasilewski, Huth (De Laet, 24), Morgan; Albrighton, Drinkwater, Cambiasso, Konchesky; King (James, 19); Ulloa, Vardy (Mahrez, 77).
Unused subs: Schwarzer, Hammond, Wood, Kramaric.

Chelsea: Cech; Ivanovic, Cahill, Terry, Azpilicueta; Ramires, Matic; Willian (Zouma, 84), Fabregas (Mikel, 90), Hazard (Cuadrado, 88); Drogba.
Unused subs: Courtois, Luis, Ake, Oscar.

45

Chelsea 3-1 Sunderland
Premier League
24 May 2015

Jose Mourinho was in a different frame of mind in March 2015. This was not the manager who was beginning to lose his grip on his job at Chelsea, more it was a manager at ease with his position. He seemed comfortable, confident everything was going his way. John Terry had just signed a new one-year contract extension that would keep him at the club beyond that season and the manager was understandably full of praise. Terry was enjoying another fine campaign en route to the Blues being crowned Premier League champions and Mourinho wanted his thoughts to be known on just how vital his captain remained.

'This new contract is not to say, "thank you very much". It is because John continues to perform,' Mourinho explained. 'He is a top defender. I am happy that he completely deserves this new contract after a season where he has already played 40 matches.'

Those matches would go on to become forty-nine in all competitions, with Terry very much at the heart of everything the club achieved that season, adding the League Cup to their trophy haul.

Mourinho was not only fulfilling his mentor role in the father-son relationship that he and Terry enjoyed. There was more to it than that; he was basking in the glory of restoring Terry to what he used to be. Whereas other managers had not fully believed in him, Mourinho had. This new contract was symbolic for the wisdom of his judgements. Others were wrong to forget about Terry; he would be a Chelsea player for another season and it was because of the manager's influence. Chelsea fans could keep their 'Captain, Leader, Legend' banner up for another season yet.

Two months on and Chelsea were facing Sunderland on the final day of the season. There was that carnival atmosphere in the air that precedes any trophy presentation. It was for that reason Stamford Bridge had sold out. The fans inside had not come to watch a game that had nothing riding on it – they were present to watch the champions be crowned. It was Coronation Day.

Points on the board meant nothing. Chelsea would be finishing top regardless of what happened, but it was a bit different for Terry. He knew that if he played the full ninety minutes he would become just the second outfield player in the history of the Premier League to be an ever-present throughout the season.

The first had been Manchester United's Gary Pallister, who achieved the rare accolade in 1992/93. That it took Terry twenty-two years to emulate that feat outlines just what an achievement it would prove. Jens Lehmann and Joe Hart had done it for Arsenal and Manchester City, respectively. They were goalkeepers, though, meaning their longevity over the thirty-eight games of the season is not as valid. Goalkeepers have their role to play, yet to run thousands of kilometres over the course of a season takes a toll on the body that goalkeepers do not put on themselves. That in itself is strain enough without the physical side of the game that a central defender must deal with.

Terry had long stressed the point that even at thirty-four years old he did not feel his body was giving up on him. He was often speaking of feeling he was in peak physical condition, so to last a full nine months and play every second of Chelsea's Premier League season spoke of the levels he remained at. It was proof of what Mourinho had said a couple months earlier – that Terry continued to perform. He was still the player he had met in 2004.

When Mourinho had returned to Chelsea, Terry's career was up in the air. Injuries were seemingly getting the better of him and after Rafa Benitez seemed to cast him aside, his future did not hint at the longevity it would later have.

'The manager was straight with me from day one,' Terry recalled. 'When Jose came in, after the first week he said, "For me, nothing has changed. You're still top, you can still work and play at the top."

'He showed faith in me, and to get that arm around you is something everyone needs, even if you are one of the more experienced players in the team. At the time the manager spoke about it, I think I needed it and, when I got that from him, it not only made me feel ten feet tall, but it made me want to work even harder for the man in charge. It makes you go to that extra level – and I would give everything for the manager.'

In the same way Terry's new contract that had been signed in March was vindicating Mourinho's methods, so too was the final game of the season. It is why Terry had formed such a close bond with the manager and followed him through everything.

Six months after Mourinho had been sacked by Chelsea for a second time, he was being appointed Manchester United manager, succeeding Louis van Gaal at Old Trafford. That rankled with some sections of the Chelsea support who struggled to imagine Mourinho turning up at Stamford Bridge in red. Mourinho was their manager, not United's. It did not sit well; it felt uncomfortable. It was probably too much reality to handle, that those times of Mourinho leading the club to success were over and they were not coming back. Everyone had to move on.

Such is the relationship between Terry and his former boss, the defender was genuine in sentiments toward Mourinho in the wake of his United appointment.

'It's fantastic news for Manchester United,' he had said at the charity event that followed the conclusion of 2015/16. 'I'm sure that United's fans and players will be delighted with that because, as I've said many times before, he's the best manager I've worked under.'

It was because of the moments Terry would enjoy under Mourinho that cemented his opinion. Collectively, Chelsea have never won as much than with Mourinho at the helm, but on a personal level he had done so much to further Terry's career. From that plane journey across the Atlantic when he made him his captain, right through to helping restore his reputation in the English game, Mourinho had been the manager to squeeze every ounce of talent from Terry. Here he was, thirty-four years old and still breaking records.

'Football has changed a lot since I was first in the side, so I have had to adapt my game to suit that. I think it used to be a lot more physical when I first came into the side, in an honest way,' Terry explained in a *Chelsea* magazine interview. 'Both centre-half and striker would go for the ball and you'd both be challenging for it, whereas now a lot of strikers will try to get their body in the way so that, if you don't win the ball, you are giving a foul away in a dangerous area – even the smaller strikers get their bodies into positions where you can't get around them. So, you have to adapt your game, and I always wanted to do that as the game evolved over the years as well.'

Mourinho's influence had been a big part of Terry doing that. The pair had made history together many times before at Stamford Bridge and when Lee Mason blew his final whistle against Sunderland, it was another record to add to the long list. Terry had lasted the distance, he was joining Pallister in that elite club. Mourinho was there saluting him from the sidelines. Terry's reward came moments later when he received the Premier League trophy for a fourth time.

Chelsea: Cech; Ivanovic, Cahill, Terry, Azpilicueta; Mikel (Christensen, 78), Matic; Cuadrado (Remy, 44), Hazard, Willian; Drogba (Costa, 30).
Unused subs: Courtois, Luis, Boga, Solanke.

Sunderland: Mannone; Jones, O'shea, Coates, van Aanholt; Larsson, Rodwell, Johnson (Giaccherini, 75); Wickham, Defoe, Fletcher.
Unused subs: Pickford, Reveillere, Vergini, Cattermole, Buckley, Graham.

46

Chelsea 3-3 Everton
Premier League
16 January 2016

A big part of Chelsea's problems in 2015/16 was a failure to cope when opponents would press them in the defensive third. For a team that oozed quality throughout the squad, a lack of mettle saw them prone to errors whenever they were put under the pressure. Those uncharacteristic mistakes had become rife. Players who were usually defensively sound, comfortable in possession and commanding, seemed to wilt. They were supposed to be reigning Premier League champions, but the qualities that had got them such status had been ruthlessly stripped back in December 2015.

A hint at how things got to such a drastic position was given by Cesc Fabregas in the wake of Jose Mourinho's sacking.

'The biggest problem was [Mourinho] trusted us too much, gave us more holiday because we were champions and we let him down,' the Spaniard had explained in an interview with Sky Sports. Fabregas was talking about the extended break the players had enjoyed over the summer, which meant they had come back later than other clubs and looked undercooked by the time the season had started.

'That was the main reason he had to go and for that, myself and the team feel bad for it.'

It was an admission of Chelsea's mindset becoming focused on this sense they were always playing catch-up with those clubs around them. They were trying to catch up on their fitness; they were trying to catch up with the points they had on the board; they were trying to play catch up in games where they were falling behind to sloppy goals.

Mourinho was not even the Chelsea manager when Everton came to Stamford Bridge in January 2016. A fortnight or so had passed since his departure, but those same problems were there and Guus Hiddink was desperately trying to set things straight.

Chelsea may have been match fit by this stage, yet they were saddled with a pressure not even they were used to. It is different at the bottom of the table where teams are fighting in a different way. The points remain the same for a victory, although the way you get them is different. Seldom can sides that are just six points free of the drop zone come January play with any real sense of freedom. The situation is much too tense for that; rather than play your way out of trouble, it becomes a task more about scrapping your way out of it. Teams need to earn that right to play again and that is exactly where Chelsea found themselves.

Undefeated since the 2-1 loss to Leicester City that had sealed Mourinho's fate, Chelsea were still looking down at the table and seeing enough that made them feel edgy. Given how their season had gone, six points was not a cushion; a few stems of hay it may have been, but a bale it certainly was not. They needed something more substantial to soften any future blows.

The sense of foreboding was palpable with every home game. Chelsea supporters would not admit it publicly, but they could sense the club was flirting with a relegation battle. They were not in one yet, although it would not take much to ensure they were.

That feeling of anxiety was felt among the players as well and it made for some tense moments in west London. Now home games were being endured more than enjoyed for all involved. There have been hard times at Stamford Bridge in the past, but Roman Abramovich's wealth was supposed to have ended them. Now Chelsea were back to their mid-1990s form when it took Mark Stein and Paul Furlong to get them out of trouble.

Roberto Martinez's Everton thought they had capitalised on the growing pressure in west London when they took a two-goal lead at Stamford Bridge. Of all the players to score an own goal that afternoon, John Terry was the culprit to give the Toffees a leg up.

That is when the panic set in. From the game being a dull affair up to the interval, Everton's 50th-minute opener suddenly meant it was open season.

Their position in the table coupled with a severe lack of form meant Chelsea could not cope with conceding the first goal in matches. Such were the panic and nerves, experienced players lost their heads. Suddenly it was about getting the scores back all square immediately and it became hellish in the process.

Too often Chelsea would lose shape as players ran around the pitch without a sense of how things should work collectively. They looked around them and could not trust the look in the eyes of their teammates so opted for some ill-advised kamikaze missions forward.

Intelligent teams did not take long to spot this and despite the shortcomings of their own manager, it was not long before Everton's players had. It was six minutes in fact, with Kevin Mirallas benefitting from Chelsea's lack of defensive acumen to double the visitors' lead.

Hiddink was slumped in the dugout, clearly wondering why he had allowed his good friend Abramovich to put him through this public torture. He could been backpacking with his wife in India, but instead he was carrying a much heavier weight and seemed powerless to stop the wreckage happening in front of him.

In short, it was horrendous from a team that, as recently as May 2015, had been the toast of the Premier League. Terry's own goal and Mirallas' strike were goals number 32 and 33 conceded in the league and January was not even out. For perspective, Chelsea had conceded just 37 in all competitions in 2014/15.

Fortunately Everton were not much better at the back. For Everton's problems, read Chelsea's. Within ten minutes of that Mirallas goal, the game was back to being all square at 2-2 thanks to Diego Costa and Cesc Fabregas, not to mention some defensive mishaps by the visitors' back four.

It had become a fixture defined by a comedy of errors so when Ramiro Funes Mori came off the bench to score Everton's third in the 90th minute, there was still a sense something would happen at either end. Both sides had one more mistake in them.

'What I will say is this,' begins Pat Nevin. 'There was a lot of criticism of this Chelsea side this season, but one thing you could never level at John Terry is that he threw in the towel. Yes he struggled for form at times, just like the rest of them, but he never gave up trying. He worked his socks off every time he played.'

Chelsea were more thankful than happy Terry applied himself in the way Nevin described. The former Chelsea winger's words were said in hindsight, but they were certainly true; especially against another of his former clubs in Everton.

Having the first word with that own goal, Terry had the last when he scored Chelsea's equaliser in the eighth minute of stoppage time. Everton were crushed, especially as referee

Mike Jones had initially signaled a minimum of seven minutes would be added on. Oh, and Terry was outrageously offside when he flicked the ball beyond Tim Howard in goal.

'I'm very happy with the spirit and the ambition of the team,' Hiddink said after. For team, he could have just uttered his captain's name. The draw was as much about him as it was the circus that had seen the game finish up 3-3.

'At 2-0 it was a tremendous set-back, but I was very pleased with attitude to get back in it. We had another set-back at the end ... and I'm very happy with the attitude of the team. John was offside, but he made a beautiful, beautiful goal.'

The celebrations after said what it had meant to Terry and those inside Stamford Bridge. His booking for jumping into the Matthew Harding Stand would have felt worthwhile as it brought about a feeling of unity with the players and fans. They were only celebrating a point, yet in the grander scheme of what Terry had achieved, it stood for plenty. With the departure of Mourinho and their poor miserable defence of the title, all involved at Chelsea had been through enough grief. They needed a moment to release that tension and cheer. Terry gave it to them.

It would prove his only goal in the entire season, but Terry was showing he still had that knack for arriving at the right moment to salvage something.

Plenty lay over the horizon for him. Within a fortnight, news would break that Terry was not going to be offered a new contract to remain a Chelsea player beyond June and after he picked up an injury in February, it meant he played just four more games at Stamford Bridge after scoring against Everton.

For so many reasons more than a point, his goal had meant everything.

Chelsea: Courtois; Ivanovic, Zouma, Terry, Azpilicueta; Mikel, Matic (Oscar, 55); Willian, Fabregas, Pedro (Kenedy, 66); Diego Costa (Remy, 80).
Unused subs: Begovic, Rahman, Cahill, Loftus-Cheek.

Everton: Howard; Oviedo (Funes Mori, 71), Jagielka, Stones, Baines; Besic, Barry; Lennon (Deulofeu, 80), Barkley (Pienaar, 81), Mirallas; Lukaku.
Unused subs: Robles, Cleverley, Osman, Kone.

47

MK Dons 1-5 Chelsea
FA Cup, Fourth Round
31 January 2016

Chelsea had just cruised to victory against MK Dons, yet it was not the gathering momentum behind their FA Cup run that would be stealing the headlines in Monday's newspapers. There was another agenda.

'It's not going to be a fairy-tale ending, I'm not going to retire at Chelsea,' John Terry declared to journalists as he was departing stadium:mk.

The Chelsea captain had stopped off in the mixed zone for a chat and those in attendance had got much more than they had been bargaining for when he revealed the situation surrounding a new contract, or lack thereof, at Chelsea. His deal was expiring at the end of the season and as it stood in that moment, it was not being renewed.

Mixed zones can be frustrating places at times. A journalist can be well positioned, say all the right things, ask all the right questions, but never get the sound bites or scoop they are looking for. Sometimes players have fulfilled their media duties in the tunnel area with television broadcasters or, despite said hack waiting and waiting, the nature of the result can mean players are not always keen to stop and dissect another defeat or disappointing draw.

But then there are moments when all that disappointment has been worth it; they are the moments when a player will open up and tell you how he is truly feeling.

It was not through taking delight from Terry's pain and frustration that the journalists in Milton Keynes would have been punching the air; it was being there for what felt like a big moment in Terry's career. As professionals at the heart of such substantial breaking news, it is what drives the desire of any journalist.

The Chelsea captain had long been a respected sportsman, known for winning trophies and achieving excellence. But here he was writing headlines with all the romance of John Steinbeck. He was talking with emotion at the disappointment of him not being in a position to plan his future at Stamford Bridge. Terry was carefully selecting his words to outline the anguish at bringing his twenty-one-year Chelsea career to an end.

'I was in last week before the Arsenal game and [my contract] is not going to be extended,' Terry continued. 'It's my last run in the FA Cup so I want to make it a good one. It's a big season for me and I want to push on – not just in this competition but in the Premier League as well. I knew before the Arsenal game [when Chelsea won 1-0 a week earlier] so mentally I've kind of accepted it.'

It was clear from the initial response that Chelsea fans had not. Terry may have been thirty-five years old, yet they were not happy to see him leave, especially under the circumstances the club had found itself.

Although a 5-1 thrashing of MK Dons was reason enough for the Blues to be feeling buoyed, the campaign up to that point had told us plenty about how Terry's final season would end in west London. He wouldn't be going out with a bang, celebrating with another Premier League title or better, the Champions League.

Guus Hiddink had been back at the club for just over a month, replacing the sacked Jose Mourinho in the dugout. It had been a season of turmoil up to that point, with Mourinho's team of champions sliding down the table and seemingly unable to arrest a run of form that had left them in a relegation scrap come Christmas.

That's not overcooking the situation. The Blues were well and truly looking over their shoulder, feeling the heavy breath of the bottom three singeing the hairs on their necks. Chelsea were just three points above eighteenth-placed Swansea City on Christmas Day; whichever way we want to look at it, they were in a full-blown crisis.

The form that had got them into that position had gone on for much too long and for many other reasons besides, Mourinho was given the axe for a second time.

When Hiddink had stepped into the breach seven years earlier – in 2009 it was Luis Felipe Scolari that he replaced – things had gone much different. Chelsea had won sixteen of their twenty-two games with Hiddink in charge, losing just once. Indeed, Hiddink's impact was instant, winning eight of his first ten games to restore the equilibrium at Stamford Bridge.

With his mild manner and willingness to massage the egos of his players, Hiddink's methods were a positive influence in an the dressing room. He was respected and the players listened to him.

Fast-forward to 2016, it was a similar story. Hiddink's less confrontational ways were the antithesis of Mourinho's last days as Chelsea boss. He took the sting out of the situation, making light of bad situations in an attempt to ease the pressure.

It worked to some degree, but Hiddink's Achilles heel was the squad he had inherited. This was not the Chelsea of Terry's prime where the team all but picked itself and characters such as Frank Lampard, Michael Ballack, Petr Cech, Didier Drogba and Ashley Cole backed up their captain.

The landscape was much different, with Hiddink dealing with a group that was not built in that mould. Chelsea had taken a different direction and the doggedness of character that had got the club out of trouble in the past was not the standout quality in the modern era.

Whether it was the bad influence of Mourinho and his policies, or just a lack of mental strength, Hiddink's second coming was about dealing with shattered egos and a broken team.

It all meant that a run of form to take Chelsea to the Champions League semi-final or even win the FA Cup like he had before, was looking highly unlikely. In his first ten games in charge, Hiddink won just four, drawing the other six. In total, his record the second time out would eventually read: Won 10, Lost 6, Drawn 11.

The fall from grace had been spectacular and bullying a Championship side that would eventually be relegated back to League One after just one season was not going to paper over the cracks. Losing Terry when the club was in such turmoil just added to the bereavement of it all.

The feeling at stadium:mk as the Chelsea bus departed was that we were witnessing the beginning of the end for Terry at Stamford Bridge. Terry himself had made that much clear.

'The club will move on. No player is ever bigger than the club. Ideally I would have loved to stay, but the club's moving in a different direction,' Terry continued.

'No doubt they'll sign one or two great centre-backs. I want to come back as a Chelsea supporter in years to come with my kids and see the team doing great. Unfortunately that's not going to be with me, but I want to see the team do well. It's going to be my last year and I want to go out at the top.'

As journalists started to process the news and file their copy, the question being asked was where life without Terry would leave Chelsea. How would the club cope without him? Who would be the new captain? How do you even go about replacing a figure that has been so dominant for well over a decade?

Terry's announcement had diluted everything the club had been about since the Roman Abramovich takeover. Despite the circumstances surrounding his departure, losing Mourinho again had been a painful process for Chelsea fans and it ended that era of the club for the final time. For years they had pined for his return and after going out the way he did, there was a begrudging acceptance that it was all over for good now. Abramovich had given the supporters what they wanted and Mourinho had helped crush the dream.

To hear the news just a month after Mourinho's exit that Terry would soon be departing himself, was one blow too many. Football clubs need figureheads to cling on to – players who define what the club is about and what it represents. Not since Dennis Wise had a player done that at Stamford Bridge.

The fact that it was Wise who had helped Terry come through all the years ago seemed to legitimise his position all the more. Terry's reputation at Stamford Bridge was akin to him being the chosen one – Wise had cherry-picked him from the youth ranks and in so doing, gave his blessing that it would be Terry who would one day inherit his arm band.

Who was inheriting it from Terry? There was nobody in line, so to watch him leave in such circumstances was unfathomable. Chelsea fans had to accept his days were numbered, but few would have ever predicted he would go out like this. Not when Chelsea were on their knees, struggling at the wrong end of the table and facing an uncertain future.

Terry was supposed to leave the club in a position of power. His journey over the horizon to face the setting sun was not written with a sad ending. But here he was, giving fans the ultimate spoiler to the tale.

The end was coming soon.

MK Dons: Martin; Spence, McFadzean, Walsh, Lewington; Potter, Caskey; Hall, Carruthers (Powell, 82), Murphy (Williams, 67); Bowditch (Maynard, 76).
Unused subs: Cropper, Hodson, Kay, Church.

Chelsea: Courtois; Ivanovic, Cahill, Terry, Baba; Fabregas, Matic; Oscar (Willian, 64), Loftus-Cheek, Hazard (Pedro, 64); Diego Costa (Traore, 57).
Unused subs: Begovic, Zouma, Azpilicueta, Mikel.

48

Everton 2-0 Chelsea
FA Cup, Fifth Round
12 March 2016

Chelsea's season would end in frustrating disappointment at Goodison Park. It was perhaps fitting considering all that had come before in 2015/16 as the reigning Premier League champions' campaign had started with a whimper and ended with the sound of a death knell as they limped out of the FA Cup.

Just three days earlier they had also been knocked out of the Champions League against Paris Saint-Germain for the second season running. A hamstring injury had kept John Terry out of that game, a fact in itself that no doubt had Laurent Blanc's side relishing the prospect of getting at Chelsea's weakened defence.

Without Terry for spells in 2015/16, we saw exactly where the shortcomings were with Jose Mourinho's squad. When Hiddink took over from the Special One in December, he inherited a side much different to when he was first in interim control back in 2009.

Back then Chelsea were defined by characters like Frank Lampard, Didier Drogba and Michael Ballack. Terry was the leader of those and it was seldom they would collapse.

Hiddink revitalised their morale back then, almost taking them to a Champions League final before they lifted the FA Cup for the second time in three seasons.

Things had gone awry under Luis Felipe Scolari and things were disjointed. The character was never questioned, though. With a team containing such considerable figures, it rarely is.

This time it was different. The 'little horse' Mourinho had spoken of in 2014 was still waiting to mature, despite Premier League success that came the following season. There was a lack of substance that even with Terry in the side, was not what we had come to know in this era of Chelsea.

PSG sniffed that and capitalised. They bullied Hiddink's side, playing with all the authority and grit previous Chelsea teams had been celebrated for. It was a sobering experience that ensured the death knell would ring ever louder for that crop of players. If it had not been before then, it was suddenly clear that Chelsea's attempts to rediscover a new generation to replace the last was failing.

Three days later, Blues supporters had to go through it all again when they travelled to Merseyside to watch Everton carve up the wounded animal Chelsea had become.

With no Premier League title to chase and European qualification via the league proving an unrealistic aim, there was suddenly nothing to play for as the FA Cup dream vanished.

There was no blaze of glory to keep the fight alive, which made the loss harder to stomach for Chelsea fans. The closest Chelsea would come to showing any real passion in the game was when Diego Costa saw red for getting into a scrap with Gareth Barry. Romelu Lukaku killed Chelsea off, scoring both goals against his former employers.

Losing to Everton in the way they did should have meant the game was confined to the annals of history. It was one to forget, only John Terry never will never to be able to erase it from memory. It was his 700th game in the club's colours.

'For many years now he has given his all, both on the training ground and on the pitch. He has my full respect for this wonderful achievement,' Guus Hiddink said after.

Perhaps prior to the game the Chelsea boss did not realise the landmark occasion for Terry as he used the defender as a late substitute in an attempt to salvage something from the game. Terry was on the bench as he continued his comeback from that hamstring injury, yet featuring when he did seemed like an odd decision from Hiddink.

It was already 2-0 by that stage, so throwing Terry on as a makeshift striker seemed a pointless endeavor. The game was up for Chelsea and the afternoon was made worse with the feeling of anti-climax that marked Terry's milestone. Only two players before him had reached the 700-game mark – Peter Bonetti and Ron Harris – so that Terry did it in such disappointing circumstances did not quite deliver the sense of occasion it should have. Surely the Chelsea captain was deserving of something a little more, well, memorable.

Speaking a few days later when he started against West Ham United, Terry was rightly proud of the achievement, despite it coming when it did.

'Words can't explain how much it means to me to have reached that number,' he told the Chelsea matchday programme in an interview to mark his 700 games.

'As a 14 year-old, just the thought of playing once for this club was a dream, so to do it as many times as I've done and to have the success I have had at this football club, I'm unbelievably proud of that.

'[The] supporters believed in me from day one and to have received the backing I have from them – to hear them sing my name and support me – is all I could ever ask for as a player. I can't thank them enough for that.'

As time heals the wounds from Everton and the disappointments of 2015/16 as a whole, the result and the circumstances of it will eventually come to mean little. Defeats and crises are a reality in football, especially for a club that has tended to thrive in such circumstances in the past. When we reflect on Terry's career milestones, however, the Everton loss will always lurk in the background to serve as a reminder of the fall from grace Chelsea endured in 2015/16. For a player who achieved everything he did, the hope would have been that game 700 was remembered with much more fondness.

Everton: Robles; Coleman, Funes Mori, Jagielka, Baines; McCarthy, Barry; Lennon (Stones, 88), Barkley (Besic, 89), Cleverley; Lukaku (Niasse, 89).
Unused subs: Howard, Osman, Kone, Deulofeu.

Chelsea: Courtois; Azpilicueta, Ivanovic, Cahill, Kenedy (Terry, 85); Matic (Remy, 82), Mikel; Willian (Oscar, 73), Fabregas, Pedro; Diego Costa.
Unused subs: Begovic, Rahman, Traore, Loftus-Cheek.

49

Chelsea 2-2 Tottenham Hotspur
Premier League
2 May 2016

When a club has proved as dominant as Chelsea have against Tottenham Hotspur, the notion of a rivalry should not exist. It should feel more one-sided, with Spurs themselves sharing more animosity toward Chelsea. After all, up to the end of 2015/16 the Blues had not lost at home to their London rivals since 1990. That predates the formation of the Premier League, outlining just how Chelsea have had *it* over the north Londoners.

Yet Chelsea despise Spurs. It is a feeling that runs deep with supporters of the club, so when Maurico Pochettino brought his side to Stamford Bridge with just three games remaining of the 2015/16 season, the game had added significance.

Spurs were going for the title, clinging desperately onto the coat-tails of surprise Premier League leaders Leicester City. As coincidence would have it, Leicester were under the charge of former Chelsea boss Claudio Ranieri, which gave Chelsea an added incentive in the game.

Spurs needed a win. Anything but would give the title to Leicester with two games to spare, crowning Ranieri as a Premier League champion.

The Italian had left Chelsea in 2004 to be replaced by Jose Mourinho. He was still well regarded on the terraces, though, and after all he had done for Terry in the early part of his career, denying Spurs in his honour formed part of the motivation to get one over them.

With the disappointments they had suffered from the moment the season had kicked off, Chelsea's campaign had long been over as a contest. It was clear from as early as October that a successful defence of the title they had won so convincingly a year earlier would not happen. Paris Saint-Germain had killed their Champions League hopes for the second season running in March, with defeat to Everton in the FA Cup following on the back.

That Spurs' season could end in tears at the hands of Chelsea was inspiration enough to reignite the campaign for ninety minutes at least.

'This Tottenham-Chelsea thing came about in the sixties,' Chelsea's official historian Rick Glanvill explains. 'Firstly we lost a number of players to them – Jimmy Greaves, Terry Venables and Bobby Smith – and then mid-decade we seemed to just meet each other again and again. Players started to dislike each other, the supporters would get into fights a lot more and it reached a climax in the 1967 FA Cup Final. There were fights all over the place; it was absolute carnage.'

It was not always that way, with Arsenal being the object of Chelsea's 'affections' from their early history through to the swinging sixties.

'Older supporters I know still really dislike Arsenal more than any other club,' Glanvill continues. 'During World War Two, the club had spotters on top of Stamford Bridge during matches to spot air raids. They always like to tell me that if they had seen a bomber, they would've redirected it over Highbury. Not White Hart Lane, Highbury! They were the big rivals.'

On the back of Chelsea losing to Spurs in the 1967 FA Cup final, the clubs' paths would cross at another vital stage in their respective histories.

Chelsea and Spurs faced harsher times in the following decade. Come the end of the 1974/75 season, the pair faced each other in what's since been remembered as a relegation play-off at White Hart Lane. In front of over 51,000 fans, Spurs won 2-0 and stayed up, Chelsea dropping down into the old Division Two.

Watching highlights from the game, some of the tackles show there was little love lost between the players. At one point, Spurs' Alfie Conn even appears to use the international gesture for 'wanker' after being clattered by Gary Locke.

'It's not true that Spurs relegated Chelsea that season, though,' informs Glanvill. 'Chelsea drew their next two games [with Sheffield United and Everton] after losing to Spurs. Had they not done that, they would've had a good chance of staying up. More importantly, the fact Chelsea fans think that Spurs did relegate the club feeds into this feeling of inferiority toward them.

'Spurs won the double in the sixties and then into the eighties had the likes of Glenn Hoddle. They had a bit of swagger with Gazza and others, so they were quite a glamorous team. Chelsea were a real yo-yo side during those periods and that feeling of inferiority grew. In more modern times, Chelsea have had to unlearn it all as we've been the successful club, beating Spurs more often than not.'

All that history contributed to a fearsome London derby at Stamford Bridge. It was a game that had it all for the neutral – flying tackles, goals and controversy. It was game fed on a diet of hatred.

At the heart of it was Terry. Chelsea's captain did not play a part in the game's pivotal moments, yet it was his influence that inspired it all.

Eden Hazard, Cesc Fabregas and Pedro had used the media to push an anti-Spurs agenda that acted to inspire their teammates. Terry did not turn down the opportunity for the last word in his programme notes ahead of the game, either.

'Tonight is a huge game, a London derby against one of our big rivals,' he wrote. 'We know what this fixture means and, as with all our remaining games, we will be looking to win it.

'We know tonight is going to be a completely different type of game [to those Chelsea have before the end of the season], and we will have to battle hard to take the points from this match.'

It was the sort of fighting talk we would expect inside the dressing room. The image of Terry rounding up his players, barking out the order that they dare not lose the game.

There was too much riding on it. In that season of all seasons, when Chelsea had failed so miserably, they could not allow Spurs to wipe out twenty-six years of history. Added to that, they could not allow them to steal a march on the title.

Leicester's eight-point cushion was significant so late in the season, but had Spurs reduced it to five, the Foxes' relative inexperience in such situations would have meant anything being possible. Would they blow it in the same manner others like Newcastle United and Liverpool had in the Premier League era?

The air of unpredictability of a title run-in is why Sir Alex Ferguson would label it as 'squeaky bum time'. It comes down to which side has the character to withstand the glare of expectation that follows them. It can haunt some.

A champion four times himself, Terry did not want Leicester to be in a position to have to answer those sorts of questions against Spurs of all clubs. This was the chance to end it once and for all.

Goals from Harry Kane and Son Heung-min looked like history was being made. Spurs were two goals to the good at the interval and Chelsea looked a mess. Guus Hiddink's side lacked shape, with the battles they fought across the pitch seeming to get the better of them.

Spurs were no strangers to the dirty tricks – Kyle Walker and Danny Rose were both guilty of kicking out at times – yet it did not seem to impact the way they played.

Kane and Son's goals were typical of what we had come to expect from them throughout the year. They were team goals based on Pochettino's principles of a high press and simple, quick transitions in tight areas. Chelsea's defence could not seem to handle it and that proud twenty-six-year record was on the brink of disappearing.

Then Hazard came off the bench and the tides turned. The diminutive Belgian looked back to his Player of the Year levels, with his darting runs at the heart of the defence sending panic across the Spurs backline.

Gary Cahill pulled Chelsea back into it with a wonderful strike just before the hour, but the best was still to come.

With just under ten minutes left on the clock, Hazard picked the ball up inside the Chelsea half. He run through two opposition midfielders and broke free before finding Diego Costa. The striker sensed Toby Alderweireld to his right, so instead of taking a touch to control the ball, opened his body and swiveled beyond the Belgian. That created space for Hazard to exploit and Costa released him inside the box.

The curling shot from Hazard that nestled into the top corner of Hugo Lloris' net was exquisite in the extreme. Few players are capable of such wonders, but Hazard ranks himself in that number.

He took it in his stride, putting his body across the defender to shield the ball, before bending around Lloris. He stood no chance.

Stamford Bridge erupted into pandemonium. The upset was on, the record protected.

What had cost Spurs was their inability to see out the game. They panicked and the nine yellow cards they finished the game with proved a token of how their heads went. The difference was leadership and Chelsea had it because of Terry.

It was telling that the television cameras would pick up his instructions to his teammates late on. In the 88th minute, with the scores level at 2-2, Terry did not want Chelsea repeating Spurs' mistakes. This was a time for cool heads and he had the coolest of them all.

'If they break, make a foul,' he called out to a teammate who was off camera, pointing to an area of the pitch inside the Spurs half. Chelsea had a corner and Terry did not want a breakaway to transform the result.

It was leadership of the highest order. Deliberately making fouls will be frowned upon, yet at the highest level, it is that know-how that closes out games. We call it game management and Terry was proving he still had it.

When the whistle blew, the chaos from the ninety minutes continued as players pushed and shoved their way down the tunnel. It mattered little as Chelsea had won the fight that really mattered.

Spurs' title dream was over and Terry's Instagram post later that evening summed up the spirit of how it all went down from Chelsea's perspective.

'Great character from the players to come back from 2-0 down,' he posted. 'The atmosphere was incredible and we know how much that result means to you supporters. 27 years #notonmyshift.'

Indeed.

Chelsea: Begovic; Ivanovic, Cahill, Terry, Azpilicueta; Mikel, Matic (Oscar, 78); Willian, Fabregas, Pedro (Hazard, 46); Diego Costa.
Unused subs: Amelia, Rahman, Traore, Loftus-Cheek, Kenedy.

Tottenham Hotspur: Lloris; Walker, Alderweireld (Chadli, 89), Vertonghen, Rose (Davies, 82); Dier, Dembele; Son (Mason, 65), Eriksen, Lamela; Kane.
Unused subs: Vorm, Wimmer, Carroll, N'Jie.

Sunderland 3-2 Chelsea
Premier League
7 May 2016

And with that John Terry's Chelsea career was coming to an end. There was no new contract offer waiting for him to sign and after a disastrous campaign there would be no victory parades or trophies to lift. There would be no lap of honour on the Stamford Bridge pitch. Any dreams of a standing ovation to bid a fond farewell to the fans who had passionately stood behind him and supported Terry throughout his career, was seemingly gone. This was not a moment to remember and cherish, only the red card issued by referee Mike Jones ensured it would forever live on in Terry's memory.

A proud, victorious captain was left to walk down the Stadium of Light tunnel alone, thinking he would not be seen in a Chelsea shirt again. There were no cheers or songs of praise to cement his legend in west London; they were instead replaced with the jeers of Sunderland fans who were celebrating a much-needed three points in their bid to avoid relegation from the Premier League.

Those amplified voices will no doubt haunt Terry regardless of anything else he achieves in life. They were the regrettable final listing for the soundtrack of his Chelsea career.

Terry's departure from Chelsea was not supposed to be written like that; heroes go out on highs, not with a whimper. From a once barrel-chested captain, the sight of him crouched over on the floor, head in his hands, was cruel. There would be no mercy and he knew it.

There were just thirty seconds remaining on the clock in a game that mattered little for Chelsea. That is where the pain struck most. The club's season had passed them by and since March there had been little to play for. Drawing with Tottenham Hotspur earlier in the week had salvaged some semblance of dignity among the players, but when the time for reflection came, even ending the title hopes of a bitter rival would not see the campaign remembered fondly.

Chelsea had surrendered their champions tag in calamitous fashion in 2015/16, long before their trip to the north-east. They had made a mockery of what champions are supposed to be. That they had to take such delight in bringing others to their level spoke much about a club that had created a reputation for revelling in successes of their own, rather than the failures of others.

From Spurs to Sunderland, Chelsea had been gifted the opportunity to do that again. The Black Cats were locked in a fight against the drop with Norwich City and Newcastle United. Aston Villa were already down and three into two does not work even for primary school mathematicians, let alone multimillion pound football clubs.

The stakes were high, the task simple for the home side. They had to take maximum points to ensure their Premier League fate in the remaining two games of the season would rest solely with them.

Other than being party poopers for the second game running, Chelsea had little else to play for. They were consigned to mid-table and that fact was not changing regardless of how their afternoon went.

That was the theory at least. In practice, John Terry would not have been able to accept defeat. If we want proof to support that assertion, his red card against Sam Allardyce's men tells the story.

Having been in control for large spells, Chelsea had let their grip on the game slip. Twice they had been in front thanks to Diego Costa and Nemanja Matic, and twice they had surrendered the initiative.

When Jermain Defoe scored within three minutes after Fabio Borini had made it 2-2, the body language of Chelsea's players told us enough about how the result would finish up.

They had the best of intentions, but with twenty minutes remaining, Chelsea would struggle to draw level. They were beaten. This was not a high-spirited London derby fuelled with hate and pride on the line. It was a game that mattered only for one club – and evidently one player as it would transpire.

When the ball ran loose in midfield, there was no need for Terry to race Wahbi Khazri for possession. The game was already deep into stoppage time and the Chelsea defender was on a booking.

Those thoughts never occurred to Terry throughout his twelve years as Chelsea captain and they were not about to creep into his psyche now with the curtain close to coming down on his career.

He went for it, lunging for the ball in an attempt to win possession back for his team, knowing full well the odds were stacked in Khazri's favour. Terry had sniffed an opportunity to turn over possession for his team and regardless of the risks, he was always going to take it. To his detriment, that committed style he had become famed had now put his Chelsea farewell in jeopardy.

The last game of the season was just a week away; the referee's lips were agonisingly close to wetting the end of his whistle, but Terry couldn't accept it. The ball was there to be won and he had to do what instinct told him. He did not know any other way.

The result of his lunge would be a two-match ban that ended his season. The expectation now would be his Chelsea career would soon follow.

'It's sad,' Chelsea manager Guus Hiddink said at full-time. 'It would have been lovely to have had him in our last game at home [against Leicester City].'

Terry was last the bastion of Chelsea's golden generation. Successful teams had come and gone along the King's Road, but none had achieved what Terry's era had. Because of the achievements of Frank Lampard, Didier Drogba, Ashley Cole, Petr Cech and Joe Cole, a generation of Chelsea fans brought up on the mythology of old will now be feeding their own offspring stories of the glory days in west London as they saw them. Only this time it is better. This time the folklore features domination like never before at home and in Europe.

Terry was the leader in it all – the general marshalling his army as they conquered wherever they roamed. The Roman Abramovich Empire had broken Chelsea's chains and it extended much further than the confines of west London. Chelsea are now a global club with supporters in every territory.

Terry never turned his back or shirked the challenge laid down before him. With every title, he chased the next; with every defeat he picked his teammates up and got at it all over again. With every tackle that was there to be won, he chased the ball and committed himself to it. It sounds all very *Roy of the Rovers*, because it was.

Under the ownership of Abramovich, Chelsea rewrote the rule book for football in the modern age. Now the Premier League is awash with the mega-rich who invest lavishly in the game. For better or worse, Abramovich was the first; he started it all. In their own way, Chelsea changed the landscape of English football. They broke up the established order and that has created a behemoth.

That was all in the boardroom, a change instigated by men in suits. Out on the pitch, where it matters most, the club was led by a player who represented the finest traditions of English football. Terry was a leader of substance, a player committed to achieving greatness. He became the equal of those before him at Chelsea before eventually surpassing them. Ron Harris, Dennis Wise and Roy Bentley were all captains of significant renown and they have all been replaced by Terry's name as Stamford Bridge's finest.

For so long he had come to symbolise what Chelsea represented as a club. The sad truth was that facing Sunderland and being sent off, Terry's narrative was symbolic in itself for the road Chelsea had travelled in 2015/16. It was an anti-climax, a sobering campaign that questioned where exactly they stood as a new order threatened to engulf the Premier League in the same way they had more than a decade earlier.

After so much success in the twelve years he was their leader, Chelsea's story, like Terry's, was ending. It needed a new chapter to be written and Chelsea supporters were desperate for Terry to be a part of it. It did not appear he was going to be and the emotional farewell was being robbed from them like it had been for others in the past.

'When you've got a relationship like I've got with the football club and with the fans, and you've come through from the age of 14, there is nothing better than leading out the team to a win, to success, to titles,' Terry reflected soon after making his 700th Chelsea appearance.

'That feeling of walking out as captain, and knowing the fans trust you to do that, is the best.'

Chelsea would draw their final two games of the season 1-1 with Liverpool and new champions Leicester City. Terry missed both as he served that suspension.

It was before Guus Hiddink's final press conference of his brief return that the mood started to change. Sat in the media room at Chelsea's Cobham training ground, journalists could sniff something was awry. Some of the UK's finest hacks were there and when schedules begin to be messed with, instinct tells them something is brewing.

Hiddink should have arrived at 1.15 p.m. as the announcement a day previous had said. And the Dutchman was always on time. He was not one to keep people waiting, least of all those who had the power to shape his public persona.

The whispers were starting, the questions being asked among them. The clock was ticking well past Hiddink's expected time of arrival and still he had not shown.

The side door opened and all inside the room drew a breath of anticipation, but it was a cameraman from Chelsea TV and not the manager. A few heckles were directed his way.

Those whispers were now being replaced by the sound of keyboards working overtime. News desks were being emailed as something was clearly afoot. Then Hiddink showed his face.

'I'm sorry and I want to get this on camera,' Hiddink joked, getting into his chair. 'It is his fault,' he said, pointing at the media officer who had accompanied him. 'I like to start on time, but he is going to start the press conference today.'

After a few laughs, the Chelsea press officer in question was asked if there was any reason for the delay to proceedings.

'Yes, there is a reason,' he started. 'We're sorry for starting late and for starting Guus' final press conference late. I'm sure you will have quite a few questions on the rumours and speculation going around regarding John Terry. I can say on behalf of the club that Marina Granovskaia and Bruce Buck met with John and his agent this week and offered him a one-year contract extension.'

You could feel the excitement in the room. It was MK Dons all over again, but this time it was a different outcome for Terry. The story had changed; his Chelsea future was back in his hands.

'Obviously coming so late in the season, it is a big decision for John and his family. It is something they are now considering.'

It took Terry less than a week to make up his mind – five days, in fact. The announcement was made on the Friday and by Wednesday he was signing the deal that would bring his Stamford Bridge career into a twenty-second year. The red card at Sunderland could be forgotten. Victory was coming out of defeat.

'I'm Chelsea through and through,' Terry said in a statement that confirmed his decision. Can anyone disagree?

Sunderland: Mannone; Yedlin, Kone (O'Shea, 55), Kaboul, Van Aanholt; M'Vila, Cattermole (Larsson, 71); Borini, Khazri, Kirchoff (Watmore, 64); Defoe.
Unused subs: Pickford, Rodwell, N'Doye, Lens.

Chelsea: Courtois; Ivanovic (Rahman, 68), Cahill, Terry, Azpilicueta; Mikel (Traore, 83), Matic; Willian (Oscar, 80), Fabregas, Hazard; Costa.
Unused subs: Begovic, Loftus-Cheek, Pato, Kenedy.

John Terry in Numbers

2

Only two outfield players have played every minute of every game for a Premier League title-winning team. They are Gary Pallister and John Terry.

16

Trophies won as a Chelsea player – Premier League (4), FA Cup (5), League Cup (3), Champions League (1), Europa League (1), Community Shield (2).

40

No other defender has scored more goals in the Premier League than John Terry.

66

John Terry is Chelsea's all-time leading goalscorer (defenders).

430

The number of games John Terry has won as a Chelsea player.

703

The number of appearances John Terry has made for Chelsea.

The Competitions

Premier League
Played: 482 Goals: 40 Win Percentage: 63

FA Cup
Played: 55 Goals: 11 Win Percentage: 73

League Cup
Played: 35 Goals: 2 Win Percentage: 66

Champions League
Played: 111 Goals: 10 Win Percentage: 50

Europa League
Played: 11 Goals: 3 Win Percentage: 45